THE
OFFICIAL
CELEBRITY
REGISTRY

1993–1994

THE OFFICIAL CELEBRITY REGISTRY

1993–1994

INTIMATE INFORMATION ON THE WORLD'S MOST POPULAR MOVIE & TELEVISION STARS

SANDY STEELE

GENERAL PUBLISHING GROUP
LOS ANGELES

Publisher: W. Quay Hays
Editor: Murray Fisher
Managing Editor: Sarah Pirch
Assistant Editor: Colby Allerton
Cover Design: Deborah Daly, Daly Design
Proof Reader: Diane Woo

The publisher and authors wish to thank the following for their contributions to the book: Diane Budy, Brian and Jan Hays, Legwork - Joan Cohen and Sandy Ferguson, Mike Maclay, Scott Matulis, Tony Seidl, Kassandra Smolias and Kurt Wahlner.

For information:
General Publishing Group, Inc.
3100 Airport Avenue,
Santa Monica, California, 90405

Notice: The information in this book is true and complete to the best of our knowledge. It is offered with no guarantees on the part of the authors or General Publishing Group, Inc. Authors and publisher disclaim all liability in connection with the use of this book.

ISSN 1071-5770

ISBN 1-881-649-08-3: $9.99

Published by General Publishing Group, Inc.,
Los Angeles, CA

10 9 8 7 6 5 4 3 2 1

Bound and printed in the United States of America

TABLE OF CONTENTS

F

Falk, Peter	140
Fawcett, Farrah	142
Field, Sally	144
Fisher, Carrie	146
Fonda, Bridget	148
Fonda, Jane	150
Ford, Harrison	152
Forsythe, John	154
Foster, Jodie	156
Fox, Michael J.	158
Freeman, Morgan	160

G

Garner, James	162
Garr, Teri	164
Gere, Richard	166
Gibson, Mel	168
Gifford, Kathie Lee	170
Glover, Danny	172
Goldberg, Whoopi	174
Goodman, John	176
Griffith, Andy	178
Griffith, Melanie	180
Guillaume, Robert	182
Gumbel, Bryant	184

H

Hackman, Gene	186
Hagman, Larry	188
Hall, Arsenio	190
Hanks, Tom	192
Hannah, Daryl	194
Harrelson, Woody	196
Hart, Mary	198
Hawn, Goldie	200
Hepburn, Katharine	202
Hershey, Barbara	204
Heston, Charlton	206
Hoffman, Dustin	208
Hope, Bob	210
Hopkins, Anthony	212

Howard, Ron	214
Hurt, William	216
Huston, Anjelica	218

I

Irons, Jeremy	220

J

Jennings, Peter	222
Johnson, Don	224
Jones, James Earl	226
Julia, Raul	228

K

Keaton, Diane	230
Keaton, Michael	232
Kelly, Gene	234
King, Larry	236
Kline, Kevin	238
Klugman, Jack	240

L

Lancaster, Burt	242
Lange, Jessica	244
Lansbury, Angela	246
Lee, Spike	248
Leigh, Jennifer Jason	250
Lemmon, Jack	252
Leno, Jay	254
Letterman, David	256
Loren, Sophia	258
Lowe, Rob	260

M

MacLaine, Shirley	262
Malkovich, John	264
Marshall, Penny	266
Martin, Steve	268
Matlin, Marlee	270
McMahon, Ed	272
Midler, Bette	274
Mitchum, Robert	276

INTRODUCTION

When I embarked on this project eight long years ago, I did so to satisfy my own lifelong curiosity about the personal as well as the professional side of some of my favorite stars. I wanted to get behind the lights, make-up and sound bites and discover their individual characters—their human side. They weren't born the stars they are today, so I wanted to find out if all these celebrated, special people had some sort of common denominator. I'd have to say that if such a thing does exist, I didn't find it. But, after talking with many of them and accumulating tons of research files, a picture did begin to emerge as I discovered that their childhoods usually yielded fascinating insights into what drove them to follow the yellow brick road to fame and accomplishment.

This book is full of personal anecdotes and revelations detailing how these determined individuals marched to the beat of their own drummers and overcame such everyday human foibles as lack of self-confidence and loneliness. The stories about surviving their struggle to the top—their joy and despair—made me feel like I was right there beside them every step of the way.

In every single instance, the celebrities have shared some insight into their innermost private thoughts and feelings on every aspect of family life (and strife), career setbacks, drugs, sex, future hopes and dreams. Some of the secrets they reveal are poignant; some are totally unexpected. None of it is gossip. Every word comes from interviews with the celebrities themselves, their representatives and their closest friends, making this information even more fun.

On a lighter note, even glamorous movie stars have hobbies, but I was tickled by some of the *un*glamorous ways our screen idols fill their time away from lights and cameras.

Great thanks are extended to the celebrities and their handlers for all their kind cooperation, and to the Beverly Hills Library and the Academy of Motion Pictures Arts and Sciences in Beverly Hills for opening their files and reference documents to us.

To

the real "stars" in my life

my children

Emily and Drew

and

my husband

Rick

INTIMATE INFORMATION ON
THE WORLD'S MOST POPULAR
MOVIE & TELEVISION STARS

ALAN ALDA

REAL NAME: Alphonse D'Abruzzo
DATE OF BIRTH: January 28, 1936
PLACE OF BIRTH: New York, New York

EYE COLOR: Brown   HAIR COLOR: Dark brown
HEIGHT: 6'2"   WEIGHT: 170

Whenever you see or hear the name Alan Alda, you get that warm, fuzzy, nice-guy feeling. That's exactly what he is—but Alan's also a painfully sensitive, "new age" man committed to women's rights. In 1976, President Jimmy Carter appointed him to the Commission Overseeing International Women's Year. Explaining his image, he says, "I deliberately make lighthearted movies; I don't want my industrial-strength thinking to show." It was this intensity that shone through Alda's writing, directing and acting on the TV version of *M*A*S*H* and helped make it such a success.

After recovering from a childhood bout with polio, Alan spent his free time hanging around the theater wherever his father, actor Robert Alda, was performing. He made his first appearance on stage at age sixteen in summer stock, and later, during his junior year at Fordham University, toured Europe in performances with his father on the stage and on television. After graduating with a degree in English, Alan joined the Second City comedy troupe and the political satire comedy show *That Was The Week That Was*.

This creative venue in social commentary has always been Alda's forte and was the basis for his decision to accept the role of Hawkeye Pierce in *M*A*S*H*. Obtaining a commitment from the creator of the show that it would be more than "one of those hijinks-at-the-bat-tlefront routines," Alan saw the series as a chance to make a pro-human statement unique to standard TV fare. "The show's bias is that people count," he explains. "We joke a lot, and clown around... but we also show the audience that people are getting hurt, mangled and killed. This isn't just a bunch of guys and gals acting crazy for laughs. What they're doing is constantly fighting... the insanity of

war as best they can." Alan was able to prove his own brilliant writing talent on *M*A*S*H* and in several films such as *The Seduction of Joe Tynan*, *The Four Seasons*, *A New Life* and *Betsy's Wedding*, the latter three of which he also directed. Alda's most recent screen appearance was in Woody Allen's 1993 film, *Manhattan Murder Mystery*.

Happily married for 36 years, Alda attributes the success of his marriage to making "sex, love and marriage" the subjects dearest to his heart. It probably helped, too, that during the eleven grueling years of filming *M*A*S*H* in Hollywood, he commuted every weekend to his home and family in New Jersey. After raising three daughters, he feels like he can relax a bit now: "When you see your kids thrive, see them become happy and independent women, you feel as if you've graduated from parent school."

WOODY ALLEN

REAL NAME: Allen Stewart Konigsberg
DATE OF BIRTH: December 1, 1935
PLACE OF BIRTH: Brooklyn, New York

EYE COLOR: Brown   HAIR COLOR: Reddish brown
HEIGHT: 5'6"   WEIGHT: 120

Woody Allen is truly an icon of urban angst. His neuroses, which have been well tended by a psychiatrist for 30 years, are what make him so endearing. He claims, for example, that he rarely goes to bed at night without dwelling on death; that he has an inordinate fear of woodchucks; that he takes his temperature every two hours during the course of a day; and that he considers concentration camps a metaphor for life.

Woody and his sister were raised in a repressive Jewish household where, he says, "The basic values were God and carpeting." As a child, he hated school and preferred to hide out in his room reading comic books, following baseball, playing the clarinet and perfecting sleight-of-hand tricks. At age fifteen, he began sending jokes to newspaper columnists under the name Woody Allen and quickly got his

first job writing one-liners for a press agent. After graduation from high school, he began writing for Sid Caesar's *Your Show of Shows* and by 1961 was performing the same chores for *The Garry Moore Show*, a job he left to become a stand-up comic. Using his childhood in Brooklyn as the basis of his routine, Woody made the rounds of Greenwich Village clubs. In 1964, when he was hired to write the screenplay for *What's New, Pussycat?*, Woody fell in love with films and began writing, directing and starring in such promising pictures as *Bananas* and *Everything You Always Wanted to Know About Sex But Were Afraid to Ask*.

Woody's early efforts were pure comedies, without the thoughtfulness of his later efforts. That truly didn't come until 1977 with *Annie Hall*, a semiautobiographical relationship piece that garnered four Academy Awards. Perhaps out of habit, he cast his then love interest, Diane Keaton, in the leading-lady role, as he would do in five other films. His second wife (his first marriage, to a teacher, ended in 1959), Louise Lasser, had appeared in two of his early films. And after their romance began in 1980, Mia Farrow has co-starred in almost a dozen Allen films, including *Hannah and Her Sisters* and *Husbands and Wives*. She was replaced by Diane Keaton in Woody's most recent film, *Manhattan Murder Mystery*, when their differences over their breakup and children came to a head.

Hardly one-dimensional, Woody has recorded comedy records, authored several best-selling books and can be seen every Monday night playing his clarinet at Michael's Pub in Manhattan as a member of a semipro jazz band. Woody takes these weekly gigs very seriously. In 1978, when he won an Oscar for *Annie Hall*, he was absent from the ceremony because it was on a Monday night.

Notoriously protective of his private life, Woody has lately had to bear intense public scrutiny of his love affair with Mia's youthful adopted daughter and the resulting vicious custody battle over their biological son, Satchel, and adopted daughter, Dylan. The case was resolved in the spring of 1993, with Woody losing custody but retaining supervised visitation privileges.

Explaining his life philosophy, Woody says, "If you obsess about the big things, you are impotent and frightened, because there's nothing you can do about aging and death. But the little things you can spend days obsessing about, such as a good punch line for the third act. And this is a nice problem to obsess over."

KIRSTIE ALLEY

REAL NAME: Kirstie Alley
DATE OF BIRTH: January 12, 1955
PLACE OF BIRTH: Wichita, Kansas

EYE COLOR: Green   HAIR COLOR: Brown
HEIGHT: 5'7"   WEIGHT: 130

Overnight success? Well, almost. In 1980, Kirstie Alley left Wichita with interior design experience and $2,000 in her pocket. She was giving herself one year to make it as an actress. A year later she landed the role of Spock's Vulcan protégée in *Star Trek II: The Wrath of Khan*.

Kirstie has no complaints about her childhood; it was a comfortable, happy existence with two natural parents and a brother and sister. Not that she was an angel: In her teens she favored wild biker guys, which caused a bit of friction with her mom. Later, at the University of Kansas, she slid into a cocaine habit that continued for several years until the day in 1980 when her sister came for a visit with her children and Kirstie was so coked out she was incoherent. That was the bottom for her. She cleaned herself up and quit her decorating job: "I had spent a fortune decorating people's homes and I didn't even know what I was doing." She decided Los Angeles and

acting would be a good change of venue.

Kirstie was able to support herself by decorating while she made the usual rounds of agents and auditions. Sadly, on the day of her successful audition for *Star Trek II*, her parents were hit by a drunk driver. By the time she arrived in Wichita, her father was in intensive care, and her mother was dead. The tragedy was compounded by the fact that she and her mother had had a rocky relationship because Kirstie had been a bit of a rebel. "The biggest regret in my life," she says, "is that my mother never got to see me be successful. To her, I was always doing things backwards."

After her big break in *Star Trek II*, Kirstie continued working steadily, appearing in the miniseries *North and South*, as Gloria Steinem in the TV movie *A Bunny's Tale*, and in some stage work. When she was cast as Rebecca to replace Shelley Long on *Cheers* in 1987, the producers planned to capitalize on her exotic, sultry looks and introduce her as a tough sophisticate who could bulldoze right over the lecherous Sam Malone (Ted Danson). They weren't aware of Kirstie's zany personality. The first day she reported to the set, she wore a blond wig and demure dress a la Shelley's Diane. From that moment on, Rebecca evolved out of Kirstie's own uniquely offbeat comedic talent. Since joining the cast of *Cheers*, she's carved out a movie career for herself with films such as *Look Who's Talking, Look Who's Talking Too* and *Sibling Rivalry*. She will star again in the further sequel *Look Who's Talking Now*. Best of all, she's reaped the rewards of a little-known star perk: KISSING. She confesses: "I always knew that if you were going to be married and have only one man for the rest of your life, you'd better have a career where it's legal to smooch with other guys. I think that's why I became interested in acting—because I wanted to make out with men. I'm not kidding."

Not to worry: She and actor Parker Stevenson have been happily married since 1983 and adopted a baby boy in 1992. They live in Al Jolson's 30-room mansion along with their minizoo of 40 animals. Kirstie feels she should give something back to a life that's been good to her: She is a staunch environmentalist with the Earth Communications Office and is a spokesperson for Narconon Chiloco, a Scientology drug rehabilitation program.

POSTSCRIPT: According to Kirstie, "Ted Danson's a very good kisser. John Travolta is one of the major kissers."

ALAN ARKIN

REAL NAME: Alan Wolf Arkin
DATE OF BIRTH: March 26, 1934
PLACE OF BIRTH: New York, New York

EYE COLOR: Brown   HAIR COLOR: Brown
HEIGHT: 5'6"   WEIGHT: 150

When he was five, says Alan Arkin, "I was in my Brooklyn back-yard with some cousins, and I said, 'Let's play circus. I'll be every-thing.' " That's exactly how Alan the chameleon still thinks, acts and lives. In fact, if you were to say to him, "Alan, you're not yourself today," he'd probably say, "Thank you!"

"Being everything" started when he was a little boy and all of his childless aunts, uncles and grandparents would assemble each Sunday at the Arkin home to hear little Alan recite, sing and per-form. He was the oldest of three children born to a father who was a frustrated artist making a living as a drafting instructor and a moth-er who taught emotionally disturbed children. When he was seven, he announced he would be a great actor when he grew up.

After slogging through a detested high school and college experi-ence, taking his degree from Bennington College, Arkin joined a band called The Tarriers before joining the Compass Theater in St. Louis. In the early '60s, he graduated to the Chicago branch of the Second City improvisational comedy group in both Chicago and New York. That led to his first Broadway role in *Enter Laughing*, for which Arkin won a Tony. In full chameleon regalia, he quickly pro-ceeded to garner accomplishments in a wide spectrum of roles on stage and in film. For his screen debut in *The Russians Are Coming, The Russians Are Coming*, he was honored with a best actor Oscar nomination and a Golden Globe award. Other acclaimed films are *Wait Until Dark*, *The Heart Is a Lonely Hunter*, *Catch-22* and *Glengarry Glen Ross*.

Moody by nature, Alan is unable to perform unless he can impro-vise scenes in which he believes he is the character. "Acting," he says, "used to be a kind of therapy for me. It grew out of not being terribly happy with who I was and always trying to be someone else. But to a degree I know who I am now." After years of analysis—and tutoring by a yogi/guru—he has "found himself" through other creative outlets, mainly writing. He has produced four books, but he finds it a difficult calling, sometimes bordering on self-flagellation. "Believe me," he sighs, "I'm happier not writing. The writing process is one of

constantly giving up." Always exploring new avenues, he has taught himself to play the flute, fife and recorder, but his real passion is photography. He has been married since 1964 to author/actress Barbara Dana, with whom he has a son, Tony. Adam, his son from a previous marriage, is also an actor, appearing most recently in a recurring role on the show *Northern Exposure*.

ROSEANNE ARNOLD

REAL NAME: Roseanne Barr
DATE OF BIRTH: November 3, 1953
PLACE OF BIRTH: Salt Lake City, Utah

EYE COLOR: Brown   HAIR COLOR: Brown
HEIGHT: 5'4"   WEIGHT: 155

"I hope to God I've been through the hardest part of my life," Roseanne Arnold has said many times. Considering what she's already gone through, let's hope she's right.

Roseanne was born to Jewish parents in a city that is 60 percent Mormon. While her father sold religious icons door to door, her mother vacillated between Judaism and Mormonism: One week they went to temple and the next to church. Always a little out of step with her family and her hometown, Roseanne felt she was put on this earth to say what she thought, no matter what the consequences. She is now convinced that the physical and sexual abuse she endured as a young girl paved the way for many of her destructive lifestyle and marriage choices.

Hit by a car when she was sixteen, she experienced a near-death, out-of-body experience that changed her relationship with life. She went from being just a wisecracking clown to an "I'm going to do everything *my* way" teenager. According to Roseanne, when her behavior became more belligerent, her mother had her committed to a state mental hospital populated mostly by the criminally insane. Within a few months of her release, she became pregnant during her very first voluntary sexual encounter at the age of eighteen, and Roseanne's parents forced her to give up her baby girl for adoption. That was it for Roseanne; she never returned to Utah. She settled in a commune in Georgetown, Colorado, where she was finally in her element. Among the hippies, she was free to be herself, and nobody cared. Needing work, she took a job waitressing in a Nineteenth Century saloon where the clientele was rough, but Roseanne's stinging wit was rougher.

Between places to live, she met Bill Pentland while he was working as a night clerk in a motel, and soon they were married. She was

already formulating a comedy act out of her painful childhood, but Roseanne took a detour through motherhood and a life of still more unhappiness. Living in a tiny trailer, she had three babies within three years, making so little money that she had to make her children's clothes out of old pillowcases. Determined to rediscover the grit that had taken her this far, she resurrected her comedy career and started showing up on amateur nights anywhere there was stand-up comedy. Her lowest career point came one night in a college town when the whole room booed and badgered her off the stage; they didn't like her bitter, blue-collar housewife material, which was particularly antagonistic toward men. Afterward, she waited at the door and literally cursed each person as they exited past her. Since that time, she says she fears no audience, nor does she fear bombing out of any performance.

Inch by inch, she worked her way to Los Angeles and finally onto *The Tonight Show Starring Johnny Carson.* That one successful segment in 1985 brought her an eighteen-week stint opening for Julio Iglesias and then her own HBO special. Since the late '80s, she has starred in the number-one hit show on television, *Roseanne.* In 1989, Roseanne's autobiography, *My Life As a Woman,* detailed her struggle for happiness and success.

Many are put off by her brassy, in-your-face personality, but Roseanne is thrilled to be considered an "everywoman." "It's so easy; you just point the camera at real life, and it happens," she has said. She's happily married to Tom Arnold, whom she met while touring the stand-up circuit. After reversing a tubal ligation, she and Tom are doing everything medically possible to conceive a child of their own.

ROSANNA ARQUETTE

REAL NAME: Rosanna Arquette
DATE OF BIRTH: August 10, 1959
PLACE OF BIRTH: New York, New York

EYE COLOR: Blue   HAIR COLOR: Blond
HEIGHT: 5'6"   WEIGHT: 116

Rosanna Arquette has lived a wild life most teens would envy: living for a year with her family in a nudist colony, then on a commune with complete freedom to experiment with sex, drugs and rock 'n' roll. Explaining why she isn't messed up today, she says, "I knew what an orgasm was pretty early on; there just wasn't anything hidden from me. It's not as if my parents told me to take acid or anything. I mean when you go through your drug phase at thirteen, you don't feel as if you've missed out on anything."

Arquette came by her acting talent and lifestyle the parental way. Her grandfather, Cliff, created the radio and TV character Charlie Weaver and her father, Lewis, was an original member of the radical improv group The Committee. Both her parents were politically active, and Rosanna spent the early years of her life traveling around the country attending peace rallies with her four younger siblings. The family finally settled down on an artist's commune in Front Royal, Virginia, but Rosanna found the laid-back atmosphere too confining. When she was fifteen, she hitchhiked across country and by seventeen was living on her own in Los Angeles. Looking back on this impetuous journey, she says, "You know how it is when you're a crazy kid. No matter how hip your parents are, they're not hip enough. Every kid has to rebel against their parents."

Once landing in L.A. she began doing local theater and was acting in *The Metamorphosis* when she was discovered by a Hollywood casting director. Before long she had her first role in the TV version of *Harvest Home*. After playing Babs the hitchhiker in Blake Edwards' *S.O.B.*, Arquette got her breakthrough role as Nicole, Gary Gilmore's girlfriend in the miniseries *The Executioner's Song*. With that, her career took off, and she did two movies back to back: *Desperately Seeking Susan* and *After Hours*.

Rosanna married James Howard in 1986, but they separated two years later. Like many actresses, Arquette has appeared in *Playboy*, gracing the cover in September of 1990. She is also widely known to have been the inspiration for the hit song by Toto entitled "Rosanna," written by a member after an unrequited romance.

DAN AYKROYD

REAL NAME: Daniel Edward Aykroyd
DATE OF BIRTH: July 1, 1952
PLACE OF BIRTH: Ottawa, Ontario, Canada

EYE COLOR: Brown   HAIR COLOR: Brown
HEIGHT: 6'3"   WEIGHT: 220

For someone with a strict Catholic, middle-class upbringing, Dan Aykroyd has some pretty unusual hobbies. He goes out on crime-fighting raids with cops, riding shotgun in patrol cars; he collects police badges; and from a passionate interest in the paranormal (ghosts to us), he's amassed an extraordinary library on spectral research. His ultimate goal is to personally witness a real apparition.

He's getting close: "I once saw what could be termed ectoplasmic light, and that scared the hell out of me."

Perhaps his fetishes are genetic: His father was a Royal Canadian Mountie who subscribed to psychic research journals, and his grandparents held séances. One of two sons, Dan was a rebellious kid from the age of eight. When Dan was in the ninth grade, his father sent him to a strict Catholic seminary school, but he switched to a regular Catholic boys' school after a year while he held part-time jobs, including one as railway freight unloader. Soon he was on his way to the life of a professional academic, studying psychology, political science and criminal sociology at Carleton University in Ottawa. While there, in addition to his studies, he worked as a radio personality and was active in the school's drama guild. Fortunately for us, in 1972, at the age of twenty, the comedy bug bit Aykroyd, and he left school to join the Toronto branch of Second City.

He cut his comedy teeth with the troupe both in Toronto and Chicago for two years before being selected as one of the original cast members of *Saturday Night Live*. He stayed with the show as one of its most popular members until 1979, winning an Emmy award for his writing in the process. He and *SNL* buddy John Belushi then toured the country as The Blues Brothers, a semicomedic, semiserious music act whose album, *Briefcase Full of Blues*, won a Grammy and sold two and a half million copies. Aykroyd got his big break in the wacky film *1941* and continued to pursue acting, starring with Belushi in a movie version of the *The Blues Brothers* in 1980. It was from his desire to proselytize parapsychology that he wrote the megahit *Ghostbusters* (originally entitled Ghostmasters) as a vehicle for himself and Belushi. After Belushi's death from a drug overdose, Bill Murray stepped in and the film was a bona fide smash. Since then, Aykroyd has had continued success both as a writer and as a versatile actor with movies such as *Driving Miss Daisy*, *Ghostbusters II*, *Doctor Detroit* and *Trading Places*. In 1993, Dan starred in *Coneheads*, a movie spin-off of the popular *Saturday Night Live* skits. Lately, he has immersed himself in owning a string of old-time blues bars around the country in which the remaining Blues Brother delights in performing.

In between ghost busting and police raiding, he prefers to lead a quiet life with his actress wife, Donna Dixon, and their two baby girls in the Santa Monica hills.

ALEC BALDWIN

REAL NAME: Alexander Rae Baldwin III
DATE OF BIRTH: April 3, 1958
PLACE OF BIRTH: Massapequa, New York

EYE COLOR: Blue   HAIR COLOR: Dark brown
HEIGHT: 5'11"   WEIGHT: 175

Besides being known for his drop-dead blue eyes and Black Irish good looks, Alec Baldwin has acquired notoriety as a vociferously outspoken political animal. Before George Bush lost his reelection bid, Alec, in print, called him "a CIA mass murderer and carpetbagger who is owned by the oil companies." Much to the delight of the entertainment press, his willingness to share his strong views applies to show-business politics as well as governmental politics.

Of the six Baldwin children, Alec, the eldest, was the most imbued with his father's political and competitive drive. Alexander Jr. was a political science high school teacher and football coach who insisted that his children set goals and become accomplished. He also moved them into an expensive country club community that was above their economic means. "We really didn't belong there," Alec's sister remembers, "but my father was determined that we live there." Alec agrees: "I was like Monty Clift in *A Place in the Sun*. I was from the other side of the tracks, in a way." When Alec wasn't playing lacrosse and baseball, he was either making home movies or debating political issues within the family. Intending to enter law school and then run for public office, he enrolled in George Washington University. But after a bitter defeat for student body president in his third year—which Alec maintains was rigged—he switched to his other field of dreams: movies.

He was lifeguarding the summer before graduation from the acting program at NYU when a casting agent urged him to audition for a role on the soap opera *The Doctors*. He won the part. Following his stint there, he vacillated between Los Angeles and New York, television and stage. When Hollywood began beckoning him with minor roles in film after film, he made "the move." But acclaim and success in such hits as *Working Girl*, *The Hunt for Red October*, *Miami Blues*

and *Prelude to a Kiss* were slightly tainted for him because he felt like a pariah among the Hollywood bourgeoisie. "You see these old pigs out in Hollywood," he explains. "Go to L.A. and see the people who are behind the camera. Fat, ugly people. Their whole thing is money." With his background in politics, Alec was also accustomed to debating and influencing matters important to him, especially his films, and that labeled him as a loose cannon to some within the industry. His talent and popularity compelled studio brass to over-look his attitude, even when he butted heads with Disney over differences in *The Marrying Man*, which prompted his public pronounce-ment that Disney chief Jeffrey Katzenberg was "the eighth dwarf—Greedy." The fray may have been exacerbated by the fact that his leading lady was his then live-in love, now wife, Kim Basinger (reportedly a handful on the set herself).

While Alec and Hollywood were making up, he went back to his old stomping grounds in New York and resurrected *A Streetcar Named Desire* on Broadway. The other three Baldwin boys, William, Stephen and Daniel, are also blazing the trail to stardom, just a little more quietly.

ELLEN BARKIN

REAL NAME: Ellen Barkin
DATE OF BIRTH: April 16, 1954
PLACE OF BIRTH: Bronx, New York

EYE COLOR: Green   HAIR COLOR: Blond
HEIGHT: 5'4"   WEIGHT: 108

Ellen Barkin is what you could call a "slow starter." After studying acting for sixteen years, she had to be cajoled into her first audition by a director she happened to sit next to at the Ensemble Studio Theater. But once she got started, she went for the meatiest roles, including nude ones.

When asked about growing up, she'll tell you, "Happy childhood. No divorces." That was in a middle-class Bronx family, her father a chemical salesman, her mother a housewife. At fifteen, she entered New York's High School of the Performing Arts, where, during the three years she spent there, she was often passed over for roles because she wasn't considered pretty enough. While attending Hunter College, from which she double-majored in drama and ancient history, she waitressed to support herself. For the next seven years, she kept her day job and tried to summon the nerve to plunge into acting.

Once discovered, Barkin refused to give up waitressing in order to have the financial means to pick and choose the roles she really wanted. Her feelings on this are deeper than on seeking career success: "I'd hate to be in a movie that I didn't want to go see. I feel kind of responsible for not insulting people's intelligence." She began with appearances on the stage, in TV movies such as *Kent State* and on the soap opera *Search for Tomorrow*. Another of her choices has been to pursue parts that are different in every film, in order to avoid the typical typecasting pitfall. In *Diner* she was the downtrodden wife; in *Tender Mercies* she portrayed the feisty daughter; in *Desert Bloom* she played a promiscuous aunt; in *The Big Easy* she was a prim D.A.; and for *Harry and Son* she wore a pregnancy pillow on and off the set to get the walk just right. *Siesta* and *Sea of Love* involved some racy sex scenes. Her feelings on nudity are simple:

"You take your clothes off as an actress so you can't really cry 'Foul' when they show your breasts or whatever. Because if you don't want them to show your breasts, you don't take your shirt off." In 1991, Ellen kept her shirt on by playing a man in a woman's body in Blake Edwards' film *Switch*.

It was during the filming of *Siesta* that she met her husband, actor Gabriel Byrne, whom she wed in 1988. They take respite in their home in Ireland along with their two small children. In order to maintain her compact figure, Ellen works out daily whether filming or not. Home and family have cast a new angle on Ellen's choices now. "I care about what I do," she says. "But I think if someone told me I could never act again, I wouldn't blow my brains out or anything."

DREW BARRYMORE

Real Name: Drew Blyth Barrymore
Date of Birth: February 22, 1975
Place of Birth: Los Angeles, California

Eye Color: Blue   Hair Color: Blond
Height: 5'2"   Weight: 110

"My mother says I'm a drama queen," giggles Drew Barrymore. Her mother should know, having struggled with her only daughter through a childhood of alcohol, drugs and attempted suicide.

When actress Georgiana Drew wed vaudevillian Maurice Barrymore in 1867, they unknowingly launched a dynasty of talented but tragic people. Fifth in lineage, Drew's substance abuse problems are carrying on the family tradition. All of her forebears, including the incredibly talented and prolific Lionel, Ethel and John, died of drink and drugs. Feeling that he had failed to measure up to the "Barrymore acting tradition," her father, John Jr., was sinking into an alcoholic/drug quagmire before Drew was even born. Her Hungarian mother, Ildiko Jaid, left him while still pregnant and raised Drew by herself. She has seen her father only a handful of times in her life, and they were not pleasant. To her credit, Drew is charitable and forgiving when she speaks of him. "He had heavy, heavy problems for many, many years, but he's mellowed out lately." She also has a stepbrother named John Barrymore whom she has rarely seen or spoken to.

Drew made her acting debut at eleven months in a dog-food commercial. In 1982, at age seven, she burst into stardom as Gertie, *E.T.*'s earth friend. "All of a sudden it was like this earthquake," she recalls. "People wanted things from me and expected me to be so much older. It was very frightening." Being a celebrity also made Drew a Hollywood party commodity, and her mother unwittingly escorted her on these forays, where Drew cut her teeth on champagne. By age nine, she was a full-blown alcoholic; at ten, she was smoking pot; two years later she graduated to cocaine; and at the age of fourteen, she tried to kill herself with a kitchen knife. By this time, she had been in and out of rehab twice and strained her mother's

patience and sanity to the limit. Why did she mimic the destructive Barrymore lifestyle? Was it genetic? Drew doesn't take that cop-out. From the beginning, she says, "People in Hollywood would say, 'Oh no, what's this Barrymore kid like? I hope she's not like the rest of her family.' There's a lot of Barrymore baggage you have to carry around. But I put all that pressure on myself."

During the five years she spent in and out of hell, Drew still continued to show up on the set. She appeared in *Firestarter, Cat's Eye* and *See You in the Morning*. In 1990 she put her life's experience on paper in *Little Girl Lost*. Her dream goal has always been to play Lolita, and she says that she got her chance in *Poison Ivy* in 1992 in which she French-kisses actress Sara Gilbert. She played the scene with such enthusiasm that everyone was aghast. "I thought, Great! I really got into the shock value of it," she says. She's been receiving a lot of shock value ever since pictures of her frolicking nude in a swimming pool with other nude girls appeared in *Interview* magazine. Drew appeared in the short-lived TV show *2000 Malibu Road* and recently played the infamous Amy Fisher (in one of three productions) on the small screen. She is further expanding her professional repertoire as a model for the Guess? clothing line. "You know, when you become sober, you don't own a halo. You've just got to do the best that you can," she counsels. Drew is maintaining her sobriety on a daily basis and looking forward to a long career—and even longer life.

KIM BASINGER

REAL NAME: Kim Basinger
DATE OF BIRTH: December 8, 1953
PLACE OF BIRTH: Athens, Georgia

EYE COLOR: Blue   HAIR COLOR: Blond
HEIGHT: 5'8"   WEIGHT: 125

In conversation with Kim Basinger, the two words that repeatedly come up are "power" and the "plan." For the "power" to control her career she draws upon beauty, sexuality and raw talent. The "plan" is to have so many creative and business things going on outside of films that she can do whatever she wants.

Kim comes by her beauty and talent naturally. Her mother was a model/actress and her father a classically trained musician. Both forfeited show-business careers in order to raise their five children in a rural Georgia setting. As the middle child, Kim kept busy in ballet, gymnastics, scuba diving, piano and guitar. All the while she remained a withdrawn, detached child. But in order to overcome that shyness, her father encouraged her to enter the Junior Miss contest in her hometown of Athens, Georgia, which she won. After attending a couple of semesters at the University of Georgia, she set off for New York and the Ford Modeling Agency. She quickly became very successful but says she "never was a model, never felt like one," and developed a cruel mental condition known as agoraphobia, which causes paralyzing anxiety attacks when she's outside her own home. During those five years, even while she was making tons of money, Kim used to pray, "Oh, my God, help me to not be in this business forever."

So she threw her portfolio off the Brooklyn bridge and drove to Hollywood to audition for a part. In her first TV jobs as an actress, *Katie: Portrait of a Centerfold* and *From Here to Eternity*, she played a centerfold and a prostitute, respectively, and guested on *Charlie's Angels*. In 1983, during an actor's strike, she appeared in an eight-page *Playboy* spread, which her agent insisted would ruin her career. Quite the opposite. She was immediately offered roles in several feature films. Kim still considers *9 1/2 Weeks* her most challenging role:

"I became emotionally honest from A to Z. There is no part I can't play after that." But many who really know her will say that the soft-hearted, hick hairdresser she played in *Nadine* is really Kim Basinger. She certainly creates an intriguing dichotomy for audiences, wearing her insecurities like a badge of honor while deliberately seducing you with her hot sexuality, as in *Batman*.

Since Kim is terrified of personal appearances or interviews, it's rare that she's asked to comment on her relationships with men, particularly Prince and Alec Baldwin. But when asked, she sticks by her hard-and-fast rule to "never talk about him because he's not here in this room." She does acknowledge being married for six years to makeup artist Ron Britton, until 1988. And it was announced that in August 1993, she finally married Alec.

To continue carrying out the "plan," Kim is now concentrating on two things: finishing her rock album and developing her town of Braselton—which she purchased in 1989 for $20 million—into a tourist attraction. She is also working to come up with the $7.4 million she was unexpectedly ordered by the courts to pay Main Line Pictures after she was sued for dropping out of the movie *Boxing Helena*. This forced her to declare bankruptcy in May 1993.

KATHY BATES

REAL NAME: Kathleen Doyle Bates
DATE OF BIRTH: June 28, 1948
PLACE OF BIRTH: Memphis, Tennessee

EYE COLOR: Blue/green   HAIR COLOR: Brown
HEIGHT: 5'4"   WEIGHT: 145

When asked to describe herself, Kathy Bates says, "Persistent, intuitive, and open-minded—to the point of confusion." Hollywood uses a different adjective: heavy.

She has admittedly always had a weight problem. "I never was an ingenue. I've always just been a character actor." The youngest of three girls born to a mechanical engineer father and a homemaker mother, she was a very intense and serious teen who stayed home alone playing guitar and writing music and poetry that centered mostly on death. "It was awful," she says. "I didn't go out on one date." She went on to earn a Bachelor of Fine Arts degree as a drama major from Southern Methodist University in Dallas. A year later she went to New York armed only with $500 and her own burning ambition. She was able to support herself as a singing waitress in the Catskills and as a cashier in a gift shop until she got her first part in a Milos Forman play.

In 1983, she received a Tony nomination for a role in the Pulitzer Prize-winning play 'night, Mother, in which she played a suicidal daughter. But the role was so emotionally demanding that Kathy began to have trouble distinguishing between the play and her own life. She has since used that experience to prevent a recurrence, although it hasn't been easy for her. Her Obie-winning portrayal of Frankie in the off-Broadway play Frankie and Johnny in the Claire de Lune gave her the credentials to move to Hollywood and establish a film career. But Hollywood was blinded by the fact that Kathy didn't fit the slender, glamorous mold, and she was passed over for many parts she felt she deserved. So she had her bitter moments, but she forged ahead. "Women in the real world seem very different from women on the screen," she says. "As the people who make movies change, the movies themselves are going to change."

Kathy managed to land some small roles in decent films, but it was her frightening portrayal of psychopath Annie Wilkes in *Misery* that put her on the map. Once again, she became enveloped by her part. James Caan, who co-starred with her, said, "It didn't take much

acting for me sometimes, like where I think she's going to smash that thing on my head. She'd scare the hell out of you anyway." It obviously worked, because she received an Oscar for that role. She has since pursued diverse roles in *At Play in the Fields of the Lord*, *Fried Green Tomatoes* and *Used People*.

Kathy is engaged to her longtime boyfriend, actor Tony Campisi. Although no date has been set, she confides, "We've been together thirteen years, so I feel like it's OK."

WARREN BEATTY

REAL NAME: Henry Warren Beaty
DATE OF BIRTH: March 30, 1937
PLACE OF BIRTH: Richmond, Virginia

EYE COLOR: Blue/green   HAIR COLOR: Brown
HEIGHT: 6'   WEIGHT: 175

Sometimes it's hard to tell where Warren the actor/producer/ director and Warren the legendary Don Juan begin and end. You'd have to be blind to deny his steamy good looks, but more than 40 Oscar nominations garnered by his films can't be wrong either.

As a child, when the other kids taunted Warren because he preferred books and piano, his tomboyish sister, Shirley MacLaine, would come to his rescue. Both siblings were tutored in acting by their mother, Kathlyn, who was a drama coach and director. Their father was principal of the local high school and, according to Warren, often drunk and abusive at home. Although a shy youngster,

by the time he graduated from high school, Warren was a top-notch football player as well as president of his class. To everyone's surprise, he turned down football scholarships and enrolled at the School of Speech and Drama at Northwestern University in Evanston, Illinois. He explains his decision: "When I was young, I watched my mother direct theater, my father play the violin and my sister dance, but I never thought of getting up to perform. I was interested in the theater as a place to control, to manipulate."

That summer he went to Washington, D.C., and harangued the manager of the National Theater to give him any job at all that would afford him access to the backstage area. The man let him guard the backstage door to prevent rats from scurrying in. After one year at Northwestern, he dropped out and moved to New York, enrolling in classes with Stella Adler and supporting himself with odd jobs such as laying bricks, dishwashing, construction and playing in a piano bar. In 1959, after a brief appearance onstage in *A Loss of Roses*, playwright William Inge recommended him for the role of Bud Samper in the movie *Splendor in the Grass*. With an Oscar nomination and the film a success, Beatty achieved overnight stardom. He saw quickly that the "power to control and manipulate" was held by producers and directors; actors were really just the hired help. So in 1967 he both starred in and produced the hit *Bonnie and Clyde*, which won ten Oscar nominations. He continued writing, directing and producing with *Shampoo*, *Reds*, *Heaven Can Wait*, *Dick Tracy* and a few turkeys such as *Ishtar*. As fast as his career was ascending, his reputation as the sexiest, most sought-after lover by many of Hollywood's desirable leading ladies rose even faster. He explains his numerous involvements this way: "My mother was an actress of sorts—she taught acting. My mother's mother taught acting. My sister is an actress. I understand actresses; I love actresses."

Making *Bugsy*, in 1991, Warren finally fell really in love—the kind where two people make a baby and even get married. His co-star, Annette Bening, inspired him to say, "For me, the highest level of sexual excitement is in a monogamous relationship." They married in 1992 and have a daughter, Kathlyn. The two are even collaborating on a remake of the 1939 film *Love Affair*, already remade once as the teary classic *An Affair to Remember*. On marriage, Warren says, "I felt that if you didn't have the stamina to stay in it for life, then you really shouldn't make the promise." So far, so good.

ANNETTE BENING

REAL NAME: Annette Bening
DATE OF BIRTH: May 29, 1958
PLACE OF BIRTH: Topeka, Kansas

EYE COLOR: Blue   HAIR COLOR: Brown
HEIGHT: 5'7"   WEIGHT: 118

After all of Annette Bening's studying, hard work and impressive accomplishments on Broadway and in films, her most renowned (and fascinating) part has turned out to be as the wife of Warren Beatty and the mother of his child.

Her years from birth to present were remarkably smooth. "I'm afraid there's nothing in my background that is either twisted or amusing," she tells reporters. Her father sold insurance and taught Dale Carnegie courses while her stay-at-home mom sang in the church choir and raised the four Bening children. After moving to San Diego into a house by the sea at the age of seven, Annette did well in school and school plays. She was also athletic and excelled in scuba diving. In order to help finance her college education, she spent a full year as a cook on a charter boat prior to entering Mesa College. She wound up graduating with a degree in theater arts from San Francisco State University.

It was during her ensuing five-year stint at the American Conservatory Theater in San Francisco that she met and married actor Steve White in 1984. They spent a couple of years doing more regional theater work in Denver, but Annette found it too sparsely populated and "creepy," as she called it. She lit out for New York and within a year had earned a Tony nomination for her first Broadway performance in *Coastal Disturbances*. Modest to the point of self-effacement, Annette says, "There's nothing mysterious about me. I moved to New York, and the first play I did happened to go to Broadway. And that's when I got a Tony nomination, in 1986."

For the next couple of years she stayed busy with some TV work (*Miami Vice*) and more stage work. Then, from 1989 until 1991, she went on a filmmaking binge, cranking out solid roles in five serious pictures: *Valmont*, for director Milos Forman, *The Grifters* as the lovable slut, which earned her an Oscar nomination, *Guilty by Suspicion* alongside Robert De Niro, *Regarding Henry* as Harrison Ford's long-suffering wife, and *Bugsy* as the gangster's feisty mistress (and Beatty's real-life love interest). She also found time to throw in a couple of smaller, scene-stealing character parts in *The Great Outdoors* and *Postcards From the Edge*. Annette characteristically sloughs off high praise for her talent in a few words: "You try not to check yourself. You try to act with abandon and self-trust and go full bore with your choices." After a brief maternity sabbatical, she will return to the screen as Warren's co-star in *Love Affair*, a resurrection of the 1939 film of the same name that was remade with Cary Grant and Deborah Kerr as *An Affair to Remember* in 1957.

Getting to know Annette beyond the vital stats is like extracting teeth. When interviewers start touching on personal subjects, such as her divorce from Steve White in 1990, they are stonewalled with answers like, "I don't want to talk about it," "personal stuff" or "I wouldn't tell you that." Since it became public fodder that Beatty had retired his playboy mantle for fatherhood and marriage, they have both circled the wagons around their home and family. Relenting a little, though, she allows this summation of where she is now: "I used to see marriage as some kind of limitation, a concession. Now I'm trying to balance the personal instincts of being a woman, which have to do with having children, and supporting your partner and loving well, being there for them."

CANDICE BERGEN

REAL NAME: Candice Bergen
DATE OF BIRTH: May 9, 1946
PLACE OF BIRTH: Beverly Hills, California

EYE COLOR: Blue   HAIR COLOR: Blond
HEIGHT: 5'9"   WEIGHT: 120

"My dream, always, since I was a kid, fourteen or fifteen years old, was to do really broad, flat-out comedy. But it just would have been seen as the ambition of an insane person, in my body, to want to do that sort of thing," says Candice Bergen, alter ego of the wildly funny and successful Murphy Brown.

Growing up in Beverly Hills as the daughter of ventriloquist Edgar Bergen, Candice was overshadowed by her sibling rival, Charlie McCarthy, the dummy who dominated her father's comedy act. There were few photos of Candice as a child without Charlie in them—even in her crib. His bedroom was bigger and grander; he even had more clothes than she did. Young Candice grew up harboring an unrequited love for her father that she truly felt had been bestowed upon Charlie. She does enjoy, however, a close relationship

with her mother, Frances, and her brother.

At fourteen, Candice was sent to an exclusive Swiss finishing school, but her rebelliousness and partying didn't set well with her parents, so she was reeled back home to finish high school. She flunked out of the University of Pennsylvania after two years and became a successful Ford model in New York as well as a photojournalist. Her screen debut was as a lesbian in the 1966 film *The Group*. For the next few years she split her time between acting and photojournalism, appearing in movies such as *The Sand Pebbles* and traveling around the world on glamorous magazine assignments. In 1971, after her portrayal of a college coed in the movie *Carnal Knowledge*, she began to be taken seriously as an actress. Meanwhile, she was building a reputation as a photographer, getting such plum assignments as shooting the 1976 Democratic Convention.

Another event in 1976, turning 30, was a bit traumatic for Candice. She admitted to herself that she wasn't taking photojournalism, acting or life seriously, wasn't enjoying success and was going nowhere fast. In a deep depression, she entered psychoanalysis. "I just didn't like the way I was, and I knew if I didn't get on it, then I wouldn't like who I was for the rest of my life. So I just hunkered down." That meant one thing: examine and deal with the father/daughter relationship she never knew. For the next six years, she focused on therapy and translated it into her autobiography, *Knock Wood*. Today, she credits that experience with saving her life. In 1987, she aggressively campaigned for the title role in *Murphy Brown*, and she and the show have gone on to win both Emmys and accolades. The hand slap by Vice President Dan Quayle over Murphy's decision to have an illegitimate baby stole headlines from the 1992 presidential election.

Her husband, French director Louis Malle, and their six-year-old daughter, Chloe, are the ultimate priority for Candice now. Since she and Louis live on different continents and see each other only every few months, preserving their relationship requires a unique commitment. Having grown up herself under the roof of a star, Candice also works diligently to shield Chloe from the "fame trap" familiar to many children of show business. Candice has learned that values and family ties—not money or fame—are what really matter. "All of this could be over tomorrow, so I don't take anything for granted, but my family is what I love most in my life."

MARLON BRANDO

REAL NAME: Marlon "Bud" Brando Jr.
DATE OF BIRTH: April 3, 1924
PLACE OF BIRTH: Omaha, Nebraska

EYE COLOR: Blue   HAIR COLOR: Brown/white
HEIGHT: 5'8"   WEIGHT: 243

Brando's godlike stature as an actor and his overwhelming aura intimidate even the most seasoned veterans. Jack Nicholson warned one journalist before an interview that "whatever you imagine Brando is going to be, in person he is going to be a lot more."

With his mother an acting coach and actress, it's no wonder that Marlon and his two sisters chose to pursue the arts. Though he was a chemical salesman, his father was also involved in the more cultural aspects of life. Marlon says, "It used to bother me very much that they didn't act like other parents. They played undignified games, and Mother was always interested in the bizarre and anything exotic." During high school in Libertyville, Illinois, Marlon was a better athlete than student. When he wasn't on the field, he was in his room playing the drums; sometimes he even took them to school. Disciplinary problems forced his father to send him to the Shattuck Military Academy in Faribault, Minnesota, but the school did nothing to curb Marlon's rebellious ways, and he was expelled several weeks short of graduation. After a short stint as a tile fitter, Brando moved to New York to give acting a try.

Staying with his sister Frances, who was attending art school, Marlon took acting classes at the New School for Social Research. He made his professional debut on Broadway in 1944 in *I Remember Mama*. While studying with Stella Adler, he landed the coveted role of Stanley Kowalski on stage in *A Streetcar Named Desire*, and his brutishly sexual interpretation has yet to be matched. He went on to star in the film version in 1951 and four years later won his first Oscar for *On the Waterfront*.

During the '50s and '60s, Marlon ricocheted between notoriety and seclusion, periodically exiling himself to his private island near Tahiti. His work on the screen also became ambiguous; it was brilliant in one film and stilted in another. He received more Oscar nominations for *Viva Zapata!*, *Julius Caesar*, *Sayonara* and *Last Tango in Paris* before winning again for *The Godfather* in 1972. In an attempt to punish Hollywood for its indecent and inaccurate portrayal of American Indians, Marlon sent an Indian actress as an emissary to decline the award and make a speech on his behalf. It's his love/hate feelings about the movie business that confound his fans and fellow actors. He has said, "Acting has absolutely nothing to do with anything important, and what's the point of being an actor unless you can help some cause or other?"

Brando's most recent films include *A Dry White Season* (for which he received his eighth Academy Award nomination),*The Freshman* and *Christopher Columbus: The Discovery*.

He's the father of nine children—one, Christian, by first wife actress Anna Kashfi, and the others by various lovers. His second marriage, in 1960, lasted less than a year with no children. Until Brando was forced to immerse himself in son Christian's murder defense and daughter Cheyenne's emotional problems, he remained active in many political and human rights movements. At home, he still plays the drums to relax. He's currently working on his autobiography, but his plans for future films are unknown since he has proclaimed retirement many times. Marlon sums up his weariness with acting like this: "You have to upset yourself. Unless you do, you cannot act, and there comes a time when you don't want to anymore."

BEAU BRIDGES

REAL NAME: Lloyd Vernet Bridges III
DATE OF BIRTH: December 9, 1941
PLACE OF BIRTH: Los Angeles, California

EYE COLOR: Blue   HAIR COLOR: Brown
HEIGHT: 5'11"   WEIGHT: 175

With his father, Lloyd, and brother Jeff, Beau is one of the fabulous Bridges boys. Since Jeff has the more glamorous, high-profile career, it's ironic that Beau was the one who persuaded his younger brother to forget a music career and try acting.

Born in Los Angeles, the elder son of actor Lloyd Bridges, he was affectionately nicknamed Beau after Ashley Wilkes' son in the classic film *Gone With the Wind*. After making his film debut at age four in *The Red Pony* and his stage debut two years later in *All My Sons*, he regularly appeared in his father's TV series, *Sea Hunt*, and became a regular on *Ensign O'Toole*. Throughout school, however, acting was secondary to athletic pursuits such as baseball and basketball, and after graduation, he spent six months with the U.S. Coast Guard Reserve. He then studied creative arts at UCLA, where he played basketball as a freshman, and English at the University of Hawaii, where he surfed a lot of waves.

Eventually he dropped out of school to make his Broadway debut in a production of *Where's Daddy?* In 1967, he made his major motion picture debut in *The Incident* and from then on has enjoyed a successful career on the big screen in such films as *The Iron Triangle*, *The Hotel New Hampshire*, *The Other Side of the Mountain*, and the one that made him a star, *The Fabulous Baker Boys*. About that movie, Beau jokes, "The only way my brother agreed to play in a movie with me was if I shaved my hair and stuck out my stomach." In the 1991 HBO movie, *Without Warning: The James Brady Story*, he played presidential press secretary James Brady, who was shot during an assassination attempt on Ronald Reagan and has been confined to a wheelchair ever since. In fall 1993, Beau returns to television in the new series *Harts of the West* with his father.

Curiosity about how the three Bridges get along has always been a constant. "Everyone wants to know about competition between us," says Beau. But sharing the same profession creates a source of levity that seems to ease normal family tensions for them. Beau has been married to Wendy Peerce since 1984, and they have a son and daughter. His first marriage, which ended in 1978, produced two sons, the older of which was a black child whom they adopted. Beau says he is particularly proud of his adopted son, Casey—now a film student at USC—because "I didn't want a baby who looked exactly like me."

JEFF BRIDGES

REAL NAME: Jeff Bridges
DATE OF BIRTH: December 4, 1949
PLACE OF BIRTH: Los Angeles, California

EYE COLOR: Blue   HAIR COLOR: Dark blond
HEIGHT: 6'2"   WEIGHT: 175

Born into a show-business family that includes his father, Lloyd, and his brother Beau, it seems only natural that Jeff Bridges became an actor. Veteran film critic Pauline Kael describes him as "the most natural and least self-conscious screen actor who ever lived." Since he achieved stardom in 1971 with *The Last Picture Show*, he has appeared in more than two dozen films, including *The Fabulous Baker Boys*.

Jeff made his motion picture debut at the age of four months in *The Company She Keeps*. At eight, he appeared with his father in the TV series *Sea Hunt* and, at fourteen, toured New England with him in a summer stock presentation of *Anniversary Waltz*. Describing those wonder years, he recalls that he saw acting as "just a way to skip school and earn money to buy toys." A teen disciplinary problem, Jeff was sent to military school but later returned to Los Angeles, where he found gratification in writing music and accompanying himself on the guitar. When he was only sixteen, he sold two of his compositions to music producer Quincy Jones. After conquering a marijuana addiction, he graduated from University High School in Los Angeles and set off immediately for New York to study acting at the Berghoff Studios.

Following a short tour of duty in the Coast Guard reserves, he dove right into films and made his debut in 1970 in *Halls of Anger*. He won an Oscar nomination for his first co-starring role in 1971's *The Last Picture Show* and great reviews for his third, *Thunderbolt and Lightfoot*. Bridges' career has included the box office smashes *Against All Odds*, *Jagged Edge*, *Tucker* and *Starman* (for which he won another Oscar nomination), as well as *The Fabulous Baker Boys* (which also starred the other fabulous Bridges boy, Beau). In 1993, Jeff released two new films, *The Vanishing* and *American Heart*, and will complete another one, *Blown Away*, which also features his father.

When he's not acting, Jeff spends time with his wife, photographer Susan Gaston, and their three daughters on their 900-acre Montana ranch where he keeps a complete array of musical instruments for jams with old school buddies. He is a prolific songwriter, having composed more than 200 pieces. In addition to cofounding the End Hunger Network and serving other causes, he also finds time to enjoy painting, photography and surfing.

LLOYD BRIDGES

REAL NAME: Lloyd Vernet Bridges II
DATE OF BIRTH: January 15, 1913
PLACE OF BIRTH: San Leandro, California

EYE COLOR: Blue   HAIR COLOR: Gray
HEIGHT: 6'2"   WEIGHT: 180

Whether playing tennis or skimming the ocean bottom, it seems that Lloyd Bridges has sailed through his career and the fathering of two famous sons without a wrinkle. Anything but!

Before his parents' divorce when he was a small boy, he enjoyed unlimited free hours at his father's nickelodeon movie house where his desire to be in movies grew. But then his mom moved him and his sister to Sonoma where she struggled to support all of them by working in factories. When she remarried during his senior year in high school, he felt it was safe to leave home and began working his way through UCLA. While dabbling in school plays, he met Dorothy, and they married in 1938 in New York, where he was appearing in a play. As struggling newlyweds, he made records for the blind, and she sold gloves in Sears until a legitimate acting job for Lloyd came along. He still refers to those years as "the bottom of the barrel."

Within a few years, though, the Bridges were in Hollywood. Lloyd says, "I got every role anyone of any importance refused to do, but I didn't care." About 100 films later, he was rewarded in 1952 with a part in the four-Oscar western, *High Noon*. Then, in 1957, he won the bread and butter of his entire career: the TV series *Sea Hunt*. Since his retirement from that series, Lloyd has given memorable performances in movies such as *Home of the Brave, A Walk in the Sun, The Rainmaker* and *The Sound of Fury*. He's also turned out to be quite a comedian in *Airplane, Airplane II, Cousins* and *Hot Shots!* Never straying far from television, he's also done miniseries such as *Roots, East of Eden* and *The Blue and the Gray*. 1993 will see him complete filming *Blown Away*, which stars his son Jeff, and return in a new TV series called *Harts of the West* with his other son Beau.

Another beloved item on his list of credits includes being father of the fabulous Bridges boys, Jeff and Beau. He got their feet wet in acting as youngsters on his *Sea Hunt* series, and they took to it like ducks to water. But their relationship hasn't always been trouble-free. During the '70s, father and sons were alienated from each other, and it was painful for both parents. Enjoying a rich closeness with them now, Lloyd can look back and say, "We never forced our kids to do anything they didn't want to do. We handed out too much to them without exacting any sort of payment in return. I worked hard and battled my way to where I am. So did Dottie. And I can't imagine why we didn't inculcate our kids with the same spirit we had." Lloyd also has a married daughter, Cindy, who is not in show business.

At 80, Lloyd is in great shape. Far from retired, he still plays tennis in celebrity events and serves as spokesman for CARE while supporting environmental groups.

DAVID BRINKLEY

REAL NAME: David McClure Brinkley
DATE OF BIRTH: July 10, 1920
PLACE OF BIRTH: Wilmington, North Carolina

EYE COLOR: Brown   HAIR COLOR: Gray
HEIGHT: 6'2"   WEIGHT: 180

In his typically understated style, David Brinkley sums up an unparalleled 50-year career in journalism by saying he's "done the news longer than anyone on earth."

Descending from generations of physicians and Presbyterian preachers, David lost his father, a railroad employee, when he was eight. Much younger than his four siblings, he felt remote and lonely and turned to books for companionship. With characteristic humility, he says, "If there is anything worth knowing about me, it is that at the age of ten or twelve I became a semipermanent fixture at the Wilmington public library. I would go every day after school and stay till it closed … that's really where I learned what little I know." In high school, David applied himself only to English, because he "liked to write and was pretty good at it," and dropped out of high school in his senior year to write for the local newspaper. From 1940 to 1943, he served in the Army and was a traveling stringer for United Press International. To enhance his writing technique, he studied part-time at the University of North Carolina and Vanderbilt.

It was only by a fluke that NBC became David's home for the next four decades. CBS offered him a job writing radio broadcasts in their Washington office, but when he reported for work the first day, no one knew who he was or who had hired him. "So I walked across the street to NBC and got hired in five minutes," he recalls. After a few years on the typewriter for other broadcasters, he tried his wings on a novelty that no one was really watching: television. The first regular news program, hosted by John Cameron Swayze, was fifteen minutes long and included a brief report by a young journalist named David Brinkley. When television began to take off during the '50s, CBS came along with Walter Cronkite. In order to best its competitor in coverage of the Republican and Democratic national conventions of 1956, NBC paired Brinkley with Chet Huntley, whose solemn directness played off Brinkley's cadenced speech and wry sense of humor. The union was magic and replaced the NBC News as the *Huntley-Brinkley Report*, which aired for fourteen years.

When Huntley retired in 1970, Brinkley semiretired to become a commentator and traveling speaker, and in 1981 he left NBC to launch a new Sunday morning news and political discussion show for ABC News, *This Week With David Brinkley.*

While reading is still his favorite pastime, he also works off steam as a carpenter and enjoys the outdoors. He lives with his second wife of nine years and her grown daughter. Of his three sons from a previous marriage, one has gone into journalism and received a Pulitzer Prize, and one is a respected author and historian at Columbia University.

David Brinkley hasn't just survived in a business known for its high emotional mortality rate—he's thrived. The secret, he says, "is not to be terrified of it. Most of the news just isn't that important. In fact, very little of it is. And I think the proper attitude is to not be awed by it."

TOM BROKAW

REAL NAME: Thomas John Brokaw
DATE OF BIRTH: February 6, 1940
PLACE OF BIRTH: Webster, South Dakota

EYE COLOR: Brown   HAIR COLOR: Brown
HEIGHT: 6'   WEIGHT: 165

The son of an Army Corps of Engineers foreman and a housewife, Tom Brokaw says that growing up in Yankton, South Dakota, "There is so little around you intellectually that you reach out for broader sources of material. I was known as the town talker. I was always involved in whatever arguments were going, agitating things constantly, always had an opinion on everything."

Originally intending to become a lawyer, he changed his mind because of his admiration for the hosts of the *Huntley-Brinkley Report*, Chet Huntley and David Brinkley. At fifteen, he began his career as a newsman with an after school job as an announcer at a local radio station. He was also active in student politics in high school and was a three-sport letterman. After graduation, he spent a short stint at the University of Iowa and then transferred to the University of South Dakota, working his way through school as a reporter. Tom got his degree in 1962 and took a job as a reporter and morning news editor at a station in Omaha, Nebraska. Three years later, he moved to Atlanta, working as a news anchor and contributing stories on the Atlanta civil rights scene to the *Huntley-Brinkley Report*. Next came a seven-year run in Los Angeles with KNBC-TV that ended in 1973 when Brokaw was sent to Washington to cover the Capitol for NBC even though it meant a pay cut. A self-confessed "news junkie," he stayed in Washington during the Watergate scandals. Recalling the controversy of the period, he said, "They called it adversary journalism, but adversary is too weak a word. It reached the heights of hostility, and I'm not sure that either side—the press or the President—was well served." He took over as host of the *Today* show in 1976, a position he held until being made anchor of the *NBC Nightly News* in 1982. Many media critics believe that Brokaw's success is owed to his penchant for extracting the most

information out of hard-news interviews. "The best interviews are those that leave people with a sense that they have learned something," he says.

A member of the Sierra Club and a jazz devotee, Brokaw maintains his youthful physique as a "sports nut" through a variety of activities, foremost among them skiing, tennis and jogging. He now makes his home in New York with his three daughters and his wife since 1962, former Miss South Dakota, Meredith Auld. A one-time English teacher, she currently owns a toy shop called Penny Whistle in Manhattan.

CHARLES BRONSON

REAL NAME: Charles Buchinsky
DATE OF BIRTH: November 3, 1920
PLACE OF BIRTH: Ehrenfeld, Pennsylvania

EYE COLOR: Brown   HAIR COLOR: Dark brown
HEIGHT: 5'11"   WEIGHT: 165

The star of the violent *Death Wish* films, Charles Bronson is one of the action adventure genre's most respected stars. And although Bronson will go down in American film history primarily as a tough guy who blew away legions of bad guys, he is a gentle soul who has endured poverty and death much of his life.

Born in a Pennsylvania mining town to Russian-Lithuanian immigrants, Bronson grew up the eleventh child of fifteen in a ramshackle house a few feet from the coal mining tracks in Scooptown. Describing the harsh living conditions in that hard-luck town, he has said it was a place "where you had nothing to lose because you'd already lost it all." His father's death when Charles was ten left the family more destitute than it already was. As one of the youngest, his only clothes were hand-me-downs, but worse, what he received came from his immediately older sisters, and he went to school many times in dresses. At sixteen, he joined his brothers in the mines, where he was paid 10 cents for every ton of coal he dug. Drafted into the U.S. Army at twenty, he served for three years. Determined never to return to the mines, he then embarked on a string of odd jobs as onion picker, cook and bricklayer. It was in 1948, while working in Atlantic City, that Bronson became interested in acting and joined the Philadelphia Play and Players Troupe. After a marriage to a co-performer brought two children and ended in divorce, he moved to California to study speech and dialogue at the Pasadena Playhouse.

His first role was *You're In the Navy Now* with Gary Cooper in 1951, and he spent the rest of the decade playing supporting roles in a long series of films. He worked even more in the '60s, making an indelible impression as a featured player in such films as *The Magnificent Seven*, *The Dirty Dozen* and *The Great Escape*. Unhappy, however, with being typecast as a tough character actor,

Bronson left the United States and worked in Europe for several years. With films like *Rider in the Rain*, he became popular everywhere except the United States and in 1972 was voted the biggest box office star in the world. He didn't become a true star in America until *Death Wish* in 1974. Although he still often plays dark, ethnic types, Bronson has nurtured a career based as much on his gentle sexual mystique as his formidable physicality.

An event that finally brought him happiness was his marriage in 1969 to actress Jill Ireland, and they had a daughter in 1971. When Jill died of cancer in 1990, Charles went into seclusion for a year. While making a TV movie in 1991, he explained his return to work: "A strong man doesn't allow himself to break down. If a man can't withstand what's happened to his life in a strong way, if he breaks down, that, to me, is a little wimpy." Charles maintains homes in Bel Air and Vermont and shuns a "Hollywood" social life. Instead, he paints and keeps fit by working out on the punching bag.

MEL BROOKS

REAL NAME: Melvin Kaminsky
DATE OF BIRTH: June 28, 1926
PLACE OF BIRTH: Brooklyn, New York

EYE COLOR: Brown   HAIR COLOR: Gray
HEIGHT: 5'4"   WEIGHT: 146

One either loves or hates Mel Brooks' sense of humor. *The New York Times* has called him "America's current patron saint of going too far."

The roots of his outrageous sense of humor are in a mostly Jewish section of Brooklyn, then called Williamsburg. The grandson of Russian Jewish immigrants, he lost his father when he was only two years old, and although he was adored by his mother and older brothers, Mel grew up feeling deserted by his father. "I think that, unconsciously, there's an outrage there. I may be angry at God, or at the world, for that," he says. "And I'm sure a lot of my comedy is based on anger and hostility. Growing up in Williamsburg, I learned to clothe it in comedy to spare myself problems—like a punch in the face."

Mel starting doing impressions as a child to entertain his mother, and spent many hours watching plays and vaudeville acts on Broadway. Early on, Mel wanted to become either a pilot or a scientist, until a neighborhood kid named Buddy Rich taught him to play the drums, and Mel began making money as a drummer after school and during the summer. After high school, he spent one year at Boston College and then joined the Army, where he participated in the infamous Battle of the Bulge in 1944. After his discharge, he took the name Mel Brooks and supported himself as a drummer and comedian in the Catskills borscht belt. There he met Sid Caesar, who, in 1949, hired him as a writer for his show, *Broadway Review*, and a year later for *Your Show of Shows*, which ran for eight years as one of the most popular comedies on television. For a year and a half after it went off the air, Brooks' career stalled until he resurfaced on a series of comedy albums with Carl Reiner called *The 2,000-Year-Old Man*. The two manic comics made three albums in all and were so successful that Brooks was hired to do commercials as the 2,500-Year-Old Brewmaster for Ballantine Beer. In 1965, Brooks teamed with Buck Henry to create the smash TV spy spoof *Get Smart*. He then went on to write and direct his first feature three years later, *The Producers*, which won him an Academy Award for best original screenplay. Since then, he has produced and directed a string of comedy classics that include *Blazing Saddles*, *Young Frankenstein*, *Silent Movie* and *High Anxiety* as well as these acclaimed works of drama: *The Elephant Man*, *Frances* and *The Fly*. 1993 saw him release the spoof *Robin Hood: Men in Tights*.

Mel's marriage to actress Anne Bancroft in 1964 gave them a son in 1972, and he has three children from his earlier marriage to Florence Baum.

DELTA BURKE

REAL NAME: Delta Ramona Leah Burke
DATE OF BIRTH: July 30, 1956
PLACE OF BIRTH: Orlando, Florida

EYE COLOR: Blue   HAIR COLOR: Dark brown
HEIGHT: 5'5 1/2"   WEIGHT: 150

In recent years, Delta Burke, who shot to stardom as Suzanne Sugarbaker on *Designing Women*, has gotten almost as much publicity because of the fluctuations in her weight as she has for her success as an actress.

Raised in Florida by her mother and adoptive father, Delta has never met her real father. She began taking modeling classes at the age of twelve, and began entering and winning beauty pageants while still in high school. Her first title was as Miss Flame for the local fire department. She followed up that win with more than a dozen pageant victories, including Miss VFW Post 8207 and Miss All-American Girl. At seventeen, she won the 1974 Miss Florida Pageant and embarked on a statewide tour during which she had a terrifying experience. While relaxing beside a hotel pool, a man began taunting her with threats that he was going to kill her. When she fled to the safety of her room, he followed and physically accosted her. Her screams brought help, but she was left with unshakable fears of all men. Traumatized, she gave up modeling and fled to England with the scholarship money she'd won and spent the next two years taking acting lessons.

After returning to the United States, she moved to Hollywood with her grandmother and began auditioning for roles. Within a year, she had appeared in the TV movies *Charleston* and *A Last Cry for Help* as well as an HBO production, *The Seeker*. She then joined the HBO comedy series *First and Ten*, playing the owner of a football team. While there, Linda Bloodworth-Thomason, with whom Burke had worked on the TV series *Filthy Rich*, offered her the part of Suzanne Sugarbaker on her new sitcom, *Designing Women*. Burke grabbed it and enjoyed wide popularity until feuding with the producers over her creative contributions escalated.

Delta felt slighted on the show despite her star status and began gaining weight, to the dismay of the producers. Both parties began suing each other and Delta gained more weight. She thought her weight gain enhanced her character and told Barbara Walters in an interview that "I was fat—and the character worked." Press coverage of the battle over her weight (she at one time reached 210 pounds) led indirectly to her Emmy nomination for the *Designing Women* episode *They Shoot Fat Women, Don't They?*, which was written by the show's producers in response to the enormous media coverage. As the infighting reached a crescendo in the press, she finally left the show after the 1990-91 season to the relief of all involved. In 1992, she went blond and became the producer of her own sitcom, *Delta*. After it went off the air in 1993, she reconciled with Linda Bloodworth-Thomason and the two are planning to work together again in the near future.

Burke married actor Gerald McRaney in 1989 and, with him, produced the TV movie *Love and Curses and All That Jazz*.

CAROL BURNETT

REAL NAME: Carol Creighton Burnett
DATE OF BIRTH: April 26, 1933
PLACE OF BIRTH: San Antonio, Texas

EYE COLOR: Brown   HAIR COLOR: Reddish brown
HEIGHT: 5'7"   WEIGHT: 112

"I never learned anything from success. Success is whipped cream," said Carol recently. "I have always grown from my problems and challenges, from the things that don't work out. That's when I've really learned."

She's had plenty of opportunities to learn, beginning in earliest childhood, when both parents were alcoholics, on welfare and separated half the time. When they worked, her father was a movie theater manager and her mother wrote publicity releases. After they divorced in 1939, Carol, their only child, went to live with her maternal grandmother in a one-room apartment in Hollywood down the hall from her mother. In 1944, Carol's mom gave birth out of wedlock to another daughter, whom Carol and her grandmother took in to raise. To escape their sad circumstances, the three went to a movie

every day; then Carol would come home and act out scenes for friends. "In those movies," she explains, "there were always happy endings. The bad guy got his comeuppance, the poor person made it from rags to riches. That was drummed into me. So why shouldn't I have a happy ending?"

At Hollywood High School, she edited the school newspaper and had hopes of becoming either a journalist or a playwright. After receiving a scholarship to UCLA, Carol studied journalism for a while, but when forced to act during a playwriting class, she turned her sights toward acting. During her junior year, Carol performed at a society party in San Diego along with other students and so impressed one of the guests that he staked her and her actor boyfriend, Don Saroyan, $2,000 with which to start their careers. With money in her pocket, Burnett dropped out of UCLA and moved to New York to become an actress. She soon appeared as a ventriloquist on Paul Winchell's children's show, during which she tugged her left ear as an affectionate greeting to her grandmother at home, a gesture that became her trademark sign-off. She soon began doing regular guest spots on *The Garry Moore Show* and in three years had the lead in an off-Broadway production of *Once Upon a Mattress*, which went to Broadway the next year. She continued to appear both on stage and on television and in 1966 debuted with *The Carol Burnett Show*. In all, the show and Burnett won eighteen Emmy Awards. During the '70s and '80s, she appeared in several films, including *The Front Page* and *The Four Seasons*. Then, in 1990, after being away from the small screen for many years, Carol returned to television for a short time with *Carol and Company* on NBC and in the fall of 1993 will produce a new sitcom, *Burnett*, about the backstage intrigues of a soap opera.

Carol has also known the ups and downs in her married life. After her seven-year marriage to Saroyan ended in 1962, she wed Joe Hamilton the next year. Since he was the producer on *The Garry Moore Show* and married with eight children when they met, Carol experienced an onslaught of negative publicity. They went on to have three daughters of their own but were divorced in 1984. Less in the spotlight now, she has time to waterski, swim and sketch. A true survivor, she reflects: "I wouldn't want to change anything. The good and bad things happen for a reason. If you live through the bad times, you've learned how to survive."

JAMES CAAN

REAL NAME: James Caan
DATE OF BIRTH: March 26, 1939
PLACE OF BIRTH: Queens, New York

EYE COLOR: Blue   HAIR COLOR: Sandy brown
HEIGHT: 5'10 1/2"   WEIGHT: 165

After being one of Hollywood's hottest stars, James Caan dropped out of the limelight during the '80s, only to re-emerge triumphantly in the 1990 film *Misery*.

The third child of Arthur and Sophie Caan, owners of a kosher meat market, Jimmy grew up in the Sunnyside section of Queens, which he describes as "not conducive to the arts." He was an all-around athlete and tough guy who was kicked out of five high schools before catching on at Rhodes, a Manhattan prep school, where he played basketball and baseball and was elected class president before graduating at sixteen. He earned a football scholarship to Michigan State University, but after a shaky freshman year, dropped out and enrolled at Hofstra University in Long Island. Finding no

interest in any of the possible majors, he dropped out again, this time floating among a succession of odd jobs: deliveryman for his father, waiter and counselor at a boys' camp. Recognizing that he was going nowhere fast, he joined Sanford Meisner's Neighborhood Playhouse Theater in New York.

In 1961, he made his Broadway debut in a revival of *La Ronde* and his film debut in *Irma La Douce*. While working on the New York stage, he also began making TV appearances on such shows as *Naked City* and *Dr. Kildare*. Moving to Los Angeles in 1964, he struggled for eight long years trying to make it as a film actor. The big break came when his portrayal of Brian Piccolo in the TV movie *Brian's Song* won him an Emmy nomination in 1972. That same year, he was nominated for the best supporting actor Oscar for his role as Sonny Corleone in the smash hit *The Godfather*. Caan has explained his approach to acting simplistically: examining a character's physical traits and then "waiting for osmosis to take over." During the '70s, Caan went on to become one of Hollywood's biggest draws, appearing regularly on the big screen in films such as *Comes a Horseman*, *Hide in Plain Sight* (which he also directed) and *Rollerball*. His career stalled during the '80s, however, following the devastating death of his sister, who was also his manager, from leukemia. During that period, he recalls, "There are pictures I made that I still haven't seen. I was depressed when I was making them." His personal life was further rocked by divorce from his second wife, model Sheilah Ryan, and by cocaine addiction. But it was revived in 1990 with the release of *Misery*, in which he played opposite Kathy Bates as writer/hostage Paul Sheldon. On a roll again, that same year he also made *For the Boys* with Bette Midler, and in 1992, co-starred in the hit comedy *Honeymoon in Vegas*.

Caan's five-year first marriage, to dancer Dee Jay Mattis, produced one daughter, and his two-year second marriage, to Sheilah Ryan, produced a son who still lives with him. In 1990, he wed pastry chef Ingrid Hajek from his Bronx neighborhood, and they had a son a year later.

Still a sports nut, Caan enjoys baseball, racquetball and football as well as boxing and the martial arts. He is also an expert horseman who has competed on the professional rodeo circuit roping steers. Caan and actress Cathy Moriarty are partners in the Mulberry Street Pizza restaurant in Beverly Hills.

NICOLAS CAGE

REAL NAME: Nicolas Coppola
DATE OF BIRTH: January 7, 1964
PLACE OF BIRTH: Long Beach, California

EYE COLOR: Brown   HAIR COLOR: Brown
HEIGHT: 5'10"   WEIGHT: 175

The nephew of director Francis Ford Coppola and actress Talia Shire, Nicolas Cage grew up wanting to be a writer, not an actor. At fifteen, though, the motivation to meet girls changed his mind.

His mother was a former ballet dancer, and his father, Coppola's brother, is currently the dean of creative arts at San Francisco State University. But Nicolas didn't take after either parent. As a child, he hated and was expelled from elementary school, spending much of his time reading the classics and making Super 8 films with his brother. His parents divorced when he was twelve, and Cage moved to San Francisco with his father. Three years later, he moved in with his uncle in the Napa Valley and enrolled at San Francisco's American Conservatory Theater. After this stint, Cage returned to Los Angeles, and while he was still a student—at Beverly Hills High—landed a role in the TV movie *The Best of Times*. In 1981, he dropped out of high school and took a job as a movie theater usher in order to gain an understanding of what an audience wanted from a film. Two years later, he made his feature debut as Smokey in his uncle's 1983 film, *Rumblefish*. Before auditioning for *Valley Girl*, he decided it was time to change his last name in order to escape the "Coppola" mystique that always confronted him on interviews. He took it from composer John Cage and his favorite comic-book character, Luke Cage. Nicolas still considers *Valley Girl* his favorite movie because, he says, "It was a situation I'd gone through in Beverly Hills High School. I was taking the bus there, and other guys were driving Porsches. If there was a beautiful girl and I wanted to take her out, I couldn't do it, she just wouldn't go for it."

Although *Valley Girl* was your basic cult film, it got the attention of bigger filmmakers, and his resume today, at age 29, reads like a veteran's, with a list of nearly twenty solid films that includes *Moonstruck, Peggy Sue Got Married, Raising Arizona, Wild at Heart* and *Honeymoon in Vegas.*

By ex-girlfriend Christina Fulton, Cage had a son in 1991. In addition to an affinity for motorcycles, Cage keeps at home a collection of cats, large exotic mounted bugs and an aquarium filled with sharks and octopuses.

MICHAEL CAINE

REAL NAME: Maurice Joseph Micklewhite Jr.
DATE OF BIRTH: March 14, 1933
PLACE OF BIRTH: London, England

EYE COLOR: Blue   HAIR COLOR: Blond
HEIGHT: 6'   WEIGHT: 175

Michael Caine spent his early years in the slums of London. Soon after his birth, his father, a fish porter, lost his job, and the family was forced to move into a two-room flat without electricity where they lived for six years while his mother scrubbed floors to support the family. Michael recalls that his father—"an extraordinarily strong man, very big and tough"—taught him "a lot about survival." He also taught his son the value of hard work: He made his son go along on holidays and weekends when he went back to work at the fish market. During the war, his father served with the British Army, and when the war ended, Michael managed to receive a quality education attending Wilson's Grammar School and then a Jewish parochial school near where he lived. In order to escape the miseries of tenement life and class struggle, Michael immersed himself in films. He was greatly influenced by Humphrey Bogart, who embodied Michael's own contempt for the Establishment, and he decided to drop out of school at sixteen. He worked for several years as a pie maker, drill operator and then "tea boy" for a film producer who encouraged him to try acting. But first he spent two years in the British Army, including one on the front lines in Korea.

Re-entering the civilian world, Caine became stage manager for a Sussex repertory company. He was also given small parts and, performing them well, developed a reputation as an actor. He changed his name first to Michael Scott and then to Michael Caine—after seeing the movie *The Caine Mutiny* on a marquee—and worked in the British theater until he was cast as a British military officer in his first feature role in *Zulu*. His performance earned favorable reviews, as did his even larger role in the spy movie *The Ipcress File*. Since then, believing that the only way to remain successful is to work constantly, Caine has appeared in dozens of films from high drama to comedy, the most notable among them *Sleuth, Educating Rita* and *Dirty Rotten Scoundrels.* In fact, hardly a year has gone by since 1966, when he starred as a libidinous Cockney in *Alfie,* that Michael has not been on film or stage; so far he's starred in 66 films. Along the way he has received four Oscar nominations and took home the best supporting actor award for *Hannah and Her Sisters* in 1986. In 1993 he starred in *Blue Ice,* an HBO movie.

An accomplished cook, Caine is also part owner of the London Brasserie. He is also a passionate gardener, art collector, and most recently, in 1992, the author of a well-received autobiography, *What's It All About?,* which he wrote without a collaborator. From a brief marriage to actress Patricia Haines in 1955, Michael has a 37-year-old daughter. After a rowdy single period, he married model Shakira Baksh in 1973, and they had a daughter the next year. Blissfully content with his life today, he reflects that the poverty of his youth fueled a "workaholic" mentality and drained all of the anger from his system. Now, he works for the sheer enjoyment of it.

JOHN CANDY

REAL NAME: John Franklin Candy
DATE OF BIRTH: October 31, 1950
PLACE OF BIRTH: Newmarket, Ontario, Canada

EYE COLOR: Brown   HAIR COLOR: Brown
HEIGHT: 6'3"   WEIGHT: 280

Modest and unwilling to discuss himself, John Candy rarely grants interviews. But he was quoted on one occasion as saying that "I use what little I have in my work. It's more developing a sense of confidence about yourself, which carries over into your work. And these days a sense of humor is like a security blanket—you're doomed if you don't have one."

John's father died a few years after his birth. An only child, he was raised by his mother, aunt and grandparents in Toronto. To entertain himself, he spent hours in front of the television set or in theaters, always watching comedies. In Catholic parochial school, he was an average football and hockey player and didn't begin acting until the late '60s while studying journalism at a community college. Graduating to commercials and plays in 1971, he was soon firmly entrenched in Toronto's underground theater scene. To support himself, he found odd jobs mixing paint in a factory and working in a sporting goods store.

Starting out in a children's theater group, he worked his way into television. His early acting credits include the satirical review Creeps and several low-budget Canadian films. In 1971, he became friends with another struggling actor who was part-timing as a mail sorter for the Canadian postal service: Dan Aykroyd. Dan persuaded John to audition for the new Toronto off-shoot of the renowned Chicago Second City comedy troupe, and John's superb audition allowed him to bypass the Toronto branch and go straight to Chicago, where Aykroyd later joined him and fellow troupers John Belushi, Bill Murray and Gilda Radner. He would later star in the group's TV show S.C.T.V. where, during the eight years that followed, he was nominated twice for ACTRA awards for his writing. When the show moved to NBC, John earned Emmy awards for writing in 1982 and 1985. But since his first real feature role in the Steven Spielberg film *1941*, he has moved from portly comedian to huge star. Among his 30 films are hits such as *The Blues Brothers, Spaceballs, Planes, Trains and Automobiles, Only the Lonely*, and *JFK*. He's also captured the children's market with a TV cartoon show called *Camp Candy* starring John.

Along with Los Angeles Kings owner Bruce McNall and hockey star Wayne Gretzky, Candy is co-owner of the Toronto Argonauts. Married since 1979 with two children, he divides his time between Toronto and Los Angeles.

JOHNNY CARSON

REAL NAME: John William Carson
DATE OF BIRTH: October 23, 1925
PLACE OF BIRTH: Corning, Iowa

EYE COLOR: Hazel   HAIR COLOR: Gray
HEIGHT: 5'10"   WEIGHT: 175

The undisputed king of late-night television, Johnny Carson started out as a funnyman and grew into an American institution. Since taking over *The Tonight Show* more than 30 years ago, Carson has fought off every challenger and brought in ratings other hosts can only dream about. A country boy at heart, Carson grew up with his brother and sister in Norfolk, Nebraska, where his father worked for a utility company. At around twelve years old, he sent away for a magic kit and soon The Great Carsoni was performing not only for friends but at local parties and street festivals. Not surprisingly, he was well-known for being able to make people laugh even then and during high school wrote a humor column for the school newspaper. After graduation in 1943, Carson joined the Navy, after which he earned a degree in radio and speech from the University of Nebraska, where he became an announcer at a local radio station.

By 1951, he was in Los Angeles with a half-hour TV show called *Carson's Cellar*. After it left the air in 1953, Carson went to work as a writer on *The Red Skelton Show*. When Skelton suffered a concussion during a rehearsal, Carson filled in for him to rave reviews, and CBS gave him his own show. But *The Johnny Carson Show* went up against stiff competition and lasted only 39 weeks. From there, Carson's career stalled—only to revive in 1957 with an opportunity to host the game show *Who Do You Trust?*, which was a solid hit for five years. Then came the big break, when Carson was tapped to replace Jack Paar as the host of *The Tonight Show* in 1958. He hit the ground running. On his first night, Carson was introduced by Groucho Marx and went on to interview Joan Crawford, Rudy Vallee, Tony Bennett and Mel Brooks. The rest is TV history, and three generations of Americans went to sleep looking at Carson between their feet. He finally handed *The Tonight Show Starring Johnny Carson*

over to Jay Leno in 1992. An avid tennis fan, Carson travels each year to New York and London to watch the U.S. Open and Wimbledon. Now in his fourth marriage, Johnny has three sons from his first marriage; however, he lost one son, Chris, in a car accident two years ago.

DANA CARVEY

REAL NAME: Dana Carvey
DATE OF BIRTH: June 6, 1955
PLACE OF BIRTH: San Carlos, California

EYE COLOR: Brown   HAIR COLOR: Brown
HEIGHT: 5'9"   WEIGHT: 165

Behind Dana Carvey's innocent grin lurks a wicked wit that he's honed each week on *Saturday Night Live* since joining its cast in 1986.

The son of two schoolteachers, Carvey grew up in the suburb of San Carlos, California, with three brothers and one sister. He was an introverted youth who entertained himself by creating voices and characters to replace the friends he never made in school. He kept his family on their toes by imitating such celebrities as Larry Holmes, Jacques Cousteau and Lyndon Johnson, whose subtle mannerisms and speech patterns he used to create elaborate caricatures, a technique he has since perfected.

In high school Carvey realized he wanted to be a performer; he idolized Rich Little. To that end, he enrolled at San Francisco State University, studying radio and television broadcasting. He avoided embarrassing drama classes, instead practicing his delivery and quick wit only on close friends. Carvey finally mustered enough courage to make a successful debut at a Berkeley comedy club in 1978 with a Howard Cosell impersonation and off-color Star Trek jokes. After college he hit the stand-up circuit by night and worked odd jobs by day, including busing tables at a Bay Area Holiday Inn. In 1981, Carvey moved to Hollywood to break into television and films. He spent a frustrating five years playing bit parts in movies and wrong parts on television until returning *SNL* producer Lorne Michaels discovered Carvey at Igby's Comedy Cabaret in Los Angeles in 1986.

The character that launched Carvey's successful run on *Saturday Night Live* was the Church Lady, which he developed for his stand-up act and performed in drag for the first time on the show. She was a composite of several women at the Lutheran church his family had attended who expressed righteous indignation at the Carveys' irregular attendance and less-than-complete commitment to the church. Carvey based another character, Garth Algar, Wayne Campbell's sidekick in the "Wayne's World" sketches and movie, on two people. From his brother Brad, he took Garth's tightly curled upper lip and shifty eyes. Garth's insecurity and emotional extremes come from Carvey himself. His other characters include Hans of Hans and Franz, the obsessive fitness gurus, and the Grumpy Old Man on Weekend Update.

In addition to his original characters, Carvey performs scathing celebrity impersonations, including the best Johnny Carson around, and during the 1992 presidential campaign, his take on candidates George Bush and Ross Perot seemed, at times, more real than the real thing. He left *SNL* in 1993 to concentrate on his film career, beginning with the sequel to *Wayne's World*.

Carvey plays the drums in his spare time and in some of the musical skits on *SNL*. He has incorporated this interest into Garth, who often clutches a pair of drumsticks in "Wayne's World" sketches. In high school, Carvey was an all-conference cross-country runner, and he still stays in shape by running every day. He and Paula, his wife since 1985, have a son and split time between their homes in Manhattan and the San Fernando Valley in California.

RICHARD CHAMBERLAIN

REAL NAME: George Richard Chamberlain
DATE OF BIRTH: March 31, 1935
PLACE OF BIRTH: Los Angeles, California

EYE COLOR: Blue   HAIR COLOR: Light brown
HEIGHT: 6'1"   Weight: 170

Famous for his roles in TV miniseries such as *Shogun* and *The Thorn Birds*, Richard Chamberlain is also a classically trained actor. He left the security of a career in Hollywood to become the first American since John Barrymore to play Hamlet on the British stage. "One must never allow oneself to become comfortable," he explains.

The second son of a manufacturer, Chamberlain grew up in Beverly Hills, where he attended Beverly Hills High School. Despite his dyslexia, he majored in art at Pomona College in Claremont, California, ran track and took bit parts in campus theater productions. Until he started acting, he recalls that his college days were miserable: "I was a hermit. I sat in my little room and I painted pictures. I was in some sort of cocoon. Then I discovered acting. The stage seemed like a place where you could escape from the cocoon.... It seemed like a way to have fun without getting involved in real life." Once graduated, he was drafted into the Army and spent two years as a company clerk in Korea.

Returning to civilian life, he settled in Los Angeles, taking acting, singing and dancing lessons and supporting himself with odd jobs such as grocery clerk, chauffeur and construction work. In 1959, he got his first part as a bit player on *Gunsmoke*. This led to other TV parts and eventually to a seven-year contract with MGM, which cast him in the role that would make him famous: Dr. James Kildare. During its five-year run, *Dr. Kildare* was a huge hit, and Chamberlain was TV's golden boy. He gave it all up in 1966, however, moving to London and staying there to study acting for three years. He became associated with the Birmington Repertory Theater and, in 1969, was glowingly reviewed as Hamlet on the stage. In 1971, he returned to the United States and continued to do stage work, including two disparate interpretations of Richard II and a highly acclaimed portrayal of *Cyrano de Bergerac* for the Center Theater Group. Chamberlain then began mixing plays with television and motion pictures. In 1978, he did his first miniseries, the genre of which he would become king, with a role as Alexander McKeag in *Centennial*. He followed that in 1980 with the lead in *Shogun*, a role for which he received an Emmy nomination. He did not return to the stage until 1987 in a Broadway revival of *Blithe Spirit* and in 1993 began touring with another Broadway revival, *My Fair Lady*. His motion picture roles include *The Three Musketeers*, its sequel *The Four Musketeers* and *The Towering Inferno*.

Dividing his time between homes in Beverly Hills, Hawaii and New York, he says that he is still "addicted to exercise" and runs every day. He also paints and makes stained-glass windows for relaxation. Years of therapy have enabled him to establish and sustain personal relationships, but he says that he prefers to keep his private life very private.

CHEVY CHASE

REAL NAME: Cornelius Crane Chase
DATE OF BIRTH: October 8, 1943
PLACE OF BIRTH: New York, New York

EYE COLOR: Brown   HAIR COLOR: Brown
HEIGHT: 6'4"   WEIGHT: 185

Though for years he was recognized mainly for his zany pratfalls on *Saturday Night Live*, Chevy Chase was originally hired by *SNL* as a writer and won an Emmy for it in 1975.

The younger of two sons, he grew up in a privileged literary atmosphere. His father was a writer and publisher, and his mother was a plumbing heiress. Named Cornelius after his wealthy maternal grandfather, he never saw his inheritance because his granddad divorced his wife to marry a Zen Buddhist and left his money to a monastery. During high school, Chevy excelled at sports and was named the class valedictorian. After graduation from Bard College in New York, he held a variety of part-time jobs such as magazine writer, piano player with a rock group, tennis pro, bartender and truck driver. During this same period, he also took a course in audio engineering and, along with a couple of friends, began videotaping lampoons of various TV productions. The best of his skits were incorporated into the 1974 film *The Groove Tube*. He also wrote for the *National Lampoon Radio Hour*, *Mad Magazine* and *The Smothers Brothers Show*.

After meeting Lorne Michaels, the producer of *Saturday Night Live*, while waiting in line for a movie, Chase became a writer on *SNL*. He eventually persuaded Michaels to let him perform as well, which he did with hilarious results, until leaving the show in 1976. Explaining his own style of comedy, he believes it's the contrast between his collegiate exterior and his off-the-wall antics. "I guess I just look so straight and normal," he said, "nobody expects me to pick my nose and fall." Post-*SNL*, Chase did some TV specials and starred in his own show, *The Chevy Chase Show*. He has since become one of America's favorite comic actors and has appeared in numerous films such as *Spies Like Us*, *Caddyshack*, *National*

Lampoon's Vacation and *Fletch.* In September 1993, Chevy will launch his own late-night talk show on the Fox network which, judging by his previous efforts, promises to deliver.

In his down time, Chase enjoys playing tennis and fooling around at the piano. Currently in his third marriage—with three daughters—Chevy has finally adapted to his success and to Los Angeles

(which he refers to as a "cow town that doesn't deal with anything except TV"). His philosophy is: "We've all got that one thing in common: We are all surely going to die. So, hey, while we're on our way, why not try and go out a star?"

CHER

REAL NAME: Cherilyn Sarkisian La Piere
DATE OF BIRTH: May 20, 1946
PLACE OF BIRTH: El Centro, California

EYE COLOR: Brown   HAIR COLOR: Black
HEIGHT: 5'8 1/2"   WEIGHT: 110

In the years since she first appeared on the music scene as the better half of Sonny and Cher in 1964, Cher has gone from singing star to movie star to celebrity sensation to queen of the infomercials.

Her striking looks harken back to an eclectic ancestry: Cherokee Indian, Armenian, Turkish and French. Cher's mother was married eight times, three times to the same man. After her mother, a former model, divorced her bank manager father, Cher and sister Georgeanne were raised in Los Angeles by her mother and many stepfathers. By the time she was sixteen, Cher knew she wanted to become an actress. Dropping out of school during her junior year, she began taking drama lessons and soon landed a gig singing back-up at Philles Records. She met Sonny Bono, who was a young song-writer and record producer, on a blind date. Then in 1964, when she was eighteen, the two eloped in Tijuana, Mexico. Impressed with Cher's unusually pitched voice, he persuaded her to concentrate on singing instead of acting, and as a duo, the two began doing night-club gigs. Their first song, "Baby Don't Go," didn't make the charts, but their third song, "I Got You, Babe"—released in 1965—became a major hit, and they became music's newest, hottest thing. Unfortunately, fame was fleeting and their next album bombed.

Attempting to win back their young audience, they made two films, *Good Times*, which was modestly successful, and *Chastity* (named after their daughter, born in 1969), which wasn't. After retooling their act on the nightclub circuit, Sonny and Cher began guesting on TV shows and in 1971 headlined their own variety series, *The Sonny and Cher Comedy Hour*. With Sonny playing fall guy to Cher's sarcastic zingers, the show was a hit, and they were on top again until it went off the air in 1974. A year later they were divorced, and after a brief try at a show of her own, Cher began singing solo.

She also returned to motion pictures, debuting in *Come Back to the Five and Dime, Jimmy Dean, Jimmy Dean* in 1982 and went on to win respect as an actress in films such as *Silkwood, Mask* and *The Witches of Eastwick*. In 1988, she was awarded an Academy Award for best actress in *Moonstruck*.

In addition to Chastity, Cher has a son, Elijah Blue, born in 1976 by rock singer Gregg Allman, whom she married three days after divorcing Sonny. In 1975, Cher discovered she was dyslexic while having Chastity treated for the same condition. A maverick fashion plate, she is known for wearing provocative outfits by Bob Mackie and for several strategically located tattoos, which those outfits often fail to conceal. In 1992, after a year battling chronic fatigue syndrome and boyfriend problems, she said, "Loneliness is not the worst thing that can happen to you." More than receptive to the idea of marrying again, however, she added, "I'd consider having another baby in a heartbeat."

DICK CLARK

REAL NAME: Richard Wagstaff Clark
DATE OF BIRTH: November 30, 1929
PLACE OF BIRTH: Mount Vernon, New York

EYE COLOR: Brown   HAIR COLOR: Brown
HEIGHT: 5'8"   WEIGHT: 143

Although he has produced more than 200 TV specials and more than twenty movies, Dick Clark is best known—even today, at 63—as the perennially youthful host of the TV show *American Bandstand*. On *Bandstand*, Clark has introduced the country to a horde of soon-to-be-famous bands and singers, including Buddy Holly, Chubby Checker, Fabian, James Brown, Neil Sedaka and The Supremes. Modest about his enormous wealth and success, he says, "I can't sing or dance. I just talk."

By the age of five, Dick was writing and editing his own neighborhood newspaper. At A.B. Davis High School in Mount Vernon, Clark tried to emulate his athletic older brother, who had died in World War II. He failed as an athlete but found his metier as a member of the school's drama club. Still afflicted with loneliness, however, he tended to stay in his room and submerge himself in radio shows. That's when he decided that this was what he wanted to do when he grew up. A few months before he entered college, Dick moved to Utica, New York, where his father became general manager of radio station WRUN, and spent the summer helping out around the station, even getting some air time as a replacement for one of the FM deejays. He entered Syracuse University in 1946, and while studying advertising became involved with the student-run radio station, WAER-FM, working through his senior year as a weekend announcer and disk jockey at radio station WOLF. After graduating with a degree in advertising and a minor in radio, he worked for a while at a local TV station in Utica and then moved to Philadelphia, where he eventually landed his own radio show, *Dick Clark's Caravan of Music*.

Caravan had a TV counterpart called *Bandstand*, and, after filling in as a substitute once on that show, Clark was made permanent host in 1956. During the late '50s, he decided he wasn't making enough money on *Bandstand* and began to produce TV shows, forming several music publishing companies along with a record label under the auspices of Dick Clark Productions. In addition to hosting *American Bandstand* and countless TV specials, Clark has appeared in several films and spent fifteen years as the host of the Emmy-winning game shows *The $25,000 Pyramid* and *The $100,000 Pyramid*. While Dick refers to his conglomerate as an "entertainment boutique," a former president of entertainment at NBC characterized it as "the McDonald's of television."

Seemingly immune to aging, Clark stays in shape by lifting weights and swimming and, he says, has "an open mind and a closed refrigerator." Dick has had three marriages with three children from the first two. Dedicating his time and talents to worthy causes, he hosted the Live Aid concert in 1985. "There's so much I want to do," he says. "Most of all I want to be remembered as a hell of a lot more than some guy who did Clearasil commercials on the damn tube."

GLENN CLOSE

REAL NAME: Glenn Close
DATE OF BIRTH: March 19, 1947
PLACE OF BIRTH: Greenwich, Connecticut

EYE COLOR: Blue   HAIR COLOR: Blond
HEIGHT: 5'4"   WEIGHT: 110

Nominated for a best supporting actress Oscar for her film debut in *The World According to Garp*, Glenn Close has continued to receive reviews for her work that few actors or actresses ever match in the course of a career. In all, she has been nominated for five Academy Awards in nine years.

Born one of three children into one of the founding families of Seventeenth Century Greenwich, she spent her earliest years living on her grandparents' 500-acre Connecticut estate. Describing herself as a "wild little tomboy," she used her imagination to entertain herself by playing dual roles she had seen in TV movies. At seven, she was determined to become an actress, hopefully for Disney. In 1960, her parents moved to the Congo to work as missionaries in a clinic, and for several years, Glenn alternated her time between the Congo and Swiss boarding schools. Upon returning to Connecticut, she attended her family's alma mater, the prestigious Rosemary Hall school, where she organized a theater group called The Fingernails: The Group with Polish. After high school she spent five years in what she calls "the blank period" of "her lost life." A trained lyric soprano, she desperately wanted to sing and joined Up With People, traveling around the country performing at military bases for several years. In 1969, she married rock guitarist Cabot Wade, but they divorced in two years. At 22, she enrolled at the College of William and Mary and took her degree there, a Phi Beta Kappa, in drama and anthropology.

That same year, 1974, she made her Broadway debut in a New Phoenix Repertory Company production of *Love for Love*. Her stage career continued for several years and reached its pinnacle with a Tony-nominated performance as Charity in the smash musical *Barnum*. That role led to her film debut as Jenny Fields in the movie *The World According to Garp*. She has continued to work steadily in

film ever since, with consistently acclaimed performances in such films as *The Big Chill, The Natural, Fatal Attraction, Dangerous Liaisons* and *Reversal of Fortune*. Her TV work includes *Sarah Plain and Tall*, which she also executive produced, and *Something About Amelia*, for which she received an Emmy nomination.

"You have to find the emotional center," she says about her acting technique, "and that means being open, taking chances. When I finally find the character, that's the payoff for all the agony. When the character finally begins to crack the shell of her egg, that's the joy." Close will have the opportunity to find another payoff when she opens the musical version of the tragic film classic *Sunset Boulevard* late in 1993 after filming is completed on *The Paper*.

Close has sung the national anthem many times before Mets games at Shea Stadium in New York. An avid equestrian, she often rides her horse through New York's Central Park. She was wed in 1984 to James Marlas, a venture capitalist, and they have a daughter. However, they decided to separate last year.

JOAN COLLINS

REAL NAME: Joan Henrietta Collins
DATE OF BIRTH: May 23, 1933
PLACE OF BIRTH: London, England

EYE COLOR: Gray/green   HAIR COLOR: Brown
HEIGHT: 5'6"   WEIGHT: 120

Along with Linda Evans and Jane Fonda, Joan Collins is living proof that being a sex symbol after 40 is not an impossible dream. A veteran actress, she spent 30 years in films, with varying degrees of success, before landing her biggest role as Alexis on the prime-time soap opera *Dynasty*. "I love playing a villain—it's so very juicy," she says.

Born in England, Collins and her sister, best-selling novelist Jackie Collins, were the daughters of a vaudevillian booking agent and a housewife. They enjoyed a comfortable early life with many "interesting" houseguests—their father's clients. Attending the Francis Holland School for Girls in London, she began dancing in a school play at the age of three and made her stage debut as an actress at age thirteen in a West End production of *A Doll's House*. Throughout her childhood, she says, she was a "gawky, spotty, shy, boy-hating and introverted" girl who often went to the movies three times a day. Enrolling at the Royal Academy of Dramatic Arts, she promised her father that if she didn't succeed as an actress, she would enter secretarial school. To supplement her income while at the Academy, Collins took on modeling assignments, and one of them led to a contract with the film company Rank Organization, Ltd.

After making her film debut in 1952 as a bit player in *Lady Godiva Rides Again*, she spent the next twenty years appearing in films, mostly in "pretty girl" roles. In the early '70s, Collins, then in her forties, gained a small dose of celebrity as the star of several "sexploitation" films including *The Stud*, *Homework*, and *The Bitch*. Referring to this soft-core period, she explains, "I looked pretty good. I thought I was really a good actress, better than people had given me credit for—and they always noticed my looks more than what I was doing, and I wanted to have it again, the career. So... " By the end of the decade her career was on the upswing with films like *The Big Sleep*, and in 1981, she shot to stardom after joining the cast of *Dynasty*. Her character, the superbitch Alexis Carrington, added a touch of sex and sizzle to the show that helped make it a solid ratings success. Collins played the part until the show ended in 1989. Multi-talented, she penned her autobiography in 1978 and her own *Joan Collins Beauty Book* in 1980.

Joan is also multi-married: from 1952 to 1957 to British actor Maxwell Reed; from 1963 to 1970 to British actor and singer Anthony Newley (producing a son and daughter); from 1972 to 1983 to producer Ronald Kass (another daughter); and from 1985 to 1987 to Swedish businessman Peter Holm.

A great cook, Collins maintains her figure by constant exercise. Her hobbies include photography, collecting antiques and making home movies.

SEAN CONNERY

REAL NAME: Thomas Connery
DATE OF BIRTH: August 25, 1930
PLACE OF BIRTH: Edinburgh, Scotland

EYE COLOR: Brown   HAIR COLOR: Black
HEIGHT: 6'2"   WEIGHT: 185

Sean Connery became a star as agent 007 in a series of action-packed James Bond films. But the image of a gun-toting womanizer isn't one he is fond of. "I don't really suppose I'd like Bond if I met him," he said. "He's not my kind of chap at all."

Even more unlike the suave Bond is Connery's own background. Born in a slum section of Edinburgh, Scotland, to a truck driver and a maid, Sean grew up during the Depression and, at seven, pitched in by delivering milk. At thirteen, he dropped out of school and became a drifter, working at menial jobs such as bricklaying, plastering, coffin polishing and ushering, until he was conscripted into the Royal Navy four years later. Connery remained on duty for three years before being discharged because of ulcers. A civilian once more, he embarked on a second series of odd jobs, including lifeguard, and spent much of his free time lifting weights. In 1950, he even represented Scotland in London's Mr. Universe competition. While he was there, needing some money, he tried out for and won a part in the chorus of a touring production of *South Pacific* and spent the next eighteen months on tour. When Connery returned to London, he joined a small repertory group. That's when he was "hooked," he admits, adding that he "couldn't think of any job but show business again."

He spent the rest of the decade appearing in a series of mostly forgettable films. In 1961, the *London Daily Express* ran a contest to see who should be cast as James Bond, and Connery won the most votes. The producers met with him, hired him without a screen test, and cast him in the first Bond film, *Dr. No*. When it was a smash hit, Connery appeared in several more, including From *Russia With Love*, *Goldfinger* and *Thunderball*. Tired of being typecast, he quit to pursue a successful career as a dramatic actor, and then, in 1983, after twelve years of making non-Bond films, he reprised his role as 007—wearing a toupee—in *Never Say Never Again*. More recently, Connery has starred in such blockbusters as *The Untouchables* (for which he received an Academy Award for best supporting actor), and won applause for his varied roles in *The Russia House, Indiana Jones and the Last Crusade* and *The Hunt for Red October*. His latest accomplishment is starring in the film adaptation of Michael Crichton's bestseller *Rising Sun*.

With painting, reading and golf among his leisure pursuits, Connery is remarkably unpretentious and lives very frugally. The man that *People* magazine named the Sexiest Man Alive in 1990 is now happily married to a French painter whom he met in a golf tournament. He was married once before, for twenty years, to actress Diane Cilento, and their son, Jason, is also an actor. Taking work as it comes, he says about the future: "I suppose more than anything else I'd like to be an old man with a good face, like Hitchcock or Picasso.... They know that life is not just a popularity contest."

FRANCIS FORD COPPOLA

REAL NAME: Francis Ford Coppola
DATE OF BIRTH: April 7, 1939
PLACE OF BIRTH: Detroit, Michigan

EYE COLOR: Brown   HAIR COLOR: Brown
HEIGHT: 6'   WEIGHT: 190

When all is said and done, he may be remembered as another Orson Welles: a cinematic genius who created with his right hand and destroyed himself with his left. But Francis Ford Coppola has said recently that his best work is yet to come: "I've been 'promising'

all my life. First, I was a 'promising writer,' then I was a 'promising director.' Well, maybe at 50, I'll fulfill the promise."

The son of a traveling flutist, Coppola was born in Detroit and grew up mostly in Queens but attended 22 different schools before finishing. His middle name comes from the *Ford Sunday Evening Hour* radio show on which his father was performing during his birth. He recalls a warm and happy family life with his brother and sister, actress Talia Shire. But at eight, he contracted polio and spent an entire year in bed, where he entertained himself creating storylines for his puppets and playing with gadgets. "I became interested in the concept of remote control," he said. "I'm good with gadgets, and I became a tinkerer. I think what I really am is an inventor." At nine, he made his first film, spliced together from home movies. In 1959, at Hofstra University, he became president of the school's drama and musical comedy club, and after graduation moved west to study for his master's in film at UCLA. While enrolled there, he took a job as an assistant with independent producer Roger Corman and, at 24, made his first feature, *Dementia 13*.

He then began a long association with Seven Arts as a scriptwriter. It wasn't until four years after *Dementia 13* was released that Coppola directed his second feature, *You're a Big Boy Now*. On the strength of that film, he was hired to direct Fred Astaire in *Finian's Rainbow*. In 1969, Coppola formed the American Zoetrope studio and, through it, produced George Lucas' films *THX 1138* and *American Graffiti*. Since then, Coppola has written and directed a multitude of legendary films, including *The Godfather* (for which he won best screenplay and best picture Oscars), *Apocalypse Now*, *The Godfather Part II*, and his most recent extravaganza, *Bram Stoker's Dracula*. He made a departure into children's entertainment with *The Secret Garden* in 1993.

He and his wife, Eleanor, have two sons, one of whom, Gio, was killed in a boating accident, and a daughter, Sofia, who appeared in *Godfather III*. A walking contradiction in terms, Francis defines himself by vowing to finance his own films because, he says, "I'm really quite wealthy and can afford to do what I want;" the next day, he's doing battle in bankruptcy court.

BILL COSBY

REAL NAME: William Henry Cosby Jr.
DATE OF BIRTH: July 12, 1937
PLACE OF BIRTH: Philadelphia, Pennsylvania

EYE COLOR: Brown   HAIR COLOR: Black
HEIGHT: 6'   WEIGHT: 185

Since he became the first black actor to star in a nationally broad-cast TV series in 1965, Bill Cosby has been one of the media's most popular and powerful stars, and certainly its wealthiest. He has also been openly critical of the trend toward vulgar sexual and racial themes on television.

Cosby grew up poor in the Philadelphia housing projects he would later use as the setting for his animated hit, *Fat Albert and the Cosby Kids*. The eldest of three sons born to a Navy mess steward and a maid, Bill shined shoes and delivered groceries to supplement the family's income. At Germantown High School, Cosby was tested as having gifted intelligence, and he excelled in track, basketball, baseball and football. But his grades were lacking, and after flunking the tenth grade twice, Cosby left school without graduating and joined the Navy. During his four-year tour, he earned his high school equivalency diploma and, upon discharge, enrolled at Temple University on a track scholarship. Besides running track, Cosby played football and began working as a stand-up comedian at local Philadelphia clubs. By the end of his sophomore year, his comedy career was going so well that he dropped out of college to hit the club circuit full-time. He remembers his first job in New York at The Gaslight Club: "The boss offered me $60 a week, and I was thrilled to death. Then I realized that out of that $60 a week I had to pay for a place to stay. The boss offered to let me sleep in the upstairs storeroom. All it had was a cot. No bathroom."

In 1965, he was cast as Alexander Scott opposite Robert Culp in *I Spy* and earned three consecutive lead actor Emmy awards. It was then that he was given *The Bill Cosby Show*, which ran for two years. Bill's next two TV shows, both of the one-hour variety type, failed, but his career revived in a big way with his megahit, *The Cosby*

Show, which went off the air last season after eight record-breaking seasons in the top ten. He didn't fare so well in films, but a few of them did fairly well: *Uptown Saturday Night*, *A Piece of the Action* and *California Suite*. Cosby is also considered a premier commercial pitchman and over the years has done commercials for Coca-Cola, Jell-O, Kodak and many others.

To stay in shape, Cosby still runs track, although by his own admission he's not as fast as he was in his college days. The father of five by Camille, his wife since 1964, he has used much of his own family life as material in all facets of his career, especially in *The Cosby Show*, now in syndication. His latest project, in 1993, was hosting a revamped version of Groucho Marx's old *You Bet Your Life* TV game show. The show was canceled because of low ratings after only a few months on the air, but he went on to appear in the film *Meteor Man* the same year.

KEVIN COSTNER

REAL NAME: Kevin Costner
DATE OF BIRTH: January 18, 1955
PLACE OF BIRTH: Lynwood, California

EYE COLOR: Blue   HAIR COLOR: Brown
HEIGHT: 6'1"   WEIGHT: 180

For many years, Kevin Costner fought his desire to become an actor. "I always had this gut feeling, deep down inside, about acting," he explains, "but growing up with my family, acting seemed like pure escapism, something that no one in my family would even consider. It wasn't that they would have stopped me—it was more that it never appeared as a real possibility."

Due to the nature of his father's job as a utilities executive, Costner and his older brother spent their early childhood in a variety of California locations and attended four different high schools. He recalls that "I supplanted my own personality just to get along. I was thrown into so many situations that I quit trying. I think I lost a lot of confidence in who I was." In addition to playing baseball, basketball and football at Villa Park High School, Costner sang in the church choir. Without a firm idea of what he wanted to do with his life, he enrolled as a marketing major at Cal State Fullerton University. But while there, he became interested in acting, joined the South Coast Actors' Co-op and began appearing in community theater productions. Costner graduated from Fullerton in 1978 and after a miserable month and a half in the business world, quit to try his luck as an actor.

Moving to Los Angeles, he eventually got a job as a stage manager at Raleigh Studios and supported himself there for three years while taking acting classes and building a career in films. In 1981, he had a feature role in the low-budget thriller *Stacy's Knights*. Although he successfully landed parts, several of his early roles, including Alex, the suicide victim in *The Big Chill*, were cut during filming. His performance in the buddy movie *Fandango* was well received, but his big break didn't come until he was awarded the role of Eliot Ness in *The Untouchables*. By the time he had finished *No Way Out* and *Bull Durham*, he was a major star. Using his newfound clout, he defied the conventional wisdom about westerns as a box office fiasco and made his directorial debut with the epic *Dances With Wolves*. It swept the Oscars in eight categories in 1991. In 1992, he starred in *The Bodyguard* with Whitney Houston, who made her acting debut.

Married since 1978 to his college sweetheart, they have three children. Kevin confesses that the sex symbol image that has recently been bestowed upon him is just a mirage. "I guess I live out all my fantasies in the films. Once I get home, I'm rather domestic." He adds that he tends to be a loner, too: "I don't offer up everything there is, on-screen or in life."

WALTER CRONKITE

REAL NAME: Walter Leland Cronkite Jr.
DATE OF BIRTH: November 4, 1916
PLACE OF BIRTH: St. Joseph, Missouri

EYE COLOR: Blue   HAIR COLOR: White
HEIGHT: 6'   WEIGHT: 190

In this era of disrespect for the media, Walter Cronkite is that rarity: a newsman people trust. It's a reputation he's earned during his three-decade run with CBS News.

The only son of a dentist, Cronkite grew up in Kansas City, Missouri, and then in Houston, Texas, where he ran track at San Jacinto High School. By the time he got involved with the school newspaper and the yearbook, he had already decided to become a journalist. He'd caught the bug after reading a short story about the adventures of a foreign correspondent in *American Boy* magazine. In 1933, Cronkite enrolled at the University of Texas to study political science and economics. In addition to his studies, Walter continued athletics, appeared in college plays and worked as a sports announcer for a local radio station and as a student correspondent for *The Houston Post*. Dropping out of school in his junior year to work full-time for that paper, he said that "Covering the state capitol was a lot more exciting than studying political science in school. Besides, I never went to classes, so I got awful grades."

After jockeying around on different assignments for the paper and on different radio stations, he joined the United Press International in 1939. Covering World War II for UPI, he took part in the invasion of Normandy by parachuting into the Netherlands with the 101st Airborne Division. Afterward, he stayed in Europe reporting on, among other things, the Nazi war crime trials in Nuremberg. Upon his return to the United States in 1948, Cronkite covered Washington for a group of Midwestern newspapers before joining CBS in July of 1950. He served in a number of capacities on a variety of shows and, in 1962, became the anchor of the *CBS Evening News*. By the time he handed over the reins to Dan Rather in 1981—after covering every major news story from the JFK assassination to

Vietnam and Watergate—Cronkite was the best known, most respected and highest rated news personality in the country, and had won nearly every news award in existence.

A former car racing fan, Cronkite gave up that dangerous hobby for a tamer pastime, sailing, in which his family could participate. His family includes his wife since 1940, a former columnist and editor for *The Kansas City Journal*, and three children, who are now grown. Referring to himself as "the original Walter Mitty," Walter still reports that "I'm a journalist 100 percent, and I consider myself a lucky man because I do exactly what I want to do. Journalism is such beautiful, beautiful work, though it's so painful at times, especially these days."

TOM CRUISE

REAL NAME: Thomas Cruise Mapother IV
DATE OF BIRTH: July 3, 1962
PLACE OF BIRTH: Syracuse, New York

EYE COLOR: Green   HAIR COLOR: Brown
HEIGHT: 5'9"   WEIGHT: 155

With his sizzling performance in 1986's top grossing film *Top Gun*, Tom Cruise served notice that he was one of Hollywood's most gifted young actors. In one hit after another since then, he has grown into one of the country's top box office stars and perhaps its reigning sex symbol.

Cruise's childhood was neither typical nor easy. The son of an electrical engineer, he moved often and attended many different schools. The third of four children, he was dyslexic and often found himself in remedial classes, a fact that made the transition to so many new schools even tougher. He recalls that when he was learning to read, it was a struggle because he couldn't tell "whether letters like C or D curved to the right or the left." Ironically, his mother was a special teacher for dyslexic and hyperactive children and was dyslexic herself, as were all her other children.

At sixteen, he moved with them to Glen Ridge, New Jersey, where he was an all-around athlete, competing in several sports, including wrestling. During his senior year, however, Cruise was sidelined by an injury and turned his attention to acting. Winning the lead in a student production of *Guys and Dolls*, he enjoyed the rush of being on stage so much that on opening night he announced to his parents that he felt "at home on stage," and that he had found a way to express himself. Eager to pursue his newfound love, he left high school before graduation and moved to New York.

Working as a busboy, Cruise took acting workshops, and his first audition, for a bit part in the film *Endless Love*, led to his first professional acting job. He got another bit part in the movie *Taps*, but the director was so impressed with his intensity that he made Cruise one of the leads. After that, he played a greaser in Francis Ford Coppola's *The Outsiders* and, while it was filming, he won his breakthrough role in the surprise hit *Risky Business*. With each new film came better and meatier roles: *The Color of Money, Rain Man, Born on the Fourth of July, Far and Away, A Few Good Men* and his most recent release, *The Firm*.

A Scientologist, Cruise also loves driving fast cars, to which his *Color of Money* co-star Paul Newman introduced him. Divorced from actress Mimi Rogers, he is married to Aussie actress Nicole Kidman, who has appeared with him in two films, and they adopted a child in 1993. Producer Don Simpson explains Tom thus: "He's the youngest patriarch I've ever encountered. His road was never paved; it was always full of potholes, and he jumped over them all." This compliment is not uncommon among those who have worked with Tom who note that in spite of his super stardom, he is unfailingly polite and deferential.

BILLY CRYSTAL

REAL NAME: William Crystal
DATE OF BIRTH: March 14, 1947
PLACE OF BIRTH: Long Island, New York

EYE COLOR: Hazel   HAIR COLOR: Brown
HEIGHT: 5'6"   WEIGHT: 130

"I'm comfortable being old... being black... being Jewish. And I look very good in dresses," says Billy Crystal. "I like twisting my face and my voice and my mind into different characters. But... when I'm in trouble, under pressure, I fall back on being old and Jewish. I rattle phlegm... I feel good."

Billy's family influence was more musical than comic. While his mother craved the stage and performed in plays at temple, his uncle founded Commodore Records, and his father, who managed Gabler's Commodore Music Shop and produced jazz concerts, used to bring home black jazz musicians at Passover: "We had swinging seders." Billy also says that "we had this mixture of black jazz men and Jewish ethnic people with great love and a sense of humor—all at the bar mitzvah together." Unlike many comedians, Crystal wasn't a class clown during high school. He emceed the school's annual variety show, played football and soccer and was captain of the baseball team. After earning a baseball scholarship to Marshall University in West Virginia, he played one year before transferring to New York's Nassau Community College, where he majored in theater and spent three seasons with the school's alumni theater group. He then studied television and film directing at NYU, and after graduation formed an improv group called Three's Company with two of his NYU friends. They spent four years making the rounds at colleges and coffeehouses, and when it broke up, Crystal embarked on a solo career as a stand-up comic.

He appeared at Catch a Rising Star in New York and, after moving to Los Angeles, at the Comedy Store. TV producer Norman Lear saw him perform and gave him a guest shot on his sitcom *All in the Family*. He then gave him the role of Jodie Dallas, television's first openly gay character, on *Soap*. After four years, Crystal spent an

Emmy-winning season on *Saturday Night Live* and parlayed his success on that show into a Grammy-nominated album, *You Look Mahvelous*. In 1978, he made his film debut as a pregnant man in *Rabbit Test*, and since then he has become one of Hollywood's hottest attractions, starring in such films as *When Harry Met Sally...*, *City Slickers* and, most recently, *Mr. Saturday Night*, which he also wrote and directed. He has also served, along with Whoopi Goldberg and Robin Williams, as co-host of several HBO Comic Relief specials since 1986 and has earned a new niche as host of the Oscar ceremonies.

When Billy wants to wind down, he kicks back with his wife and two daughters. For exercise, he enjoys tennis and is the first one on the softball field if you show up with a ball and bat.

MACAULAY CULKIN

REAL NAME: Macaulay Culkin
DATE OF BIRTH: August 26, 1980
PLACE OF BIRTH: New York, New York

EYE COLOR: Blue   HAIR COLOR: Blond
HEIGHT: Growing   WEIGHT: Gaining

Left home alone in his big-screen breakthrough, in real life
Macaulay Culkin is rarely without a parent and/or one of his six siblings. "Mack" Culkin comes from a theatrical family: His father
Christopher was formerly a stage actor, his aunt is Bonnie Bedelia
and three of his brothers and sisters act on stage and in films. His
parents introduced him to the theater when he was very small when
at the end of a play's run at the Light Opera of Manhattan, the whole
family would pitch in to help strike the set. The Culkin kids and their
friends often played in the darkened theater after performances.

At the age of four, Macaulay began taking ballet lessons at the
92nd Street YMCA Dance Center, which led to his first stage role in
Bach Babies and other theater projects. He continued studying at
George Ballanchine's School of American Ballet and has appeared in
the New York City Ballet's production of *The Nutcracker*. He'll also
be starring in the film version as the Nutcracker Prince. Despite his
youth, Culkin is already a veteran of eight films, including his debut
in *Rocket Gibraltar*, his scene-stealing performance in *Uncle Buck*
and the *Home Alone* movies. He enjoys acting and considers his
most challenging moment on screen the death scene from *My Girl*.
In that same film Macaulay had his first screen kiss, which he didn't
enjoy quite so much, because it took fifteen takes to get it right from
every angle.

Macaulay has recently discovered girls and has already had his
first date and girlfriend. He attends the Professional Children's
School in Manhattan and is tutored while on a film set. He entertains
himself by playing practical jokes on the cast and crew—like putting

double-sided tape on the toilet seat. Macaulay earns money to supplement his five-dollar-a-day allowance, not only winning $50 dollars playing poker with the crew of *Home Alone 2*, but collecting $200 from the adult stars of *My Girl*, Jamie Lee Curtis and Dan Aykroyd, after he and co-star Anna Chlumsky initiated a "swear jar" to which everyone had to contribute when they swore. Macaulay has befriended pop star Michael Jackson, who took him on a trip to Barbados, and with whom he has gone toy shopping in disguise. He even appeared in Jackson's "Black or White" video. When he's at home with his family, he says he likes to walk his dog, a bearded collie named Bishop, play Nintendo and follow pro wrestling.

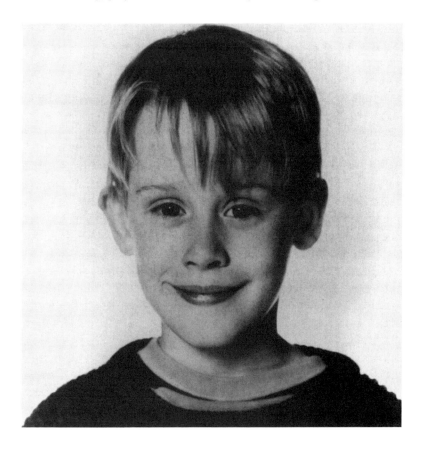

JAMIE LEE CURTIS

REAL NAME: Jamie Lee Curtis
DATE OF BIRTH: November 22, 1958
PLACE OF BIRTH: Los Angeles, California

EYE COLOR: Blue   HAIR COLOR: Dark blond
HEIGHT: 5'5"   WEIGHT: 115

This ex-scream queen has parlayed roles in horror movies like *Halloween* into a successful career in both movies and television.

In the late '70s, Jamie was looking for direction in her life in all the wrong places but found it in the new genre of "slasher" movies: "When I was a teenager, nobody was making teenage movies. It was a time when actresses like Barbra Streisand and Sally Field were in their late twenties and thirties. No one knew what people were doing at age eighteen. That's why a horror film came out that reinvented the teenage audience."

The daughter of Tony Curtis and Janet Leigh, Jamie grew up in Los Angeles with her mother. She was an active and athletic child who played piano and guitar and enjoyed putting on plays for the neighborhood kids. She attended Beverly Hills High School and the Westlake School in Bel Air until 1975, when her mother's new career on stage moved them back east. After graduation from the Choate School in Connecticut, she returned home intending to study law at the University of the Pacific, but lasted only three months. Falling in with an older crowd that was into cocaine, she recalls herself "just blowing around. It was a really lost time." In an attempt to reconcile with a father she had hardly known, she spent a few years with him, but they ended up doing little together but coke.

After extricating herself from that situation, she began taking acting classes and appearing on such TV shows as *Columbo* and *Quincy*. It was in 1978 that she made her motion picture debut as a teenager terrorized by the boogie man in *Halloween*. Her next pictures, *The Fog*, *Prom Night*, *Road Games* and *Halloween II* were all variations on the same theme. She broke out of that mold in 1983, giving a hip performance as Dan Aykroyd's prostitute girlfriend in the comedy hit *Trading Places*. After building a solid film career with hits such as *A Fish Called Wanda*, Jamie made the move to television as Richard Lewis' co-star in the sitcom *Anything But Love*. Although the show suffered from shaky ratings, it was a darling of the critics, and she won a 1990 Golden Globe award as outstanding female performer in a comedy. Jamie is currently shooting *My Girl II*, the sequel to *My Girl*.

Jamie has been married since 1984 to writer-comedian Christopher Guest, and they adopted a daughter in 1986. Now that everyone in the family seems to be drug-free, she says that life has evened out, and her relationship with both parents is smooth. "I used to be wildly, chronically insecure," admits Jamie, "But, yes, I have come of age. It's really my time. Jamie's time."

TED DANSON

REAL NAME: Edward Bridge Danson III
DATE OF BIRTH: December 29, 1947
PLACE OF BIRTH: San Diego, California

EYE COLOR: Brown   HAIR COLOR: Brown
HEIGHT: 6'2"   WEIGHT: 185

"My father," says Ted Danson, "is director of a museum dedicated
to the natural history of Arizona and the arts and crafts of the Hopi
and Navajo Indian tribes. So there were a lot of Hopis and Navajos
and ranchers' kids in my life. It was really an idyllic growing-up."
And it was playing "cowboys and Indians" with the local Indian boys
that gave him his first taste of acting.

At thirteen, Ted decided on a change and attended Kent, a prep
school in Connecticut that was affiliated with the Episcopal church.
While there, he acted in his first real play and also went out for basketball. Without any real goal or direction, he transferred to Stanford
University in California, where "I just played around, didn't know
what I wanted to do." Then one day, while trying to figure it out, a
good-looking waitress caught his eye, and he decided to follow her,
"just to be near her," he says. She happened to be an aspiring actress
on her way to an audition, and while he was there, he got caught up
in the spirit of things and won a part himself.

Now that he knew what he wanted to do, Ted moved to
Pittsburgh to join the Drama Department at Carnegie-Mellon
University. After earning his drama degree, he moved to New York
and worked in commercials and two soap operas, *The Doctors* and
Somerset. Moving to Los Angeles in 1978, he taught at the Actor's
Institute, did some more commercials, and landed an occasional
guest spot on TV shows like *Laverne and Shirley* and *Magnum, P.I.*
He also appeared in several films—including *Body Heat* and *The
Onion Field*—but didn't get his star until the producers of *Cheers*
picked him to play libidinous bartender Sam Malone. It became the
role for Ted, and although he went on to star in films such as *Three
Men and a Baby*, Sam may be the role for which he seems destined
to be remembered. But he is now pursuing a movie career in earnest

with his recent hit *Made in America* and *Getting Even With Dad*, which is in production and co-stars Macaulay Culkin.

Divorced from his college sweetheart, Ted was at an EST seminar in 1977 when he met interior decorator Casey Coates. They were married that year; then, in 1979, she suffered a massive stroke during childbirth. After three years of therapy, she recovered, and they adopted another daughter. In 1987, they founded the American Oceans Campaign, a lobbying organization dedicated to cleaning up sea pollution. Ted also raises money to help educate American Indian children in the Southwest. Shortly after the release of *Made in America*, Ted and his wife agreed to split up, and he began a much publicized romance with Whoopi Goldberg, his co-star in that movie.

GEENA DAVIS

REAL NAME: Virginia Davis
DATE OF BIRTH: January 21, 1957
PLACE OF BIRTH: Wareham, Massachusetts

EYE COLOR: Brown   HAIR COLOR: Brown
HEIGHT: 6'   WEIGHT: 135

In her high school yearbook, Geena Davis wrote this caption underneath her picture: "Plans to go to Hollywood and become a movie star." Though she went on to win an Oscar for her portrayal of Muriel the dog trainer in *The Accidental Tourist*, it took the phenomenal success of her female Easy Rider role in *Thelma and Louise* to really make her a movie star.

One of two children born to a civil engineer and a teacher's aide, Geena and her brother were raised in Wareham, Massachusetts. As a child, she studied the piano and the flute and aspired to become a concert pianist while putting on one-girl plays for her friends and family. She competed in both the hurdles and the high jump at Wareham High and was considered something of a class clown, claiming to have had only one date before spending her senior year as an exchange student in Sweden. That's where she had her first real boyfriend. "Suddenly nobody was noticing I was tall. They liked me there," she has said. And it was there that she decided to become an actress.

Returning to the United States, Geena spent a year at New England College before entering the professional actor's training program at Boston University. While there, she spent summers acting at the Mount Washington Repertory Theater Company in North Conway, New Hampshire. After taking her degree from B.U. in 1979, she moved to New York and, between auditions, supported herself as a model. She made her feature film debut as a half-dressed girl in Dustin Hoffman's dressing room in the 1982 film *Tootsie*. In addition to her movie career, which has ranged from *The Fly* (her first starring role) to *Beetlejuice* and *Thelma and Louise*, Geena spent the 1983-84 season opposite Dabney Coleman on the short-lived sitcom *Buffalo Bill*. Following her role in the hit *A League of Their Own* in 1992, she is currently filming *Angie, I Says*.

Geena has said that the key to success in life is "independence." Her divorce from second husband, actor Jeff Goldblum, and becoming a movie star have certainly made her independent.

DANIEL DAY-LEWIS

REAL NAME: Daniel Michael Blake Day-Lewis
DATE OF BIRTH: April 29,1957
PLACE OF BIRTH: London, England

EYE COLOR: Green   HAIR COLOR: Brown
HEIGHT: 6'2"   WEIGHT: 160

Known for his on and off-screen intensity, Daniel Day-Lewis has grown beyond playing eccentric characters to emerge as a true leading man.

Daniel was raised by his father, English poet laureate Cecil Day-Lewis, and mother, actress Jill Balcon. The family, which includes his older sister, Tamasin, often enjoyed visits from literary luminaries such as W.H. Auden. Daniel went to a state school in his youth because the elder Day-Lewis was a Communist who felt his son should have experience with people and institutions outside the family's wealth and privilege. When he was eleven, he was sent to Sevenoaks Academy, an all-boys boarding school, where he felt so out of place that he became willful and obstinate and began drinking and stealing. His only relief came from participating in the school's theatrical productions. But after two years, he ran away to Bedales, his sister's arts-oriented coed school, and stayed on to pursue both acting and woodworking with a passion. Daniel's father saw him perform only once on stage before his death in 1972 of pancreatic cancer. Day-Lewis now regrets not only having been such a disagreeable young man during his father's last days but that his father never lived to see his son make a success of his career.

At the age of sixteen, Daniel accidentally overdosed on migraine medication, suffered uncontrollable hallucinations for two weeks, and was mistakenly admitted to a mental hospital as a heroin addict. To escape confinement, Daniel had to play what he called his "greatest performance of sanity." He jokes that since then he has suffered no migraine pain. In between roles, he travels through Europe with his watercolor set. To keep in shape and maintain his emotional balance, he runs five miles a day.

Day-Lewis has earned high praise from his peers for choosing such diverse roles and for the energy and dedication he pours into them. He transforms himself physically for each new character and is almost unrecognizable from film to film. As the street tough in *My Beautiful Laundrette*, he sported spiky bleached hair. His next role was the uptight English nobleman in *A Room With a View*. His portrayal as the crippled Christy Brown in *My Left Foot* earned him an Academy Award. For that role, Day-Lewis learned to write, paint and eat with his foot, and kept so in character that on breaks he remained in his wheelchair and had to be fed and carried around by the crew. He played the prolific lover, Tomas, in *The Unbearable Lightness of Being*, but it wasn't until his dashing performance as Hawkeye in *The Last of the Mohicans* that Daniel Day-Lewis finally emerged as a sexy leading man. He is following up with Martin Scorsese's *The Age of Innocence* in 1993.

ROBERT DE NIRO

REAL NAME: Robert De Niro Jr.
DATE OF BIRTH: August 17, 1943
PLACE OF BIRTH: New York, New York

EYE COLOR: Brown   HAIR COLOR: Brown
HEIGHT: 5'9"   WEIGHT:148

Robert De Niro is one of the few actors who has won not only the applause of critics and the respect of colleagues, but widespread box office appeal as well. His ability to immerse himself completely in a part, losing or gaining weight, seemingly getting taller or shorter, older or younger, have made him a legend in the acting community.

Robert, an only child, was two years old when his artist father and mother separated. Raised in Greenwich Village and the Lower East Side's Little Italy, he attended several high schools, including the High School of Music and Art. But his mother recalls that "his idea of high school was just not to show up," and he dropped out at sixteen to take acting classes with famed acting coach Stella Adler. Explaining his decision to explore acting at a young age, Robert has said, "At first, being a star was a big part of it. When I got into it, it

became more complicated. To totally submerge into another character and experience life through him, without having to risk the real-life consequences—well, it's a cheap way to do things you would never dare to do yourself."

Landing small parts at first, he acted off-off-Broadway and in workshops and then, in 1968, was cast in *Greetings*, an underground film by the then unknown underground director Brian De Palma. He worked with De Palma again two years later in *Hi, Mom!*, playing the part of Jon Rubin, the same character he had played in *Greetings*. Although he worked steadily during his early days as an actor, De Niro did not attract any real attention until 1972 when he played Bruce Pearson, a baseball catcher dying of Hodgkin's disease in the film adaptation of Mark Harris' novel, *Bang the Drum Slowly*. Never having been a baseball fan, Robert went to the Cincinnati Reds Florida camp to train for the part. "I enjoyed the experience as research for a movie, but it didn't increase my interest in the game," he said in one interview. He also spent a few weeks in south Georgia cultivating a backwoods accent and tobacco spitting. After starring in Martin Scorsese's *Mean Streets*, De Niro hit the big time as the young Vito Corleone in *The Godfather Part II*. De Niro studied Marlon Brando (who played Corleone as an old man), spent six weeks in Sicily, again perfecting his accent, and was rewarded in 1974 with an Oscar for best supporting actor. Success continued in 1976 with his portrayal of Travis Bickle, the psychopathic cab driver in *Taxi Driver*. He went on to win a best actor Oscar in 1980 for his portrayal of Jake LaMotta in *Raging Bull*. Choosy about his roles, De Niro often takes smaller character parts over full-blown leads just to experience the intricacies of what makes that character tick. His recent appearances include roles as Satan in *Angel Heart*, Al Capone in *The Untouchables*, a seedy Los Angeles skip tracer in the hit *Midnight Run*, and most recently as the abusive stepfather in *This Boy's Life*. De Niro made his directorial debut in 1993 with *A Bronx Tale*.

He was married in 1976 to actress Diahnne Abbott, and they have one son but are now divorced. On the rare occasions that Robert grants interviews, he sequesters his personal life and discusses only his work. Interestingly, for an actor of his reputation and accomplishment, De Niro reportedly never rehearses, preferring to develop the scene as the camera rolls. As he explains, "That's the only time it's real."

GÉRARD DEPARDIEU

REAL NAME: Gérard Depardieu
DATE OF BIRTH: December 27, 1948
PLACE OF BIRTH: Châteauroux, France

EYE COLOR: Green   HAIR COLOR: Brown
HEIGHT: 6'3"   WEIGHT: 225

"I was born in a family in which people didn't speak much and drank a lot," says the French actor. Young Gérard would come home to find his father, an illiterate and often unemployed sheet-metal worker, sprawled out drunk on the sidewalk across the street from his house. His mother, Liliette, always reminded him that his birth as the third of her six children dashed her ambition to leave them and travel. An athletic boy, he played soccer on the school team and did a little amateur boxing, as his crooked nose still bears witness. But because his family was held in such low esteem by the neighbors, Gérard had few playmates. To kill time, he stole cars and dealt in black-market whiskey and cigarettes at the nearby American Army base.

At the age of twelve, he dropped out of school and left home, living with two prostitutes. He soon took to the road, working odd jobs like selling soap for the blind and brushes door to door. But petty theft, assault and robbery were his way of life. Depardieu has also admitted that he participated in numerous rapes during these years, stating that, "It was absolutely normal in those circumstances. That was part of my childhood." His delinquency sent the young Depardieu to jail. During this period, he lost his ability to speak. "When you're young and afraid, you lose the habit of talking," he says. A prison psychologist sent him to a speech therapist who diagnosed Gérard's problem as overly sensitive hearing. To overcome his disability, he read works of literature and acted them out. Through therapy he also discovered and developed his photographic memory.

Acting intrigued him so much that, at sixteen, he auditioned for and was accepted to the Theatre Nationale Populaire in Paris. Taking a wide variety of roles, Depardieu earned a loyal following in his early days and has since become the best, most popular and most prolific

French actor of his generation. His first major film role was *Nathalie Granger*, in 1971, and his breakthrough was in *Les Valseuses* (Going Places) in 1973. To date, he has starred in more than eighty films— about four to six a year. But he says, "At least sixty of them were boring. About ten were very, very good. When it comes down to it, ten out of eighty isn't bad." Among the most notable are *The Return of Martin Guerre*, *Jean de Florette*, *Camille Claudel* and *Cyrano de Bergerac*. All of them were in French, until he learned English specifically for his role in *Green Card*, the 1990 romantic comedy that was his first American film.

He and wife Elisabeth, herself an accomplished actress, have been married more than twenty years and have two children, Guillaume, also an actor, and Julie. Depardieu has become something of a businessman, financing and producing several films. He also owns two wineries in France and is proud of the fact that on his passport, the occupation listed is no longer "actor" but "winemaker."

JOHNNY DEPP

REAL NAME: John Christopher Depp II
DATE OF BIRTH: June 9, 1963
PLACE OF BIRTH: Owensboro, Kentucky

EYE COLOR: Brown   HAIR COLOR: Brown
HEIGHT: 5'9"   WEIGHT: 145

A reluctant sex symbol, Johnny Depp received more than 10,000 fan letters a month while he was starring in the TV series *21 Jump Street*. Ironically, in his youth, Depp's aspirations tended toward music; acting never entered his mind. His engineer father and waitress mother moved the family to Miramar, Florida, when he was seven years old. Johnny saw a gospel group perform and knew music was for him. At twelve he bought his first electric guitar for $25 and taught himself to play. True to his ambition, he began living out the stereotype of the young rocker, learning to smoke at twelve, later drinking and eventually experimenting with harder drugs. Petty theft and fighting led to some scrapes with the police, and at one time, Depp was suspended from school for mooning a teacher. Of this rebellious drug phase and his eventual withdrawal from it, he says, "I saw what was happening to me. And I saw people I was hanging around with and I realized this wasn't for me." His parents divorced when he was sixteen, and soon afterward he dropped out of high school. A loyal friend, he moved into a car with his best friend, Sal, who had nowhere else to live, so that Sal wouldn't feel abandoned.

Of the fifteen bands Depp played in while pursuing a music career, The Kids were the most successful, opening for bigger groups at their Florida gigs. At twenty, Depp wed one of his bandmate's relatives, Lori Anne Allison, moving with her and the rest of the band to Los Angeles in 1983 in search of a record deal. Instead, he found himself selling ballpoint pens over the phone to make ends meet, among other odd jobs.

Within two years, the band and his marriage broke up. Alone in Los Angeles, he befriended actor Nicolas Cage, a fan of The Kids, who suggested he try acting and sent Depp to his agent. Within a week, he auditioned for and got a role in the first *Nightmare on Elm*

Street, and a small part in the acclaimed *Platoon* soon followed. Not wanting to do television, Depp first rejected the role of Tom Hanson on *Jump Street*, but later rethought and signed on because he didn't think it would last a year. It became a hit, and Depp grudgingly stayed for four years, enduring the adoration of fans and hoping that the position and power it gave him in Hollywood would eventually bring him roles with more artistic integrity. When his contract expired, he pulled out, believing the show's quality had eroded. He moved on to films, winning his first leading role in *Cry-Baby* in 1990. His leading-man status, as well as his skill as an actor, was solidified by his portrayal of the title character in *Edward Scissorhands* in 1991 and his 1993 film *Benny and Joon*.

In addition to his unflagging interest in music, which he has turned into a commercial venture with half-ownership in a Sunset Strip nightclub called The Central and an appearance in Tom Petty's video "Into the Great Wide Open," Johnny reads voraciously and has a passion for the works of J.D. Salinger and Jack Kerouac. Several tattoos adorn his body, including one which says "Winona Forever" on his right shoulder that he got during his relationship with his former fiancée, actress Winona Ryder.

LAURA DERN

REAL NAME: Laura Elizabeth Dern
DATE OF BIRTH: February 10, 1967
PLACE OF BIRTH: Santa Monica, California

EYE COLOR: Blue   HAIR COLOR: Blond
HEIGHT: 5'10"   WEIGHT: 120

Fated to become an actress, Laura Dern hails from a theatrical family: Father Bruce Dern and mother Diane Ladd are both Academy Award-nominated actors, and her maternal cousin was playwright Tennessee Williams. But when her parents were reluctant to let their daughter follow in their footsteps, Laura pursued an acting career of her own. Explaining what influenced her decision, she says, "I think passion attracts me, and I grew up with two people who were completely passionate about their work. Seeing your parents come home at night and feeling satisfied with what they do—how can you not be attracted to it?"

Laura's parents divorced when she was only two years old, and she grew up with her mother. Bruce and Diane had lost an eighteen-month-old girl in a drowning accident before Laura was born, and her father felt the loss deeply. Fearing a repeat of his pain, he distanced himself from his second daughter, and the physical separation created by the divorce was coupled with an emotional chasm that took years to bridge. At her prompting, he and Laura finally reconciled when she was twelve. She had gained a second family through her mother's remarriage to a stockbroker and lived with them for two years in New York.

By the age of nine she had discovered her desire to act. Laura made her film debut opposite her mother as an extra (eating an ice cream cone) in *Alice Doesn't Live Here Anymore*, and soon after began taking acting lessons in earnest, pedaling her bike to classes with Lee Strasberg for two years and attending summer programs first at Harvard, then at the Royal Academy of Dramatic Arts in London. She won her first substantive film role in *Foxes* when she was eleven under the pretense that she was fourteen. But her breakthrough was *Mask*, in which she gave an astonishingly convincing performance as a blind girl. She has since become known for her honest portrayals of naïvely sexy young women. In *Smooth Talk*, she was a girl on the verge of womanhood, a virgin seduced by a drifter. For director David Lynch, she first played the innocent Sandy in *Blue Velvet*, then the intensely sensual Lula in *Wild at Heart*. Her performance as a love-starved, emotionally deprived young girl in *Rambling Rose*—again opposite her mother—earned each of them an Academy Award nomination—the first mother-daughter team nominated in the same year. Laura went on to co-star in the megahit of 1993 (and possibly history), *Jurassic Park*.

Laura is a spiritual person, something her mother exposed her to as a young girl. When she was ten, Ladd gave her a stack of books that included the Bible and the Koran. She continues to study metaphysics and philosophy, developing her own explanation and guidelines for life. To ground herself and keep her ego in check in the emotionally and mentally demanding profession of acting, she practices yoga and meditation.

DANNY DEVITO

REAL NAME: Daniel Michael DeVito
DATE OF BIRTH: November 17, 1944
PLACE OF BIRTH: Neptune, New Jersey

EYE COLOR: Brown   HAIR COLOR: Black
HEIGHT: 5'   WEIGHT: 155

At five feet tall, Danny DeVito is living proof that successful actors come in all shapes and sizes. The youngest of three children, he spent his childhood in parochial school, terrified of the nuns. At one time or another, his father owned businesses ranging from a dry cleaners to a pool hall. Once free of high school, he became "Mr. Danny," a hairdresser in his sister's salon. Soon wanting to do more with his life, he enrolled at the American Academy of Dramatic Arts in New York to become a makeup artist. Discovering that that major wasn't offered—and since he was there anyway—he signed up for acting lessons.

After unfruitful rounds of casting directors and summer stock, he moved to Los Angeles to look for parts but wound up parking cars for two years. Returning to New York, he appeared in several off-Broadway plays, including *One Flew Over the Cuckoo's Nest*. DeVito had met Michael Douglas while acting in summer stock, and when Douglas produced the film version, he hired DeVito for the role of Martini. After minor roles in several more movies, DeVito got his big break when he won the role of Louie Da Palma in the star-making sitcom *Taxi*. Although Louie was originally intended as a supporting character, DeVito was such a hit that soon the producers began focusing entire episodes around him, and his portrayal won him a best supporting actor Emmy in 1981. During *Taxi*'s last season in 1982-83, one of its producers, James L. Brooks, cast Danny in the role of Vernon, Shirley MacLaine's unsuccessful suitor, in *Terms of Endearment*. There soon followed a string of films in which DeVito played quirky, memorable bad guys, who turned him into a box office star: *Romancing the Stone*, *Wise Guys*, *Twins* and *Ruthless People*.

In 1990, he directed and played a small part in *The War of the Roses* and, in 1992, directed Jack Nicholson in *Hoffa*.

Since 1982, DeVito has been married to *Cheers* actress Rhea Perlman, who at one time played his girlfriend Zina on *Taxi*. With three children born in the last six years, Danny says, "We've been in diapers now for almost seven years straight." He also says that they haven't lost sight of keeping their relationship tightly strung, and on a regular basis take off on weekends alone together in a hotel.

PHIL DONAHUE

REAL NAME: Phil Donahue
DATE OF BIRTH: December 21, 1935
PLACE OF BIRTH: Cleveland, Ohio

EYE COLOR: Blue   HAIR COLOR: White
HEIGHT: 6'   WEIGHT: 174

Hosting an interview show that features the most controversial issues and people of our time, Phil Donahue admits that he struggles to maintain his journalistic neutrality. "I don't feel obligated to talk down the center of every issue," he has said, "but at the same time, I think it's really important not to preach. It's arrogant, and in a pragmatic sense, it's not good television. But I reserve the right to express myself, and I feel compelled to bring a guest who speaks in grand terms down to earth."

The older son of a furniture salesman father and department store clerk mother, Phil attended a Catholic school where baseball was his main interest. Lacking the grades to enter the Jesuit high school, he attended St. Edward High in Cleveland and maintained "a largely mediocre report card," as he describes it. His broadcast career started during the summer between his junior and senior years at Notre Dame when he landed a job as a gofer at a local TV station owned by the university. Eventually he became one of the regular announcers and, after graduation in 1957, went to work as a summer replacement announcer at Cleveland's KYW-AM-TV.

For the next ten years, Donahue worked for several stations in Michigan and Ohio but was never able to break into a major market. Discouraged, he dropped out of broadcasting in 1967 and took a job as a salesman in Dayton, Ohio. Four months later, he returned to television as the host of his own morning interview show, *The Phil Donahue Show*. It was there that he pioneered the concept of audience participation, now a staple of the afternoon talk-show crowd. Phil recalls that "two or three shows in, I realized the audience was asking some very good questions during commercials. Then, on some given day which I don't even remember, I jumped out of the chair and went into the audience. A woman stood up and asked the guest a question. And that, that was nirvana." The show was picked up for syndication by the Avco Broadcasting Company, and by 1980, Phil Donahue was the most watched syndicated talk-show host in America. Today he is firmly entrenched as one of the triumvirate of daytime talk-show hosts along with Oprah Winfrey and Geraldo Rivera, and he remains the one against whom all other hosts are measured. Phil penned his autobiography, *My Own Story*, in 1980 and *The Human Animal* in 1985.

Phil has five children from his first wife, whom he divorced in 1975. In 1980, he married actress Marlo Thomas, whom he met when she was a guest on his show. Phil considers himself a reformed male chauvinist and is a strong activist for the National Organization for Women. Referring to the role of religion in influencing sexism, he says, "Women were occasions of sin. The Church taught us that. Men were so busy trying to avoid sin that we could never make friends with women, never share ideas, never care how they felt." Formally separated from the Church, he also says that "organized religion has been very unfair to God."

KIRK DOUGLAS

REAL NAME: Issur Danielovitch (Demsky)
DATE OF BIRTH: December 9, 1916
PLACE OF BIRTH: Amsterdam, New York

EYE COLOR: Blue-green   HAIR COLOR: Blond
HEIGHT: 5'11"   WEIGHT: 170

Kirk Douglas is a man of many accomplishments. Not only is he an award-winning actor, he is also a producer, best-selling author, diplomatic representative of the United States and an internationally honored citizen.

Born to Russian immigrants, the middle child and only boy of seven children, young Issur woke before dawn and sold newspapers to help his financially struggling family, and he was a mediocre student until his high school English teacher introduced him to drama. As a child, he had play-acted with his sisters for fun, but now he took it seriously, participating in oratorical contests, debates and plays. After graduation, he took his $163 in savings and hitchhiked to St. Lawrence University in New York, riding atop a manure-filled truck on the last leg of his journey. There, Douglas was an honor student in English and German, though his studies were secondary to other activities. In addition to being a state champion wrestler, Douglas found time to serve as president of the National Student Federation of America, the student body, the campus council and, in his senior year, the dramatic society.

He then moved on to the American Academy of Dramatic Arts, earning his tuition by wrestling in mock matches, bellhopping and waiting tables at Schrafft's. World War II called him into the service, and he attended the Naval Midship School at Notre Dame, then served in various venues and finally in the Galapagos, where he was injured in a submarine attack. Recuperating in a New Orleans hospital, he was visited by fellow AADA student, Diana Dill. The two married in 1943, had two sons together, and divorced in 1950. Douglas remarried in 1954 to Anne Buydens, with whom he also had two sons. All four of his sons are now involved in show business.

Douglas made his stage debut in 1941 before going to war and his screen debut in 1946. By 1949, when he received his first Oscar nomination for *The Champion*, he was a well-established star. For his work since then, he has earned two more Oscar nominations, a New York Drama Critics award and an Emmy nomination. In 1955 he became one of the first actors to establish his own production company, and has since produced, directed and starred in many of his own films. He was also instrumental in breaking the "Hollywood Blacklist" when he made it known that he had hired a famous banned writer for the epic *Spartacus*, at a time when movie producers wouldn't touch him, and others soon followed suit.

In 1988, the multi-talented Douglas wrote an autobiography, *The Ragman's Son*, which became a bestseller, and has since followed it up with two novels, *Dance With the Devil* and *The Gift*, both equally well received. In 1991, Douglas was awarded the American Film Institute's Life Achievement Award, in a ceremony held just weeks after he was nearly killed in a tragic helicopter crash that claimed two victims. At the AFI, Douglas said, "They say life flashes before you like a movie, but I was knocked out. I didn't see one thing. Thank God I got a second chance to see it all again." Kirk is currently at work shooting the film *Greedy*.

MICHAEL DOUGLAS

REAL NAME: Michael Kirk Douglas
DATE OF BIRTH: September 25, 1944
PLACE OF BIRTH: New Brunswick, New Jersey

EYE COLOR: Blue   HAIR COLOR: Brown
HEIGHT: 5'9 1/2"   WEIGHT: 150

The eldest son of screen legend Kirk Douglas, Michael Douglas has become a Hollywood superstar both as an actor and as a producer. His very first project as producer, *One Flew Over the Cuckoo's Nest*, grossed $180 million in 1975, and in 1988, he won an Academy Award as best actor for his portrayal of Gordon Gekko in *Wall Street*. Quipped his father, "Had I known he was going to be such a success, I would have been nicer to him when he was young."

Michael and his brother grew up mostly with their mother, actress Diana Dill. Since her career kept them on the move, Michael attended a variety of elementary and middle schools between the east and west coasts, including military school in Los Angeles. But he received his primary education at ritzy eastern prep schools, including the Choate School in Wallingford, Connecticut. He was accepted to Yale but enrolled instead at the University of California at Santa Barbara, where he flunked out during his first year. After eighteen months of working at odd jobs, he re-enrolled and became a drama major. While at school, Michael acted in many school productions and was named the school's best actor in 1967 for his performance in *Candida*. After graduation in 1968, Douglas moved to New York and studied acting, first at the Neighborhood Playhouse and then at the American Place Theater. He also began appearing off-Broadway and in mostly forgettable TV shows and movies. In 1972, however, he was cast opposite Karl Malden as detective Steve Keller in the series *The Streets of San Francisco*, and his career took off. The show became a solid success by the mid-'70s, and Douglas was nominated for three

consecutive Emmy awards. He left the show in 1975 to produce *One Flew Over the Cuckoo's Nest*, which his father had bought in 1963. It was a huge hit and made him a hot property. Since then, he has produced *The China Syndrome*, *Romancing the Stone* and *Starman*, among many other hits. When *Romancing the Stone* became a box office smash in 1984, Douglas became as popular an actor as he already was a producer, with lead roles in *Wall Street*, *The War of the Roses*, *Fatal Attraction*, *Basic Instinct* and *Falling Down*, all hyper-controversial films.

Married since 1977, he and his wife, Diandra, have one son. He shies away from the Hollywood social whirl and devotes time to campaigning for handgun control and other liberal causes.

ROBERT DOWNEY JR.

REAL NAME: Robert Downey Jr.
DATE OF BIRTH: April 4, 1965
PLACE OF BIRTH: New York, New York

EYE COLOR: Brown   HAIR COLOR: Brown
HEIGHT: 5'10"   WEIGHT: 150

The irrepressible star of such films as *Less Than Zero* and *The Pickup Artist*, Brat Pack actor Robert Downey Jr. was named "Hollywood's Hottest Actor" by *Rolling Stone* magazine in 1988.

Born into a theatrical family, he spent his childhood in such places as New Mexico, London and Woodstock, New York, before settling in California. He made his debut at age five in *Pound*, a movie produced by his father. Robert's sister had no interest in acting, but his actress mother also showed up in Dad's films. "He was doing these crazy films," says Robert. "Mom would pick me up at school wearing this big quilted cape. I felt like I was in a J.D. Salinger story." He appeared in three more of his father's films, *The Greaser's Palace*, *Up the Academy*, and *This Is America the Movie, Not the Country*, before dropping out of Santa Monica High School during his junior year to appear in *Baby It's You*.

Since then, his career has taken off with quirky starring roles as a teenage Don Juan in *The Pickup Artist*, a cocaine addict in *Less Than Zero* and the reincarnation of Cybill Shepherd's lover in *Chances Are*. It wasn't until 1992 that he was ready to take on his greatest challenge: playing legendary Charlie Chaplin in the 1992 biopic, *Chaplin*. He rose to the occasion, winning not only critical nods but an Oscar nomination. He said that while filming *Chaplin*, "I'd watch one of Charlie's films, but by the end of it I was wildly depressed, because I realized that what he'd done in this twenty-minute short was more expressive and funnier than everything I've thought about doing my whole life."

During his time as one of the leaders of the Brat Pack, Robert admits that "I was into pulling 360s in the Universal parking lot and disappearing for three days for things one needs blood transfusions to recuperate from." After ending his seven-year relationship with actress Sarah Jessica Parker, he married makeup artist Deborah Falconer in 1992. According to Robert, his new motto is: "Try to be thankful for the gift I've been given—the gift of genius. And try not to be a schmuck." Downey released the romantic comedy *Heart and Souls* in 1993 and is now filming *Natural Born Killers* for director Oliver Stone.

FAYE DUNAWAY

REAL NAME: Dorothy Faye Dunaway
DATE OF BIRTH: January 14, 1941
PLACE OF BIRTH: Bascom, Florida

EYE COLOR: Brown   HAIR COLOR: Brown
HEIGHT: 5'9"   WEIGHT: 119

"I was very loved when I was a child," Faye has said. To her parents, "I was the sun and the earth and the moon." Born on a farm, she grew up an Army brat; she and her younger brother spent early childhood living on military bases around the world. A beautiful child, she was doted on by a mother who provided her with dance, music and voice lessons even when they couldn't afford it. "All the time," says her mother, "I knew Faye wanted to be the best and the biggest." During her sophomore year in high school, her parents were divorced, and Faye went with her mother to live in Tallahassee. Then, after high school, she enrolled at the University of Florida on a scholarship, but dropped out after a year to join her boyfriend, a football player, at Florida State. She didn't stay there long, though, transferring to Boston University's School of Fine and Applied Arts to continue her education as an actress.

During her senior year, while playing the lead in a university production of *The Crucible*, she was seen by Elia Kazan, and on his recommendation was admitted to the actors' training program at the Lincoln Center Repertory Theater. Although she became successful both in theater and film, it was her third movie role, as the lascivious bank robber Bonnie Parker opposite Warren Beatty in *Bonnie and Clyde*, that made her a star—and won her an Oscar nomination. "Bonnie was the closest of all the characters I have played to myself," Faye says. "I was home free with that. I knew exactly where this poor little Southern girl lived. What she wanted to break out of. That was territory I really understood." Following her work in *Puzzle of a*

Downfall Child and *The Eyes of Laura Mars*, she won a best actress Oscar in 1976 for her performance as a driven TV executive in the film *Network*. In addition to her hateful representation of Joan Crawford in *Mommie Dearest*, she starred in *Chinatown, Supergirl* and *Wait Until Spring Bandini*. Her latest films are *Double Edge* and *The Temp*, and Faye makes her TV debut in a sitcom in the fall of 1993 with actor Robert Urich as her co-star.

To relax, she turns to sculpting and cooking. Divorced from singer/songwriter Peter Wolf and photographer Terry O'Neil, she has one son, who was born in 1980.

ROBERT DUVALL

REAL NAME: Robert Selden Duvall
DATE OF BIRTH: January 5, 1931
PLACE OF BIRTH: San Diego, California

EYE COLOR: Gray-green   HAIR COLOR: Brown
HEIGHT: 5'10"   WEIGHT: 170

Like Robert De Niro, Robert Duvall is a first-take actor who avoids rehearsing and prefers to act from the gut while the camera rolls. "If I have instincts I feel are right," he explains, "I don't want anybody to tamper with them. If I play a preacher, I play what's religious in me; if I play a guy with killer instincts, I find those passions in me."

The son of a Navy rear admiral, Duvall had a well-traveled childhood, moving with his family from base to base. A natural mimic, he was an astute observer of people, their mannerisms and regional accents wherever he lived. Although he was forever putting on little skits around the house as a child, Duvall was more interested in sports than in acting. When it came time for college, he enrolled at Principia College in Elsah, Illinois, as a history and government major. There, however, one of the professors noticed Duvall's acting talent and persuaded him to change his major to drama. After taking his degree, he spent two years in the Army as an enlisted man during the Korean War. Discharged in 1955, he moved to New York and studied acting for two years at the Neighborhood Playhouse under the GI Bill. Recalling the lean days when he was working the midnight shift at the post office, he says: "My roommate was Bobby Morse, and we were starving. Then one day he got the lead in *The Matchmaker*. It happened just like that for him. I also used to bum around with Gene Hackman in those days. I remember Gene used to say, 'There's a guy coming to New York you'll really like... his name's Dusty Hoffman.' We had a lot of good times then."

Robert's turn came in 1957 when he landed the lead in a one-night production of *A View From the Bridge*. His career took off, and several months later he won a lead in the TV series *Naked City*. His experience on that show led to his second big break, the role of Boo Radley in the 1963 film *To Kill a Mockingbird*. Duvall's long list of triumphs as the consummate character actor includes the roles of Major Frank Burns in the movie *M*A*S*H* and Bull Meechum in *The Great Santini*. After vaulting to stardom as Tom Hagen in the blockbuster hit *The Godfather*, Duvall has become recognized as one of America's finest actors. He has been nominated three times for Academy Awards, and in 1983 won the best actor award for his portrayal of ex-country singer Mac Sledge in *Tender Mercies*. He also returned to television for the Western miniseries *Lonesome Dove*. Most recently, he appeared as Daddy in the 1991 film *Rambling Rose*. Robert is now shooting a new film, *The Paper*, and upon its completion will begin another, entitled *Geronimo*.

Robert had been twice married before he wed dancer Sharon Brophy in 1990. When not involved in a role, he says he spends his leisure time either bird watching around his home in Virginia or watching sports on television.

CLINT EASTWOOD

REAL NAME: Clinton Eastwood Jr.
DATE OF BIRTH: May 31, 1930
PLACE OF BIRTH: San Francisco, California

EYE COLOR: Blue   HAIR COLOR: Dark blond
HEIGHT: 6'4"   WEIGHT: 198

Speaking very few lines of dialogue, Clint has squinted and sneered his way to stardom, first as the star of numerous Italian "spaghetti westerns" and then in major American films such as *Dirty Harry* and *Sudden Impact*. Trying to explain his appeal, he says: "Maybe being an introvert gives me, by sheer accident, a certain screen presence, a mystique. If I threw it all out for them to see, they might not be as interested."

For most of his childhood, Eastwood lived a life very similar to that of the "drifter" characters who would make him famous. During the Depression, he and his sister followed their father around Northern California, picking up and moving to wherever there was work to be found. "I can't remember how many schools I went to," Clint recalls. "I do know that we moved so much that I made very few friends. Moving has become sort of my lifestyle. Basically, I'm a drifter, a bum. As it turns out, I'm lucky because I'm going to end up financially well-off for a drifter." His family finally settled in Oakland, California, and Eastwood became a basketball star at Oakland Technical High School. He also taught himself how to play jazz piano, and worked for free meals at a club. After graduation, Eastwood took to the road, baling hay, lumberjacking in Oregon and working on a blast furnace in Texas, among other things, until he was drafted into the Army in 1951.

While stationed at Fort Ord in Monterey, he met several aspiring actors, including David Janssen, who persuaded him to give acting a shot. He did so, moving to Los Angeles where a screen test earned him a $75-a-week contract with Universal. For eighteen months he played small roles in small movies until the studio finally let him go. He says of those lean times: "They made a lot of cheapies in those days, a lot of B-pictures, and I'd always play the young lieutenant or

the lab technician." In 1959, digging swimming pools in Beverly Hills to make ends meet, he was on the verge of giving up acting when, while drinking coffee in a cafeteria, he was spotted by a producer and landed the role of Rowdy Yates in the series *Rawhide.* Eastwood stuck with the role for the next seven years. Then, in the summer of 1964, he appeared in his first Sergio Leone western, *A Fistful of Dollars,* as the soon-to-be-legendary "Man With No Name." The movie was huge throughout Europe, and Eastwood proceeded to play tough-guy roles in several sequels. By 1971, he was the second biggest box office draw in the United States. In addition to his work as an actor, Eastwood has directed several films, including *Pale Rider* and *Bird* and, most notably, his 1993 multi-Oscar-winning *Unforgiven,* which he considers the capstone of his career. The same year, he starred in another hit, *In the Line of Fire.*

Having served a term as the mayor of Carmel, California, and gone the Ferrari and exotic motorcycle route, Clint now prefers a good round of golf. In excellent shape, he works out in his own gym every day and remains unpretentious and pleasantly humble. His marriage to model and designer Maggie Johnson ended in the mid-'80s after twenty-plus years of marriage and two children.

EMILIO ESTEVEZ

REAL NAME: Emilio Estevez
DATE OF BIRTH: May 12, 1962
PLACE OF BIRTH: New York, New York

EYE COLOR: Blue   HAIR COLOR: Blond
HEIGHT: 5'9"   WEIGHT: 160

This good-looking, successful ex-Brat Packer recalls the most embarrassing moment in his life: While the Sheen family was visiting father Martin on location in Mexico in the late '60s, Emilio found himself eating breakfast next to his all-time hero, Art Garfunkel. Emilio says, "I idolized Art Garfunkel and actually envisioned myself being him. So I couldn't believe my good fortune. Well, my little sister [Renee] started eating butter right out of a bowl. My mother told her not to eat it because she was going to get sick. Seconds later, Renee lost it all over the table. I smelled her vomit and I puked on the floor right next to where Art Garfunkel was eating. He looked up at me and had a really disgusted expression on his face.... We walked out of the restaurant leaving behind a trail of vomit." Years later, his night-crawling tabloid years would bring still more embarrassing moments.

The eldest son of the family, Estevez took his father's real Spanish surname so that he wouldn't get any easy breaks because of his dad. Born in New York, he grew up in Malibu, attending Santa Monica High School with such notable buddies as Sean Penn and Rob Lowe. In junior high, along with brother Charlie and Sean Penn, he began playing around with a home movie camera, shooting and splicing together vignettes around the neighborhood. When he was sixteen, he began auditioning for acting roles, and on the day of his graduation got his first part in a TV movie.

After that, he landed a role in the movie *Tex*, and then, along with Lowe, was cast in the career-launching adaptation of S.E. Hinton's novel *The Outsiders*. From then on it's been all gravy for Estevez. His first starring role, as the title character in the cult classic *Repo Man*, and later roles in *The Breakfast Club* and *St. Elmo's Fire*, which is still his personal favorite, made him one of the hottest young actors around. Using his newly found clout, Estevez branched out, writing the screenplays for his next two films, *That Was Then, This Is Now* and *Wisdom*. He has since appeared with his brother Charlie in the comedy *Working Stiffs* and has portrayed Billy the Kid in *Young Guns* I and II. His career seems to have settled into a steady hum with the recent release of *Freejack*, a sci-fi flick co-starring Mick Jagger, and 1993's *Another Stakeout*. Estevez is at work re-creating his role as an ice hockey coach in *The Mighty Ducks 2*. It's a sequel to 1992's sleeper of the same name that has inspired Disney to form an ice hockey team named... The Mighty Ducks.

Deciding that he had outgrown his party period, he wed singer Paula Abdul in 1992 and has begun parenting his two children by former girlfriend Carey Salley. He recites a lesson learned from his father, which he reminds himself is the most important of all: "My job is no more or less important than someone else's. When I realize there are a billion people in China who don't know I exist, any flightiness is swept away."

LINDA EVANS

REAL NAME: Linda Evanstad
DATE OF BIRTH: November 18, 1942
PLACE OF BIRTH: Hartford, Connecticut

EYE COLOR: Blue   HAIR COLOR: Blond
HEIGHT: 5'8"   WEIGHT: 135

Blond, lithe and beautiful, Linda Evans is a genuine middle-aged sex symbol. Linda, who became a household name as faithful wife Krystle Carrington on *Dynasty*, is living proof that age and beauty are not mutually exclusive.

She came to North Hollywood with her parents and two sisters when she was only nine months old. Linda was a very shy child, dominated by her father, a painter/decorator. Recalling her formative years, she says that she learned at home to "do what people say and they will love you. So I chose most of my life to please others at all costs, and I discovered only recently that you can be loved without violating yourself." Although she took drama classes at Hollywood High School, Evans got her first part—in a soda commercial—only because she happened to accompany a friend who was trying out for the part to a casting session.

When she was fifteen, she made her debut in a TV series as, ironically, a friend of John Forsythe's daughter in *Bachelor Father*. Forsythe remembers Linda then: "She was a tall, skinny, knobby-kneed little girl when I first saw her." She then appeared on *The Adventures of Ozzie and Harriet* as well as in the film *Twilight of Honor* in 1963, but didn't achieve true stardom until landing the role of Audra Barkley on the hit series *The Big Valley*. Evans gave up the role in deference to her first husband, John Derek, who wanted her at home. He then proceeded to drop her for sixteen-year-old Bo Derek in 1973. Evans resumed her career, doing guest spots on television and getting increasingly better roles in movies like *The*

Klansman and *Tom Horn*. It was in 1980 that she accepted the role of Krystle, John Forsythe's wife, on *Dynasty*. It became a hit, and Evans went on to win a series of awards, including America's "Favorite Sex Symbol."

In order to keep in shape, Evans works out daily. She is a gourmet cook and also an expert numerologist, a skill she sometimes uses to analyze relationships. Linda had a three-year marriage to Beverly Hills realtor Stan Herman and has recently moved to the state of Washington. In 1983, she wrote a beauty book which was edited by Sean Derek, John's daughter by first wife Ursula Andress. Linda's ultimate beauty secret, she maintains, is: "To me, people look good on the outside because of how they feel on the inside."

PETER FALK

REAL NAME: Peter Michael Falk
DATE OF BIRTH: September 16, 1927
PLACE OF BIRTH: New York, New York

EYE COLOR: Brown   HAIR COLOR: Brown
HEIGHT: 5'6"   WEIGHT: 155

When he was three years old, Peter Falk's right eye was taken out during an operation to remove a malignant tumor, and he has worn a glass eye ever since. But it hasn't slowed him down a bit.

Peter remembers that he was self-conscious about it at first until he "started playing ball and going to the gym, and it became a joke." The son of clothing merchants, he attended New York's Ossining High School, where he got good grades, was elected president of his class and lettered in track, baseball and basketball. But, after school hours, he was a "genuine delinquent," by his own description, "out of some kind of craving for excitement. Some of the things we do when we rebel as kids come from a desire to put some of the dream into the real world." After graduation, he studied for a year at Hamilton College in upstate New York before leaving to join the Merchant Marines. He served for eighteen months as a cook and, after his discharge, went back to Hamilton to finish his degree. One year later, however, he transferred to the New School of Social Research, where he obtained his B.A. in political science in 1951. After getting his M.B.A. in public administration from Syracuse University, he tried and failed to join the CIA and eventually took a job as a management analyst with the Connecticut State Budget Bureau.

In Connecticut, Falk spent his free evenings acting with the Mark Twain Maskers and took acting classes with Eva Le Gallienne at the White Barn Theater. The notion that "ordinary people don't become actors," according to him, was dispelled after eavesdropping on some professional actors. Peter says, "I stopped by a theater in New Haven, and I followed Roddy McDowall, Estelle Winwood and Maria Riva to lunch just to hear what they'd talk about. The conversation was absolutely banal, and here I thought they were all geniuses."

Now that he was serious, he moved to New York and made his

professional debut in 1958 off-Broadway in *Don Juan*. In 1961, he hit the big time and received Academy Award nominations for his role in *Pocketful of Miracles* and for his portrayal of gangster Abe Reles in *Murder, Inc.* That role launched his career on both the big and little screen, and he began to appear frequently on both. He gave birth to the lovable, tough-guy detective, *Columbo*, in a TV movie in 1968. After it became a series, *Columbo* ran on NBC from 1971 to 1978, many segments of which he directed. It was brought back by ABC in 1989 and is still running today.

Falk enjoys sketching and playing golf and is a huge fan of the New York Knicks and the Los Angeles Lakers. Married since 1960, with two grown daughters, Peter still feels "more alive" when in New York, and although he has a home in Beverly Hills, he calls it "clean streets—no people—no nothing." His longtime friend and former pool hall buddy, the late John Cassavetes, affectionately described him: "He's deep. He's gentle. He's two thousand years old. He's somebody everybody falls in love with."

FARRAH FAWCETT

REAL NAME: Farrah Fawcett
DATE OF BIRTH: February 2, 1947
PLACE OF BIRTH: Corpus Christi, Texas

EYE COLOR: Green   HAIR COLOR: Blond
HEIGHT: 5'6 1/2"   WEIGHT: 112

Although she has gone on to become an accomplished dramatic actress in *Extremities* on Broadway and *The Burning Bed* on television, Farrah Fawcett may always be best known as Charlie's sexiest angel. Her famous poster, which sold over eight million copies during the '70s, was part of the sexual awakening of a whole generation of American men.

Perhaps the premier sex symbol since Marilyn Monroe, Farrah, who is one-eighth Choctaw Indian, received her early education in a Catholic parish school along with her older sister. A hard-working student and complacent daughter, she has said of her rearing, "I was always protected by my family. I liked being protected. It kept me from getting too wise too soon." Hollywood publicist David Mirisch discovered her while she was attending the University of Texas and brought her to Los Angeles. Before long she was Queen of the Los Angeles Boat Show as well as Miss Pro Tennis. She married actor Lee Majors, who would later go on to become the *Six Million Dollar Man*.

While making a respectable living appearing on various TV shows throughout the '70s, she continued to earn most of her income as a model. That changed in 1976 when Aaron Spelling cast her as crimestopper Jill Munroe on his new show *Charlie's Angels*. Until she quit the series to form a production company with Majors in 1977, Fawcett was the most popular Angel, and Fabergé even developed a line of hair care products to capitalize on her widely imitated leonine hairstyle. Rather than resting on her beautiful laurels, she went on to pursue the most dramatic roles she could find on Broadway and in TV movies. Her performances as a rape victim in *Extremities* on Broadway and a victim of wife abuse in *The Burning Bed* on television were widely applauded.

Since her breakup with Majors in 1980, she has lived with Ryan O'Neal, with whom she has a child, Redmond, and with whom she starred in the canceled TV sitcom *Good Sports*. Very athletic, Farrah is active in everything from scuba diving to racquetball. "There's more to it than looking your best," she has said. "You have to be at your best, too—bopping along all the time, happy, upbeat, friendly."

SALLY FIELD

REAL NAME: Sally Margaret Field
DATE OF BIRTH: November 6, 1946
PLACE OF BIRTH: Pasadena, California

EYE COLOR: Brown   HAIR COLOR: Brown
HEIGHT: 5'2"   WEIGHT: 100

After her tenure as a dumpling-like pixie on the TV series *Gidget* and *The Flying Nun*, Sally Field remade herself into a serious actress. As owner of her own production company, today Sally says, "My career has been a struggle from the moment I began. I thought, 'I'll win an award and all these fabulous scripts will come to my door.' Nothing came to my door."

Field's father was an actor, and her mother, Margaret, was a starlet for Paramount in the '50s; Sally grew up wanting to follow in her footsteps. But recalling a repressed Catholic upbringing, she says, "I felt very angry and sexy about things. When you were a female in the late '50s, where the hell did you put those feelings? Where did they go if you felt mean and violent and sexy? Then you let them all out and you say, 'It wasn't really me.' " She began writing and performing her own plays when she was only seven. Then, as a cheerleader in high school, she also took part in theater productions such as *Suddenly Last Summer* and *The Man Who Came To Dinner*. After graduation, she was supposed to attend Valley State College, but instead enrolled in the Columbia Pictures Workshop, where casting director Eddy Foy III auditioned her for the lead in the new TV series *Gidget*. Sally beat out 75 other actresses for the role and portrayed the boy-hungry teen for the one season *Gidget* was on the air.

Hoping for more substantial roles, Field initially balked at becoming Sister Bertrille on *The Flying Nun*, but ended up accepting it at $4,000 a week. The show became a hit, and she was catapulted into stardom at the age of 21. In an attempt to become a "serious actress," she began turning down TV offers and auditioning for meatier film roles. It paid off, and she was offered a featured part as a health spa receptionist in the film *Stay Hungry*. Reviews for the film were mixed, but Field's performance was generally well received. Her next

role, as the lead in the TV movie *Sybil*, won her an Emmy for best actress. With her career now firmly on the rise, Field appeared in a slew of movies, including the *Smokey and the Bandit* series with one-time beau Burt Reynolds. She further solidified her position as a star—and established her credentials as a dramatic actress—with two Academy Awards for her performances in *Norma Rae* and *Places In the Heart*. She returned to comedy in the soap opera farce *Soapdish*.

Her first marriage, which produced two sons, ended in 1973. After a high-profile romance with Burt Reynolds, she married producer Alan Greisman in 1984, and they have a son. Field keeps a low profile within the industry and enjoys spending time with her family, reading and playing the piano.

CARRIE FISHER

REAL NAME: Carrie Frances Fisher
DATE OF BIRTH: October 21, 1956
PLACE OF BIRTH: Beverly Hills, California

EYE COLOR: Brown   HAIR COLOR: Brown
HEIGHT: 5'1"   WEIGHT: 95

After surviving a family scarred by divorce, alcoholism, drug addiction, rehabs and pitted relationships, Carrie's take on life is: "You find me a kid that thinks he got enough affection and attention as a child and I'll show you Dan Quayle."

Carrie was two years old when her father, Eddie Fisher, left her mother, Debbie Reynolds, to marry Liz Taylor, creating a tabloid feeding frenzy. At thirteen, her mother's second marriage to Harry Karl was dead in the water, and Carrie was singing in Debbie's Las Vegas nightclub act. At sixteen, she dropped out of Beverly Hills High School and joined the chorus line of the Broadway play *Irene*, of which her mother was the star. She then embarked on a short New York acting career, did a stint at Sarah Lawrence College in Bronxville, New York, and made her film debut as a seductive teenager in *Shampoo*. She then spent a year and a half studying acting at London's Central School of Speech and Drama before being cast as Princess Leia in *Star Wars*. The film was so successful that Fisher was asked twice to reprise her role in 1980's *The Empire Strikes Back* and 1984's *Return of the Jedi*.

During this period, her drug addiction had reached a saturation point. As a therapeutic outlet, she accepted an article assignment from *Esquire* before going into rehab. Later, in 1985, she was gratified to discover that her celebrity as an actress paled next to that which she received upon publication of her first novel, *Postcards From the Edge*. Between the publicity generated by the book and the movie adaptation (for which Fisher also wrote the screenplay), she became "hot" and was soon doing supporting roles in such movies as *When Harry Met Sally...* and *The 'Burbs*. She is currently overseeing the production of two more of her books, one of which is based on the journal she kept as a child.

Carrie had a year-long marriage to singer Paul Simon in 1983. She gave birth in 1992 to a daughter by her beau, talent agent Bryan Lourd. Feeling sufficiently purged of her childhood and early adult years, she is enjoying the perks and satisfactions of accomplishment. Her attitude is: "You know, when you're hot you're just on your way to being cold. I'm living in a boomtown. It's 1849 in central California. There's just so much gold and there are too many people with tans mining for it. I'll probably crash, but hopefully not burn. I'm both phoenix and ashes. And Tucson, too!"

BRIDGET FONDA

REAL NAME: Bridget Jane Fonda
DATE OF BIRTH: January 27, 1964
PLACE OF BIRTH: Los Angeles, California

EYE COLOR: Teal   HAIR COLOR: Brown
HEIGHT: 5'6"   WEIGHT: 111

"I have an artistic impulse, and I figured that if I didn't act," says Bridget Fonda, "I'd probably be dancing on bars." So what's a third-generation Fonda to do?

When Bridget was born to actor Peter Fonda and actress Susan Brewer, both parents were enmeshed in the '60s counterculture lifestyle, and she was raised to be a free and independent spirit. But Peter's drugging and womanizing got the best of the marriage, which broke up when she was eight, and he spent little time either with her or brother, Justin, which inflicted a boil of pain that is still festering. That trauma was compounded by her mother's remarriage to Peter's former agent, and the five years they shared a home with Bridget and Justin were unhappy for all. The kids never accepted their stepdad, and he seemed determined to destroy their famous father's image. In order to wall out her pain, Bridget ignored it and tried to parent both her mother and brother: "In a strange way, I was raised to be the head of my family. You don't feel dependent on anybody." Another blow fell when Justin, at age fourteen, chose to move to Montana with his father, and Bridget felt she had been deserted once again. "It took me a long time to get over it," she recalls. "I cried for a year."

Eager to put her unhappiness behind her, Bridget abandoned her desire to become an artist and enrolled at NYU and the Lee Strasberg Theater Institute in New York to study acting. She knew from the outset that being the granddaughter of Henry Fonda and the niece of Jane Fonda would be more a burden than a benefit. She pretty much said it all when she made her 1987 movie debut in *Aria*, in which she stripped naked, had sex, then committed suicide during her eight minutes on screen with no dialogue. Since then, Bridget has lent a provocativeness to every role she tackles, large or small. Her performances in *Shag*, *Scandal*, *Godfather III*, *Singles* and *Single White Female* have put her career on a fast track. And she front-lined compellingly as the star of *Point of No Return*, an Americanized version of the French hit *La Femme Nikita*. Bridget is currently shooting a movie about a cop and a waitress who share a winning lottery ticket called *Cop Gives Waitress $2 Million Tip*. Says Bridget, "I'm very work obsessed. It's how I define myself."

Although she's satisfied with the way her career is going, no amount of success will be able to fill one empty hole in her world: "My greatest fear is that what I want for my life is not possible for me to have. I want a family, and I want a solid family. I want it to be really strong. It's really hard because it's not something I ever saw a good example of. It's fictional to me."

JANE FONDA

REAL NAME: Jane Seymour Fonda
DATE OF BIRTH: December 21, 1937
PLACE OF BIRTH: New York, New York

EYE COLOR: Blue   HAIR COLOR: Brown
HEIGHT: 5'7"   WEIGHT: 118

Before she acquired her own mantle of fame, Jane was always known as the first child of legendary actor Henry Fonda. But the maternal side of her gene pool is even more prestigious. Her mother, Frances Seymour, who was Henry's second wife, is from a very old, wealthy Canadian family of Norman-Welsh origin and includes Lady Jane Seymour as a forebear. Jane and brother Peter were born into status and wealth, but Jane, who was tossed back and forth between parents, remembers that she never quite bought into the aura of privilege because, as she said, "There was always an element of a midwestern farmer about father, something about ethics and integrity." Although she recalls Henry as being austere and unaffectionate, she remembers little about her mother, who suffered from mental illness and spent much time in a sanitarium. She died when Jane was sixteen, supposedly of a heart attack, but a year later, Jane learned the real cause of her mother's death from a movie magazine: She had committed suicide.

After attending schools in Los Angeles and New York, Jane graduated from the Emma Willard School in New York. In 1956, after a brief hiatus from Vassar to do some plays with her father, she returned to school but, as she said, "was out with boys all the time and never studied." Dropping out after her sophomore year, she started modeling, appearing on the cover of *Vogue*, while studying acting under Lee Strasberg at the Actor's Studio. The early stages of her career were spent on Broadway and doing films in America and France. In 1966, she married director Roger Vadim and appeared in several of his pictures, the most successful of which was the space fantasy *Barbarella*, in which Fonda played a sex robot.

During the '70s, Fonda combined acting with politics, traveling around the country supporting various causes and earning herself a

place on the Nixon "enemies list." In 1972, after winning a best actress Oscar for her portrayal of prostitute Bree Daniel in *Klute*, she earned the name "Hanoi Jane" by traveling to North Vietnam and going on several Radio Hanoi broadcasts to urge American airmen to stop bombing. She was promptly "graylisted" and from 1973 to 1976 hardly acted at all. Most of that time was spent supporting her new husband, Tom Hayden, in his campaign for election to the U.S. Senate. In 1977, she made her comeback with roles in the comedy *Fun With Dick and Jane* and the more serious *Julia*. By 1978, Fonda was one of America's most successful actresses, forming her own production company, IPC Productions, and producing successful films, including *Coming Home, 9 to 5* and *On Golden Pond*. In 1979, Jane began her next metamorphosis by opening her first workout studio in Beverly Hills and producing books and videos designed to get America in shape.

In addition to her daughter by Roger Vadim, Jane has a son from ex-husband Hayden. In yet another radical career change, she announced retirement from acting after marrying TV mogul and Atlanta Braves owner Ted Turner. Explaining her self-imposed retirement from making films, she said simply, "Ted isn't the kind of man you leave behind to go on location."

HARRISON FORD

REAL NAME: Harrison Ford
DATE OF BIRTH: July 13, 1942
PLACE OF BIRTH: Chicago, Illinois

EYE COLOR: Blue   HAIR COLOR: Brown
HEIGHT: 6'1"   WEIGHT: 170

Of mixed Irish Catholic and Russian Jewish parents, Harrison
Ford also has a bit of the entertainer in his blood. His grandfather
was in vaudeville, and his father produced commercials for an advertising agency in addition to doing voice-overs. As a child, Harrison
had "a real fear of facing people," especially in school. When he
entered Wisconsin's Ripon College, he had no goal in mind and put

in four years studying philosophy. Needing an elective in his junior year, he took a drama class and was shocked to find that his shyness evaporated on stage. After one season of summer stock, he was hooked and set off for Hollywood.

Ford was discovered by a talent scout while appearing at a Laguna Beach playhouse and signed to Columbia Pictures' new talent program at $150 a week. After giving him small parts in several films, Columbia gave up on Ford and dropped him, but he was immediately signed with Universal, which gave him several more small roles and some guest shots on TV shows like *Gunsmoke* and *Ironside*. After a time, however, Ford became disillusioned with the studios and dropped out for a while, making a living as a carpenter. Finding a different type of creative outlet in woodwork, Harrison said he found it "an escape from the mind-wrestling; something simple, direct, visible, palpable, possible."

Feeling more self-confident after his sabbatical, he returned to acting in 1973 as a hot-rodder in George Lucas' surprise hit *American Graffiti*. A role as a corporate hatchet man in Francis Ford Coppola's movie *The Conversation* followed, but Ford continued to be primarily a carpenter until his breakthrough role as Han Solo in *Star Wars* at the age of 35. His reprisal of the role in *The Empire Strikes Back* and *Return of the Jedi*, as well as his portrayal of globe-trotting archaeologist hero Indiana Jones in the *Raiders of the Lost Ark* series, made him one of Hollywood's top-grossing stars. Following *Witness* in 1985, *The Mosquito Coast* in 1986 and *Frantic* in 1988, Harrison was absent from the screen until his sensitive performance in 1991's *Regarding Henry* and his latest appearance as the hero in the 1992 version of Tom Clancy's best-selling *Patriot Games*. In addition to signing a contract to star in all the future Tom Clancy adaptations, he was featured in the movie version of the long-running TV hit *The Fugitive*.

Divorced from his first wife in 1978, their two sons are grown. He now lives in Wyoming with his second wife of ten years, screenwriter Melissa Mathison, and their son and has built most of the furniture in their home. Claiming to be difficult to live with, Harrison says he prefers to stay inside himself: "I just don't go to anyone for advice or for a shoulder to lean on. My questions are for me to answer out of my own experience. The Buddha said, 'Work out your salvation with diligence.' "

JOHN FORSYTHE

REAL NAME : John Lincoln Freund
DATE OF BIRTH: January 29, 1918
PLACE OF BIRTH: Carneys Point, New Jersey

EYE COLOR: Brown   HAIR COLOR: Brown
HEIGHT: 6'1"   WEIGHT: 170

At the pinnacle of a long TV career, which included a stint as America's favorite father, John Forsythe cemented his place in the TV hall of fame as Blake Carrington on the smash series *Dynasty*. Though he has always played the epitome of quiet elegance and grace, he confesses that his heart has always been on the baseball field. "As an ex-sports announcer," he says, "I've done very well."

After growing up in a New Jersey town of just over 300 people, John moved with his family to New York City when he was eleven. As a boy, he was an avid sports fan who dreamed of someday becoming a sportscaster. He won a baseball scholarship to North Carolina University but dropped out during his junior year to become a public address announcer for the Brooklyn Dodgers. That radio exposure led to dramatic roles on popular radio shows such as *Stella Dallas* and *The Romance of Helen Trent*.

As radio work trickled into stage work, he made his Broadway debut in 1942, and several roles later was signed to a movie contract with Warner Brothers, which began casting him in its films. During World War II, he joined the Air Force and was assigned to the Air Corps show, "Winged Victory." After his discharge in 1947, Forsythe moved to New York and supported himself with odd jobs and modeling assignments while trying to make it as a stage actor. He became one of the founding members of Lee Strasberg's Actor's Studio, and in 1957, debuted on television as Bentley Gregg in the series *Bachelor Father*, the show that made him a star. When *Father* went off the air five years later, Forsythe made many films before returning to television in *The John Forsythe Show*, *To Rome With Love* and *The World of Survival*. After a dozen TV movies, he played the invisible Charlie on *Charlie's Angels,* and then assumed his megastar role as Blake Carrington.

From a brief, long-ago marriage, he has two daughters and another one by his present wife of 48 years. He has also been blessed with grandchildren. When one granddaughter graduated from Vassar in 1991, he gave her a nice big check and sat her down for a talk; he said to her, "Deborah, in Hollywood I am still considered a sex symbol. Even as a grandfather, I am still considered a sex symbol. But, Deborah, I don't think as a great-grandfather I will be considered a sex symbol. So don't feel you have to rush into anything." Since a quadruple-bypass operation ten years ago, he has learned to enjoy more genteel recreation such as reading, horse breeding and attending spectator sports.

JODIE FOSTER

REAL NAME: Alicia Christian Foster
DATE OF BIRTH: November 19, 1962
PLACE OF BIRTH: Los Angeles, California

EYE COLOR: Blue   HAIR COLOR: Blond
HEIGHT: 5'5"   WEIGHT: 115

Born just a few months before her parents' divorce, Jodie was raised by her mother and rarely saw her father. "I feel lucky in a way that I never knew a father, that there was never a marital conflict in the house," she says. "I've always felt like a replacement, that I took the place of a husband, roommate or pal."

For eight years, her mother supported the family—including three brothers and sisters—by working on publicity for a producer.

She was able to quit when her son Buddy, who had been making commercials, became the breadwinner. It was on a casting call for suntan lotion that Jodie, too young to wait in the car, got the nod to enter show business when she was noticed in the studio. She became the bare-bottomed tyke who adorned the Coppertone TV ads for decades. Having taught herself to read at the age of three, she was reading scripts at five, and by the time she was eight, she'd been in more than 40 TV commercials.

She made her acting debut in 1969 on *Mayberry RFD*, on which Buddy played the regular role of Mike Jones. As a child actress, she appeared in countless episodes of countless TV shows including *Gunsmoke*, *The Courtship of Eddie's Father*, *The Partridge Family* and *Kung Fu*. She even had her own series, the short-lived *Paper Moon*. She was all of thirteen when she played Iris, a youthful prostitute, in *Taxi Driver*, for which she was nominated for an Academy Award. Because she was so young, the film's producers hired her sister Constance to double for Foster during a scene in which Iris appeared naked. But before she was given the role, the Los Angeles Welfare Board, alarmed at the nature of the role, insisted she pass psychological tests. Jodie said, "I spent four hours with the shrink to prove I was normal enough to play a hooker. Does that make sense? He asked me what kind of food I ate and would I like to get married. I said not at thirteen."

Giving the valedictory speech in French, she graduated at the head of her class from the prestigious Lycée Français in Los Angeles in 1980. Foster then put her acting career on hold and enrolled at Yale to study literature. During her freshman year, a fan, John W. Hinckley Jr., attempted to assassinate President Ronald Reagan, claiming he did it to impress Foster, with whom he said he was in love. After graduation with honors, Foster returned to the screen, winning a best actress Oscar for her role as a rape victim in *The Accused* and another Oscar honoring her work as an FBI agent in the film *The Silence of the Lambs*. She also debuted in 1991 as director of the well-received *Little Man Tate*. She shifted gears in 1993 when she starred opposite Richard Gere in *Sommersby*. She will next appear in the movie version of the hit TV western *Maverick*.

Jodie's favorite pastime is reading, sometimes in French—but she's not a bookworm. She also likes tennis, horseback riding and practicing karate.

MICHAEL J. FOX

REAL NAME: Michael Andrew Fox
DATE OF BIRTH: June 9, 1961
PLACE OF BIRTH: Edmonton, Alberta, Canada

EYE COLOR: Brown   HAIR COLOR: Sandy
HEIGHT: 5'4"   WEIGHT: 130

Many people have heard the story about how Michael J. Fox was so poor when he landed the role of Alex P. Keaton on *Family Ties* that he was using the pay phone outside a Pioneer Chicken franchise as an office. Far fewer, however, know the reason why he was so poor: The free-spending actor was thousands of dollars in debt when his first series, *Palmerstown, U.S.A.*, was canceled: "I was an idiot, trying to paint this picture in my head of a young successful guy."

Describing his happy childhood as the fourth of five children, Michael hands the credit to his parents' relationship: "My mother and father are their best friends in the world—always together—an unmovable force." He also credits his family dinner hour for developing his comic talent and his sense of humor. "The oldest form of theater is the dinner table," he says. "It's got five or six people, new show every night.... Same players. Good ensemble." While his father was in the Canadian Army, they moved frequently until Michael was in the fifth grade, and he learned to adapt to each new situation. He also learned to turn his diminutive height into a subject for jokes and won friends quickly. Planning to become a hockey player or a writer, he fell into acting when his high school drama teacher gave him a casting notice for the part of a ten or twelve-year-old character which he won. Continuing to play parts younger than himself, he found himself on the stage more than in school and dropped out in the twelfth grade.

Serious about acting, he moved to Los Angeles and quickly found small parts in television and films. When he won a major part in Alex Haley's TV series *Palmerstown, U.S.A.*, he set about spending far more than every penny he earned before the series was canceled.

Finding himself $35,000 in debt, with no income, Michael lived off macaroni and cheese and sold off his furniture piece by piece just to get by. Once his phone was disconnected, things got desperate. Then his first *Family Ties* audition for the show's creator, Gary David Goldberg, was unsuccessful. Luckily, the casting director got him a retry, and this time Fox got the part. Originally intended as a supporting character, his portrayal of Yuppie-to-be Alex was such a hit that, like Fonzie on *Happy Days*, he soon became the focal point of the show. Fox's TV success led to the role of Marty McFly in the smash hit *Back to the Future* and its two sequels, and to superstar status as one of Hollywood's most popular leading men as the star of *The Secret of My Success* and *Bright Lights, Big City*.

In 1988, he took his wife, actress Tracy Pollan, to live in rural Connecticut with their young son.

POSTSCRIPT   Although his middle initial is really A., Fox uses the initial J. in honor of Michael J. Pollard, a character actor whom he greatly admires.

MORGAN FREEMAN

REAL NAME: Morgan Freeman
DATE OF BIRTH: June 1, 1937
PLACE OF BIRTH: Memphis, Tennessee

EYE COLOR: Brown   HAIR COLOR: Black
HEIGHT: 6'2"   WEIGHT: 180

During his four years in the Air Force, Morgan Freeman learned something about himself that would become the cornerstone of his career in acting. He recalls that "I wanted to be an Air Force pilot. I ended up as a half-assed radar technician because I was aced out—racism, the Southern old-boy network. I was insolent, I called a horse's ass a horse's ass, even if it was wearin' brass. The whole thing in the service, you're supposed to look down. Never could do that." That was in the late '50s, the gestation of the civil rights movement. But he wasn't crusading; he was just being Morgan Freeman.

Morgan gives full credit for his success to the mother and grandmother who raised him, his two brothers and one sister in a one-bedroom "shotgun shack." His grandmother held nightly prayer sessions, and his mother encouraged him to enter school plays. "Boy, I'm going to take you to Hollywood," she would say. Then, in high school, they relocated to the infamous South Side of Chicago, and Morgan grew up fast. "There were gangs fighting each other and any outsider with ice picks, nails and bottles. So I stole, I conned, I passed the tests. But I was scared; I'm not the violent type." Morgan finished high school unscathed and retreated to the Air Force. When his tour was over, he fell back on something he already knew: acting.

In Hollywood, with a part-time job as a clerk, he studied drama and says it softened his thick Southern accent but not much else: "That business of peeling away layers of skin was too murky and deep for me. I think you learn acting by acting—OJT [On-the-Job Training]." His stage appearances, bouncing between New York and San Francisco, consistently earned him praise, but his refusal to portray or even read for parts that were black stereotypes forced him to sell hot dogs and wash cars in order to eat.

When he landed a role opposite Pearl Bailey in Broadway's *Hello,*

Dolly! he got the attention of critics and audiences. Moving on to play the lead in *Purlie* brought him more work than he could handle, replete with awards and a Tony nomination. Then, inexplicably, his phone quit ringing from 1980 to 1982. He had decided to put acting behind him and drive a cab when Paul Newman broke the dry spell for him with a film role in *Harry and Son*. Then Morgan landed the 1984 role of a pimp in *Street Smart*, reaching back to his own Chicago street days for a terrifying performance and earning an Oscar nomination. *Lean on Me* was déjà vu, since it was school that saved him from probable gang death. As the chauffeur in *Driving Miss Daisy*, he also knew where to find the Southern "yes'm, Miss Daisy" character that brought him another Oscar nomination. This year Morgan tried on his director's wings with the release of *BOPHA!*, a movie about racial prejudice in South Africa.

With his career battened down, Morgan now takes his calls via ship-to-shore on a 38-foot ketch that's practically never moored. His second wife and shipmate, Myrna, isn't quite as sea hardy but is "a good sport." Accompanying them is Morgan's eight-year-old granddaughter, whom they are raising for his daughter. He already has four grown children between the ages of nineteen and 30, from his first marriage and two previous lovers.

JAMES GARNER

REAL NAME: James Scott Baumgarner
DATE OF BIRTH: April 7, 1928
PLACE OF BIRTH: Norman, Oklahoma

EYE COLOR: Brown   HAIR COLOR: Brown
HEIGHT: 6'1"   WEIGHT: 205

"If you have any pride in your work, you don't go on TV," says Jim Garner, half seriously.

Part Cherokee Indian, James was one of three sons left after their mother died in 1933. While his father worked as an upholsterer in Norman, James was raised by grandparents, aunts and uncles. When his father moved to Los Angeles, he spent his high school years bouncing back and forth between there and Oklahoma, taking a year off at sixteen with the Merchant Marines. After graduation from high school, James was drafted into the Korean War, and while on active duty was wounded twice, receiving two Purple Hearts. Returning home, he ran into an old friend, Paul Gregory, who had become a movie producer. He gave Garner his first show-business job cuing Lloyd Nolan in a traveling road production of *The Caine Mutiny Court-Martial*.

When the show closed, Garner returned to Hollywood, took a screen test with Warner Brothers and was put under contract at $150-$200 a week. His big break came when he was cast as Marlon Brando's pal Bailey in *Sayonara*. He received rave reviews and in 1957 was given a supporting role in the war film *Darby's Rangers*. When star Charlton Heston quit, Garner was picked to replace him. That same year, Warner cast him as Bret Maverick on television. By 1960, *Maverick* was a huge hit and Garner was a star. With the studios determined to reinvent him as a Rock Hudson/Cary Grant crossbreed, he continued to do films throughout the '60s, mostly with Doris Day. Boomeranging back to his original venue in 1973, he accepted a TV role as L.A. private eye Jim Rockford on *The Rockford Files*. The public loved Garner as the affable detective, and he stayed with the series until ill health forced him to give it up in 1980. But during the '80s, he was well enough to turn up in TV movies from time to time as well as in feature films such as *Victor/Victoria* and *Murphy's Romance*. At the same time, his Polaroid TV commercials brought him even more popularity as well as financial independence. In 1993, he came back to the medium he loves to hate in HBO's *Barbarians at the Gate* and is making a return to westerns in the movie version of his old series *Maverick*.

Married in 1954, James separated in 1980 from his wife. He has two daughters, one of whom was adopted from his wife's first marriage. His chronically bad knees and arthritis prevent him from playing as much golf as he would like, so he relaxes at his home in Beverly Hills.

TERI GARR

REAL NAME: Teri Garr
DATE OF BIRTH: December 11, 1945
PLACE OF BIRTH: Lakewood, Ohio

EYE COLOR: Blue	HAIR COLOR: Blond
HEIGHT: 5'7"	WEIGHT: 119

Teri's found just the right amount of fame for her—she's financially secure but isn't exactly Madonna. She defines it as, "I'm just famous enough to get a good table in a restaurant, but not famous enough that people will bother me while I'm eating."

Teri is the daughter of former Rockettes dancer Phyllis Garr and actor Howard Garr, who died when she was eleven. While her mother was a wardrobe mistress at MGM in Hollywood, young Teri visited the set regularly and decided that real-life jobs were dismal compared to the excitement she saw in movies. Resolving to start out as a ballerina, she took lessons and at thirteen was dancing professionally with the San Francisco Ballet. A couple of years later she returned home and became a regular with the Los Angeles Ballet while attending North Hollywood High School.

After majoring in speech and dance at Cal State, she began dancing and acting on both coasts, earning enough to live and study acting at the Actor's Studio. She danced in a string of Elvis Presley movies, was a regular on *The Sonny and Cher Comedy Hour* and a dance double for Ann-Margret in *The Swinger*. "When you're a dancer," she recalls, "you always think you have a weight problem. I took diet pills—I did it all. But I was never happy; I was emotionally drained."

Teri decided that she could probably act just as well as the actresses in the movies she had hoofed her way through and promptly dropped dancing. Her first speaking role was in the Monkees' movie, *Head*, in 1969, a film written by her friend Jack Nicholson, whom she had met in acting classes. It was Nicholson who introduced her to Francis Ford Coppola, who in turn made her one of the original members of his Zoetrope Studios repertory company. Garr went on to stardom in films such as *The Conversation, Young Frankenstein, Close Encounters of the Third Kind* and *Mr. Mom.*

Teri has struggled through some bad relationships, but so far she's never married. "My father was an alcoholic and was sick the whole time I was growing up," she says. "After he died, it was a struggle financially for my mother. So I decided—probably subconsciously—that since my father couldn't be depended on, I'd better make sure I have a lot of money saved before I look for the right man." She's still looking.

RICHARD GERE

REAL NAME: Richard Gere
DATE OF BIRTH: August 29, 1949
PLACE OF BIRTH: Philadelphia, Pennsylvania

EYE COLOR: Blue   HAIR COLOR: Brown
HEIGHT: 5'11"   WEIGHT: 155

Richard's interviews accomplish exactly what he wants—to give away nothing of his personal self for fear of losing credibility in his acting roles. On the subject of his status as a sex symbol, however, he's very direct: "I have no interest in being anyone's icon on any level, and the least interesting of them all is the sex symbol."

With his father an insurance salesman and his mother a housewife, Richard had what he called a nice middle-class upbringing. After growing up on a farm in upstate New York, his brother became a concert pianist, and his three sisters are now a psychiatrist, a sculptor and a dancer. While excelling at gymnastics in high school, Richard also played the piano, guitar, trumpet and banjo, and composed musical scores for school productions. After earning an athletics scholarship to the University of Massachusetts in 1967, he acted in summer stock at the Provincetown Playhouse in Cape Cod. At the end of the season, he dropped out of school and joined the Seattle Repertory Theater's production of *Volpone* as a performer and a composer, but Gere soon moved to Vermont and lived in a commune of rock musicians. It took less than a year for him to become disenchanted with commune life, and he moved to New York City to seek his fortune as an actor.

His first major break came when he was asked to replace Barry Bostwick as Danny Zuko in the Broadway show *Grease*. After that, he worked for several years as a successful theater actor before making his screen debut in 1975 as a pimp in *Report to the Commissioner*. Two years later, he made his name in Hollywood as the whacked-out villain Tony Lopanto in *Looking for Mr. Goodbar*. In 1980, Gere's portrayal of a Beverly Hills hustler in *American Gigolo* and then the Navy cadet hero of *An Officer and a Gentleman* elevated him into a

bona fide sex symbol. Determined to avoid typecasting, however, he bravely played the lead in the biblical film *King David*. When it bombed, he went into a slump for several films, but the runaway hit *Pretty Woman* brought him back to the top bigger than ever.

During the '80s he took advantage of his slow period to begin following the teachings of the Dalai Lama, even going on a pilgrimage to Tibet. He is also politically astute and is attuned to problems affecting the Far East as well as the AIDS crisis. His high-profile marriage to supermodel Cindy Crawford affords him the opportunity to share the spotlight with those causes.

MEL GIBSON

REAL NAME: Mel Calumcille Gerard Gibson
DATE OF BIRTH: January 3, 1956
PLACE OF BIRTH: Peekskill, New York

EYE COLOR: Blue   HAIR COLOR: Brown
HEIGHT: 5'10"   WEIGHT: 160

On his first audition, asked why he wanted to be an actor, Mel said, quite honestly, "I've been goofing off all my life. I thought I might as well get paid for that."

Known Down Under as an Australian, Mel is actually an American. The middle child of eleven, he spent his younger years in upstate New York before his father, fearful that his sons would be drafted to fight in Vietnam, moved the family to Australia when Mel was twelve. Mel attended Catholic high school in Sydney, hoping someday to become a journalist or a chef. He took up acting only because his sister filled out an application on his behalf to the National Institute of Dramatic Art and submitted it behind his back. He went through with the audition on a lark and, to his surprise, was actually accepted.

After graduation in 1977, he joined the State Theatre Company of South Australia, where he auditioned for and two years later landed the lead role in *Mad Max*. The night before he was to show up for his first day of shooting, Mel found himself in a barroom brawl. We don't know what the other guy looked like, but Mel said he showed up for work badly beaten with his face looking "like a busted grapefruit" and expected to be fired. In a twist of fate, it turned out that his appearance was perfect for the avenging character he was playing, and the director was thrilled. It was "probably the classiest B-grade trash ever made," says Mel, and *Mad Max* became the biggest commercial success of any Australian film ever, grossing over $100 million. From there, Gibson had no trouble getting roles in other Aussie films such as *Tim*, *Gallipoli* and *The Z Men*. Once he reprised his role as Max in *Mad Max 2* (retitled *The Road Warrior* in America), Gibson became a presence in American film. His performance in *Lethal Weapon* opposite Danny Glover made him a full-blown star and the object of women's daydreams. As his popularity grew, so did the number of leading-man roles. His appearances in *Tequila Sunrise, The Year of Living Dangerously* and *Hamlet* solidified his position as a contender for Sexiest Man in America, and he was the first to be awarded that exact title in *People* magazine.

A private man, Gibson shuns the public eye and spends much of his time with his family on a ranch in Australia. Carrying on the large family tradition, Mel and his wife have six children.

KATHIE LEE GIFFORD

REAL NAME: Kathie Lee Epstein
DATE OF BIRTH: August 16, 1953
PLACE OF BIRTH: Paris, France

EYE COLOR: Brown   HAIR COLOR: Brown
HEIGHT: 5'5"   WEIGHT: 110

Kathie Lee's wholesome personality goes way back: "I've always been very approval-oriented. When I was little, I'd make cookies so people in the neighborhood would like me."

What's not to like? The middle child of a Navy officer and a home-maker, she was born in Paris and raised in Bowie, Maryland. Although her father was a nonpracticing Jew, she and her mother became born-again Christians when Kathie was eleven. During the '60s, while other girls were wearing love beads and dropping acid, Kathie Lee organized a folk-singing group and became a gospel singer at Oral Roberts University. But she felt harnessed at ORU and bolted for Hollywood.

Landing bit parts on soaps and recording gospel albums, Kathie's career was moving right along, but she took a detour in 1976 to marry a gospel composer. It ended in 1981. Luckily, *Good Morning America*'s offer to do some fill-in spots arrived about the same time, and she moved to New York. Slipping with ease into this new career, with her fresh unabashedness on camera, she won plum assignments and eventually the role of Joan Lunden's fill-in. In 1985, Regis Philbin was relocating to New York, and Kathie Lee left the security she had found with *GMA* to co-host a new show with him, *Live With Regis & Kathie Lee*. Trying to explain the show's instant success,

Kathie says, "I called Reege a jerk that first week. Nobody had ever called the King a jerk on the air."

Kathie's success seems to be everywhere. She has several big-ticket endorsement contracts, she's marketing her own line of clothes, and her high-profile marriage since 1986 to Frank Gifford seems picture-perfect. Included in that picture are their son, born in 1990, and their new baby girl, who was born in August 1993. But Kathie thinks that trappings aren't a guarantee for happiness. She says, "If you don't have a family, you have very little chance to be a happy person." In 1992, she published her autobiography, aptly titled *I Can't Believe I Said That*, and it became an instant bestseller.

DANNY GLOVER

REAL NAME: Daniel Glover
DATE OF BIRTH: 1947
PLACE OF BIRTH: San Francisco, California

EYE COLOR: Brown   HAIR COLOR: Black
HEIGHT: 6'4"   WEIGHT: 205

"Self-esteem is a little word but it means so much. Life is an ongoing process of learning how to feel good about ourselves," says Danny Glover. He's speaking from experience.

Growing up in San Francisco, Danny didn't have much success with school or with girls. One of five children born to NAACP activists, he endured the difficulties resulting from dyslexia and epilepsy. But he was a hard worker, earning money as a paper boy on the route he'd had since age eleven. After a short stint at City College in San Francisco, Glover worked as a dishwasher, first at a local women's college, then at Mount Zion Hospital. With no real plans, he drifted through life until 1966, when he began taking night classes at San Francisco State University. At the time, the school was a focal point for black activism and Glover became involved, eventually becoming the chairman of the Black Student Union. When the activism cooled off, he left school without a diploma and took a job in city planning where he would remain for eight years.

While he was still working for the city, he studied at the American Conservatory Theater and began to get interested in acting. After two years of working in local productions, Glover decided to become a full-time actor. Quitting his day job, he got his hack license, supporting his family as a cabbie and a dishwasher while attending casting calls in Los Angeles during the day. He struggled for several years in small-time theater productions before breaking into films in 1979 with *Escape From Alcatraz*. Several more features followed, then the critically praised *Places in the Heart* and *The Color Purple*. For both, Danny made a visit to his 90-year-old grandparents. "They've had the same farm in Georgia for decades," he says. "They told me about the Depression and the times when, if you were black, you had to be out of town by sundown or you could get lynched. They picked cotton all their lives. I even picked cotton on their farm when we went there for the summer, so I had a head start on the other actors." But it took teaming with Mel Gibson in the box office smash *Lethal Weapon* for Danny to gain the actor's dream—his choice of scripts. The first film he chose was the 1992 hit *Grand Canyon*, which redefined him as leading-man material.

Danny married his college sweetheart, a jazz singer, seventeen years ago, and they still live in San Francisco with their daughter. "What I want to do as a person is grow," he says. "I'm using my art as access to myself." But when he said that in a recent interview, his wife, Asake, said, "So you think you're a star? Well, you're not. Now go and wash those dishes!"

WHOOPI GOLDBERG

REAL NAME: Caryn Johnson
DATE OF BIRTH: November 13, 1949
PLACE OF BIRTH: New York, New York

EYE COLOR: Brown   HAIR COLOR: Black
HEIGHT: 5'7"   WEIGHT: 120

Even though her face and remarkable hairstyle would be recognized anywhere in the world, Whoopi still tries to keep her real name private. "I'm protecting my family," she explains. "As it is now, I can go home and live as this other person, and even though I look like Whoopi Goldberg on the street, I can whip out my driver's license and say, 'Hey, but I'm not.' "

When Whoopi's father left before she was born, she was raised with her brother in a New York City Chelsea district housing project, and her mother supported them with odd jobs, like teaching for Head Start. Whoopi attended church regularly at St. Columba and received her elementary education in that parish school. At the age of eight, she started appearing in children's plays at the Hudson Guild and developing her skills for studying people and becoming a mimic of idiosyncrasies. Whoopi said, "What it is is, I'm a real sponge in terms of seeing things and absorbing them. And with the people I have admired over the years, I've stolen from them and added things that I know instinctively." Dropping out of high school during the '60s, she settled into the hippie scene, but after a while she asked herself: "Am I going to keep doing drugs and kill myself or figure out what I'm going to do with my life?" From that point on, she immersed herself in civil rights marches and demonstrations while looking for work on the stage.

She got her showbiz start in the chorus of musicals like *Pippin* and *Hair*. In the early '70s, after her brief marriage had failed and left her with a daughter, she and the baby flew to California to visit a friend. With no reason to go back to New York, she ended up moving to San Diego, where she helped found the San Diego Repertory Theater and joined the improv group Spontaneous Combustion. While in San Diego, she coined the stage name Whoopie Cushion,

changed it to The French Whoopie Cushion, and finally settled on Goldberg. Moving to Berkeley, she lived with actor David Schein and joined an experimental theater group called the Blake Street Hawkeyes, supporting herself with a series of jobs that included bricklayer, bank teller and cosmetologist. At one point, she even worked at a mortuary dressing the hair of and applying makeup to dead people.

She finally made it to Broadway with a one-woman show entitled *The Spook Show*. Director/producer Mike Nichols caught her act and soon was producing her himself in another one-woman show called *Whoopi Goldberg*. It was when Steven Spielberg cast her as the lead in his adaptation of *The Color Purple* that Whoopi became a star. Her roles have continued to snowball with the films *Jumping Jack Flash*, *Clara's Heart*, *Soapdish*, *Ghost*, and *Sister Act*, one of the top-grossing movies of 1992. Whoopi caught the public's attention in 1993 when she co-starred with Ted Danson in *Made in America* and their on-screen relationship expanded into a real-life romance.

Always concerned with social causes, Goldberg is one of the co-hosts, along with Robin Williams and Billy Crystal, of the annual comedy benefit Comic Relief. She will complete filming of *Sister Act 2* in 1993.

JOHN GOODMAN

REAL NAME: John Goodman
DATE OF BIRTH: June 20, 1952
PLACE OF BIRTH: St. Louis, Missouri

EYE COLOR: Blue   HAIR COLOR: Light brown
HEIGHT: 6'2"   WEIGHT: 250

John Goodman, the portly actor who plays the perfect foil to Roseanne's caustic wit on her namesake show, regards comments about his sex appeal and titles like Sexiest Man insulting and cruel. Why women find him desirable, or why the media markets him that way, he doesn't understand.

After his father's death when John was two, he and his brother and sister were raised by their mother, who supported her family by waitressing and working as a drugstore clerk. At Afton High School, John served as a lineman on a football team that ended up winning only one game. He tried junior college but dropped out after a year, then moved on to Southwest Missouri State University, where he also played football until a knee injury sidelined him. During his year off from the team, he turned his energy toward a long-harbored interest in drama and began taking classes and performing in campus productions with fellow students and future stars Kathleen Turner and Tess Harper. After graduation with a B.F.A. in theater arts, he borrowed $1,000 from his brother and left for New York on August 14, 1975, a day he remembers as "hot, depressing and scary." There, he lived in Hell's Kitchen and barely made ends meet with infrequent off-Broadway stage work and dinner and children's theater, where the audiences were not only distracted but distracting, and he recalls that work as "pretty good concentration training." His Broadway debut came in 1979 in *Loose Ends* with Kevin Kline. The two became friends, and Kline took John to Café Central, a bar on the Upper West Side of New York where actors like Robert De Niro hung out and aspirants like Bruce Willis worked. He spent much of his off-time there and was inducted into the fraternity of actors.

He spent the next few years on stage in such classical productions as *A Midsummer Night's Dream*, *As You Like It* and *Henry IV*. He has always regarded this period as crucial to his development as an actor and his ability to "analyze" the many scripts that come to him. His breakthrough came in 1987 when a producer for stand-up comedienne Roseanne Arnold's planned sitcom discovered him in *Antony and Cleopatra* and cast him as Dan Conner, Roseanne's husband. He has settled nicely into this role, earning three Emmy nominations. During breaks from the show, he has found time to co-star in several films, usually in character roles as the lead's buddy, including *Everybody's All-American*, *Raising Arizona*, *Always* and *Barton Fink*. With his rise in popularity on *Roseanne*, he has moved on to leading roles in such films as *King Ralph* and *The Babe*, for which he lost 60 pounds to play the legendary Babe Ruth.

He and Annabeth, his wife since 1989, have a daughter, Molly. They split their time between their two homes, one in Los Angeles and one in New Orleans.

ANDY GRIFFITH

REAL NAME: Andrew Samuel Griffith
DATE OF BIRTH: June 1, 1926
PLACE OF BIRTH: Mount Airy, North Carolina

EYE COLOR: Blue-gray   HAIR COLOR: White
HEIGHT: 6'   WEIGHT: 180

For most of his life as an actor, Andy Griffith seems to have been playing the affable, slow-moving, Southern gentleman. In real life, it's hard to find any difference.

The only child of a factory foreman and a housewife, Griffith swept out the high school after classes in order to pay for trombone, bass horn and guitar lessons. He was raised in the Morovian faith and, at one point, enrolled at the University of North Carolina in 1944 as a predivinity student. During college, however, he became interested in acting, joining the university's drama group and the cast of the annual *The Lost Colony* outdoor pageant on Roanoke Island. After marrying a fellow student and graduating with a degree in music, Griffith taught school for three years in Goldsboro and performed monologues at local clubs. In 1955, Capitol Records released one of them, *What It Was, Was Football*, selling 800,000 copies.

Feeling ready for the big time, Andy and his wife moved to New York but were turned down everywhere. Undaunted, they returned to North Carolina and raised $1,000 to start their own troupe. After a season of performing at conventions, he got his break on *The Ed Sullivan Show* as a monologuist, and in 1955, made his Broadway debut as the homespun soldier Will Stockdale in *No Time for Sergeants*. He was a huge success and was soon tapped for two major film roles—as the guitar-playing vagrant Lonesome Rhodes in *A Face in the Crowd*, and as the reluctant sheriff in *Destry Rides Again*. It was in 1961 that he landed the title role in what would become the hallmark of his career, as the toothy, easygoing sheriff on *The Andy*

Griffith Show, which also etched out fine careers for Don Knotts and Ron Howard. After it went off the air in 1967, Griffith executive produced *Mayberry RFD* and *The New Andy Griffith Show*, both of which had brief runs. However, he maintained a screen presence in several miniseries and TV movies such as *Centennial*, *Murder in Texas*, *Fatal Vision*, *Hearts of the West* and *Diary of a Perfect Murder* until landing the title role in *Matlock* in 1986.

He and his first wife have two adopted children. Divorced from her since 1972, Griffith wed again in 1983 to Cindi Knight.

MELANIE GRIFFITH

REAL NAME: Melanie Griffith
DATE OF BIRTH: August 9, 1957
PLACE OF BIRTH: New York, New York

EYE COLOR: Blue HAIR COLOR: Blond
HEIGHT: 5'8" WEIGHT: 122

A true child of Hollywood, Melanie Griffith has had her ups and downs—both as a person and as an actress. With 20/20 hindsight, she now says, "You know, I was my own worst enemy. I had to learn to believe in myself."

The daughter of actress Tippi Hedren and Peter Griffith, an advertising executive, she moved to Hollywood with her parents when she was four years old. Shortly thereafter, they were divorced, and she grew up with her mother's second husband, Noel Marshall, a TV director and producer. A precocious child, she began reading her stepfather's scripts at age ten and critiquing them for him. Noel has said, "If she said, 'This is dumb,' I wouldn't bother to read it."

Melanie began modeling in her teen years with no interest in becoming an actress. She had only bad memories of acting because of her mother's grim experience under director Alfred Hitchcock in *The Birds*. But all that changed when she showed up at seventeen for a modeling assignment in 1974 that turned out to be an audition for a small part in the film *Night Moves*. She acquiesced and accepted the part. "After I started filming, I loved it. Mostly because I was playing a real person, not like in a commercial or something stupid like that," Melanie remembers. She came off so well in that first small part as a teenage sexpot that she quickly fell into two more similar roles, playing a man-hungry child-woman with a kittenish voice. Unfortunately, Griffith's personal problems, including a long bout with alcohol and drugs, stalled her career for some time after that. While attempting to revive her career, she studied in New York with Stella Adler and soon began landing more sexy roles in such movies as *Fear City* and *Body Double*. But it wasn't until her performance in *Working Girl*—for which she was nominated for a best actress Oscar—that she moved into the upper echelon of female stars.

Through it all, though, she continued to drink heavily and use drugs. She credits the director of *Working Girl*, Mike Nichols, for snapping her to her senses. "I got drunk on the set," said Melanie, "and they made me pay for the lost time. That got my attention. If it hadn't been for Mike, I don't know what would have happened to me." She checked herself into the Hazelden Clinic and has been a new person ever since exiting. Her last two films were *Paradise* and *Born Yesterday*, both of which co-starred her two-time husband, Don Johnson—a whole story unto itself.

When Melanie was fourteen, she visited her mother on the set of *The Harrad Experiment*. Also in the cast was a young, rakish actor named Don Johnson who was 22 years old. Griffith immediately fell in love, moved in with him at fifteen and quickly got married. They were divorced by the time she was eighteen. While studying in New York, she met and married actor Steven Bauer in 1983 and had a son, but they were divorced two years later. It was while on a plane to the Hazelden Clinic that she phoned Don and re-established their love connection. They remarried in 1989 and have a daughter of their own. Melanie has begun shooting a new film called *Milk Money* for director Richard Benjamin.

ROBERT GUILLAUME

REAL NAME: Robert Peter Williams
DATE OF BIRTH: November 30, 1937
PLACE OF BIRTH: St. Louis, Missouri

EYE COLOR: Brown   HAIR COLOR: Black
HEIGHT: 5'10"   WEIGHT: 160

"I'm a bit too shy to curry any kind of favor," says Robert Guillaume. "But because of my Cassius-like exterior, no one is really aware that I'm shy. My facade says, 'Don't mess around with me.' "

As a child, raised by his grandmother, Robert was a star soprano in his parish choir. He dropped out of high school to enlist in the military, but after his tour, he went back to win his diploma. From there, he enrolled at St. Louis University as a business major but transferred to Washington University to study opera. He eventually studied in Aspen, Colorado, with Russell and Rowena Jelliffe, the founders of the Karamu Theater in Cleveland, Ohio, where Guillaume would later serve an apprenticeship. Although he was nominated for a Tony award for his portrayal of Nathan Detroit in *Guys and Dolls* and played on Broadway in *Purlie*, *Golden Boy* and *Othello*, he experienced difficulty making the transition from singer to actor and says, "Instead of trusting my own instincts, I anticipated what other people expected of me. The problem was that I didn't really know who I was." And Guillaume was still virtually unknown when he won his first Emmy for his role as Benson on *Soap* in 1979. His dry-humored character became so popular with the show's fans that, when the series folded, Guillaume was given his own show, *Benson*, for which he won a best actor Emmy in 1985. He has since appeared in countless TV movies and several films, including *Lean On Me*, and has made two more attempts at TV series. But nothing more clicked until 1990, when he was tapped to succeed Michael

Crawford in the title role of the Los Angeles stage production of *Phantom of the Opera*. Although many people who were unaware of his singing talents were puzzled when he was given the role of the Phantom, Guillaume got rave reviews during the eight months in which he performed the part.

BRYANT GUMBEL

REAL NAME: Bryant Charles Gumbel
DATE OF BIRTH: September 29, 1948
PLACE OF BIRTH: New Orleans, Louisiana

EYE COLOR: Brown   HAIR COLOR: Black
HEIGHT: 5'9"   WEIGHT: 185

Bryant Gumbel's soft-spoken eloquence may be the result of his father's influence. "He was always there for me, stressing how important was my ability to write, to read, to listen, to speak," says Bryant.

A probate judge in Cook County, Illinois, his father worked his way through law school and sired two boys and two girls. Shortly after Bryant's birth, the family moved to the middle-class Hyde Park section of Chicago. While his mother took care of the home, his father nurtured in the boys a love of sports and the necessity of proper demeanor. In a hint of things to come, Bryant recalls that his brother's and his favorite game was playing sportscaster. "We'd grab our gloves," he recalls, "stand in front of a full-length mirror, wind up, pitch and announce entire imaginary games, taking turns every half-inning." After finishing Roman Catholic high school, Bryant went on to play baseball and football at Bates College in Lewiston, Maine, where he earned a degree in Russian history.

When a wrist injury ended his hopes for being drafted by a pro baseball team, he moved to New York and took a job as a sales rep at a paper company for $160 a week. Bryant remembers that he slid into a slump for almost a year: "I can remember one Christmas. I had a mattress, an eight-inch black-and-white TV and a light bulb. That was it," he said. "I went and bought a Blimpie sandwich and I called my folks from the corner of 46th and Eighth, collect, because I had no money." Realizing he should be doing what he really loved, sportscasting, he submitted an article to *Black Sports* magazine. On the strength of that piece, Gumbel was hired as a writer and soon became editor.

At 23, he became the weekend sportscaster at KNBC-TV in Los Angeles. By 1976, he had been promoted to sports director and was at the same time anchoring weekend events for NBC sports. Working on telecasts for major league baseball, NFL football and NCAA basketball, Gumbel became one of the most recognizable TV personalities in the country. He soon moved on to doing sports features for the *Today* show and co-hosting the network's prime-time show, *Games People Play*. He continued as NBC's NFL anchorman until moving on as full-time co-host of the *Today* show in 1982.

While Bryant has had his share of bad press from female co-workers who consider him chauvinistic and others who call him quick-tempered, his performance continues to speak for itself. As Bryant says, "My job isn't to interpret the world or prove how much I know; it's to be conversant enough to do sensible interviews, seek out the truth, and sense when people are lying." Since 1973, he has been married to his wife, a sculptor, with whom he has two children. An avid golfer, Gumbel spends much of his free time on the links.

GENE HACKMAN

REAL NAME: Eugene Alden Hackman
DATE OF BIRTH: January 30, 1930
PLACE OF BIRTH: San Bernardino, California

EYE COLOR: Blue   HAIR COLOR: Reddish brown
HEIGHT: 6'2"   WEIGHT: 184

Gene Hackman doesn't like to talk about himself much, but he has said, "Everything you do has to be important. I don't take myself seriously, but I do take acting seriously."

Growing up in Danville, Illinois, where his father was a second-generation pressman for the *Danville Commercial News*, he spent his free time in the movie house. Things seemed to be going all right in high school, where he played basketball, but Gene says that he "suddenly got the itch to get out." At sixteen, he quit school and, lying about his age, joined the Marines. That's where he dipped his toes into show business by volunteering to be the disc jockey and newscaster for his unit's radio station. Upon his release from the service—where he had earned his high school equivalency diploma—Hackman studied broadcasting in New York under the GI Bill, then went to work at various radio stations around the country. When none of these jobs seemed to hold his interest, he ended up in California studying acting at the Pasadena Playhouse. Returning to New York, he supported himself as a doorman, truck driver, salesman and furniture mover while trying to break in as a stage actor.

After several years, Hackman finally made it in 1964 with his portrayal of Cas Henderson in *Any Wednesday*. He continued to act in plays, had small parts in several films and appeared on a slew of TV shows including *The Defenders* and *Naked City*. One of the films was a box office bomb called *Lilith*, which also featured Warren Beatty, but Beatty must have liked working with Hackman because he gave him the role of Clyde Barrow's brother in *Bonnie and Clyde*, for which Hackman was nominated for a best supporting actor Oscar in 1967. *Time* magazine wrote of him: "A sort of blue-collar actor, slightly embarrassed about art but avid about craft."

It was in 1976 that he won the best actor Oscar for his portrayal of Popeye Doyle in *The French Connection*. To prepare for that demanding role, he spent many weeks on the streets of Harlem with Eddie Egan, the detective he was portraying. The bigotry and vulgarity he encountered still didn't quite toughen him up for the more violent scenes, and they required many retakes. In addition, Gene insisted on doing much of his own driving in the breathtaking car-chase scenes. After that, his career took off, and he has since appeared in countless films as a supporting actor and as a leading man. Among them: *The Poseidon Adventure, Bite the Bullet, The Conversation, Superman* and *No Way Out,* and in 1992, *Unforgiven,* for which he won an Oscar for best supporting actor.

By his first wife, Gene has three children. He and his current wife, an accomplished pianist, live in Santa Fe. He says he has never had a vacation in his life but enjoys riding motorcycles and flying rented planes.

LARRY HAGMAN

REAL NAME: Larry Hagman
DATE OF BIRTH: September 21, 1931
PLACE OF BIRTH: Fort Worth, Texas

EYE COLOR: Blue   HAIR COLOR: Reddish
HEIGHT: 6'1"   WEIGHT: 190

In typical J.R. Ewing style, Larry Hagman has said of his role on Dallas: "Something like this happens only every ten or twenty years in an actor's life, and I mean to cash in on it."

The son of actress Mary Martin and a lawyer father, Larry grew up troubled by his parents' divorce and his new stepfather, producer Richard Halliday. He divided his time between his real father in Texas, his mother and his grandmother in Los Angeles. Educated at a string of private schools, he was a constant disciplinary problem, and that problem continued until he flunked out in his first year at Bard College in New York.

After he meandered through lightweight stage jobs in Florida and New Jersey, his mother persuaded him to take a small acting role in the London production of *South Pacific*, in which she played Nellie Forbush. When the show closed, Hagman stayed in Europe, spending four years directing USO shows for the Air Force. Upon his return to the United States, he spent the late '50s and early '60s acting on and off Broadway and appearing in New York-based TV shows. It was in 1964 that he finally made his way to Hollywood for a role in the *Alfred Hitchcock Hour*. When the episode in which he was scheduled to perform was canceled, Hagman stuck around to do some auditions, and lightning finally struck: He was picked to co-star opposite Barbara Eden in *I Dream of Jeannie*. The show ran for five years and made him a star.

When *Jeannie* was canceled, he went on to appear in feature films: *Harry and Tonto, Mother, Jugs and Speed* and *The Eagle Has Landed*, among others. But two attempts at series television failed before Hagman landed the role of J.R. Ewing in 1978 in *Dallas*. Greedy, devoid of any moral fiber or conscience, willing to do whatever it takes to get his way, J.R. was a self-confident S.O.B. and a

media phenomenon. It was from his own father's oil-rich clients that Hagman brought to the role recollections of the mendacity he saw as a young man. "They had such a nice sweet smile," he remembers, "but when you finished the meeting your socks were missing and you hadn't even noticed they'd taken your boots." The final episode of the 1979-80 season—in which J.R. was shot—was one of the highest rated TV shows ever, watched by 30 to 40 million people worldwide. By the 1980-81 season, Hagman was pulling in $75,000 an episode and was one of the most popular stars on television.

A longtime resident of Malibu and its former self-appointed mayor, Larry practices regular meditation and recognizes Sunday as "a day of silence." He lives there with his wife, Maj, a Swedish dress designer who now designs hot tubs. The two have a son and a daughter who is an actress. Larry is an aggressive antismoking crusader but otherwise has adopted a very relaxed lifestyle, which he celebrates with a banner that hangs from the top deck of his home. Translated from Latin, it reads: "Life is a Celebration."

ARSENIO HALL

REAL NAME: Arsenio Hall
DATE OF BIRTH: February 12, 1957
PLACE OF BIRTH: Cleveland, Ohio

EYE COLOR: Brown   HAIR COLOR: Black
HEIGHT: 6'   WEIGHT: 175

The only son of a Baptist preacher and a housewife, Arsenio Hall decided at age five that he must escape the ghetto. A rat ran across his foot when he was in the bathroom that day: "I decided right then that my big goal was to live in a house with no rats and roaches. Me and my mother. That's all I wanted." That same year, his parents divorced, and he was raised by his mother and grandmother. But he credits watching his father preach with giving him the tools for "working a crowd." He started practicing early when he gave magic shows at receptions after the weddings at which his father officiated. "Most kids had a paper route and mowed lawns to make a little money," he says, "but I was allergic to grass, so I did magic." Arsenio had few friends and consoled himself with radio and television. His favorites were talk shows: "All-night radio and Johnny Carson were my friends."

It was after comedian Franklin Ajaye appeared at his high school that Hall decided to become a stand-up comedian, but he didn't act on his decision immediately and enrolled as a speech communications major at Kent State University, where he was active in theater and as a campus disc jockey. After graduation, he started out pursuing an advertising career, but in 1979 he finally began performing stand-up. Eventually he quit his day job and moved to Chicago, where he was discovered in a comedy club by singer Nancy Wilson. Impressed with his potential, she paid for his move to Los Angeles and soon Hall was opening for big-name acts like Aretha Franklin and Tina Turner. He began appearing on *The Tonight Show* and for a while co-hosted the show *Solid Gold*. Hall also appeared on *The Late Show* with Joan Rivers, and after Rivers was fired, was one of many guest hosts brought in to replace her. He drew such high ratings that he was given his own show, *The Arsenio Hall Show*, which went on to become a solid performer in the ultra-competitive late-night time slot. Arsenio has also made his mark on the big screen as an actor in *Coming to America*, among others, and most recently as executive producer of the new film *BOPHA!*

Arsenio has never married and spends his free time pursuing his passion for basketball, both playing and watching. He is also a committed crusader against drugs and can be seen on MTV spreading the word to young people.

TOM HANKS

REAL NAME: Tom Hanks
DATE OF BIRTH: July 9, 1956
PLACE OF BIRTH: Concord, California

EYE COLOR: Green-gray   HAIR COLOR: Brown
HEIGHT: 5'11"   WEIGHT: 155

After his parents' divorce when he was five, Tom Hanks lived with his father, an itinerant cook, moving from place to place for three years. "I think I moved every six months when I was a kid," Tom remembers. "But I had a solid core of my older brother, my sister and my dad."

Painfully shy after attending five different grammar schools, Tom also recalls, "I was the guy who'd yell out funny captions during film-strips." The family finally settled in Oakland, California, when he was eight, and at Skyline High School, Tom found an outlet for his insecurities in student plays.

He didn't seriously consider becoming an actor until 1977 when, as a student at Sacramento State University, he met Vincent Dowling, director of the Great Lakes Shakespeare Festival. Dowling invited Hanks to join the festival and Hanks accepted, dropping out of school. After three years of repertory work, he moved to New York and lived the life of a struggling actor for a while before being spotted by a talent scout from Los Angeles. That got him his big break on the new ABC sitcom *Bosom Buddies*. Although it was uneven at times, the series lasted two seasons and launched the careers of both Hanks and co-star Peter Scolari. It was after a one-shot guest spot on *Happy Days* that producer Ron Howard asked him to read for a secondary part in *Splash*, but when Howard recognized his impish, lovable little-boy quality, he handed Tom the lead opposite Daryl Hannah. When it became a hit, Hanks' career took off. Since then, he's made a string of hits, including *Big*, *Volunteers*, *A League of Their Own* and the 1993 romantic comedy *Sleepless in Seattle*. We will see him on the screen next as a lawyer with advanced AIDS in the film *Philadelphia*.

Tom is guarded about his private life, but he insists there's nothing interesting to talk about. "I have no hobbies," he says. "I don't have one of those ranches in Alberta that I disappear to for months. When I'm not working, I wake up, drink some coffee, read the papers, and get on the phone and see what's going on." He does, however, have two children from a previous marriage, and a present wife, actress Rita Wilson.

DARYL HANNAH

REAL NAME: Daryl Hannah
DATE OF BIRTH: 1960
PLACE OF BIRTH: Chicago, Illinois

EYE COLOR: Blue   HAIR COLOR: Blond
HEIGHT: 5'10"   WEIGHT: 120

She's been a cavewoman, a Manhattan interior designer, a mermaid, an android, a beautician, an astronomer and a cheerleader—and all in just one decade.

After her parents divorced when she was seven, Daryl Hannah retreated into her own never-never land and doesn't even remember the next four years. "I probably lived a little bit too much inside my imagination," she says. "I used to see witches and leprechauns and stuff. I actually still remember these things as if they actually happened, so I kind of like to leave that time alone and not rip it apart." After psychiatrists said that she was semiautistic, her mother packed her up, took her to the Bahamas and let her run free. "I'd bring my teddy bear to the beach and to dinner," Daryl recalls. "Mom let me work it all out." And when she finally said, "Mom, let's go home," they left. But Daryl's mother says that she remained reserved afterward. Daryl had been dancing since age four, but now she had a fervent interest in acting, and she appeared in her first commercial at eleven. When she was twelve, her mother remarried, this time to Chicago real estate tycoon Jerry Wexler, and Daryl's life changed radically. Daryl and her brother and sister were ensconced in a posh penthouse on Lake Shore Drive, and Daryl was enrolled at Francis Parker, the exclusive prep school. Frequent trips to Europe, the Caribbean and Wexler's estate in Colorado followed. Active in theater and track and the only girl on the school soccer team, she seemed to thrive. But because she was always tall and skinny, Daryl was saddled with nicknames like Beanpole and never dated. Throughout junior high and high school she studied at Chicago's famous Goodman Theater, then moved to Los Angeles and enrolled at the University of Southern California as a general education major. Her true motivation for being there, she admits, was to find a crack in the wall of

fame. A chance meeting on the street with a producer brought her some small roles in a few low-budget films. Then, in 1982, she put her athleticism to good use, doing her own stunts in her first major role as an evil replicant in *Blade Runner*. In 1984, in *Splash*, she played a mermaid and, refusing a stunt double, did her own underwater scenes. In the wake of that hit, parts started coming her way— some good, some bad. "After *Clan of the Cave Bear*," she has said, "I thought I'd never work again." But she went on to star in *Legal Eagles*, *Roxanne* and *Wall Street*.

Hannah is a strict vegetarian, and in order to stay in shape does gymnastics and scuba dives as often as she can. Although never married, she had a lengthy liaison with singer Jackson Browne and even played keyboard in some of his videos. Presently, the public is enthralled by her romance with John F. Kennedy Jr.

WOODY HARRELSON

REAL NAME: Woody Harrelson
DATE OF BIRTH: July 23, 1961
PLACE OF BIRTH: Midland, Texas

EYE COLOR: Blue   HAIR COLOR: Blond
HEIGHT: 5'10"   WEIGHT: 170

The easygoing, bubble-headed bartender that he plays on *Cheers* couldn't be less like the real-life Woody Harrelson. Still trying to outgrow a streak of wildness ever since childhood, he admits that "violence was almost an aphrodisiac for me. I really loved it. I would smile when I was about to get into a fight."

In 1970, Woody's father left him and his two brothers to be raised by his mother, grandmother and great-grandmother. "It wasn't a shock to me that he wasn't around," he says. "We weren't a *Father Knows Best* kind of family." His mother moved them to Lebanon, Ohio, where she worked as a legal secretary. Although he was constantly in scrapes as a boy (he even kicked a teacher), Woody was also deeply religious and wrote poetry. But in his freshman year at Indiana's Hanover College, his father was convicted of murdering a federal judge and sentenced to life in prison—and Woody proceeded to turn his back on religion. In college, however, he devoted himself to his drama courses, appearing in 26 productions, and graduated with degrees in theater and English.

Eighteen months later in New York, he was waiting tables, short-order cooking, and doing everything else but acting. He had his bags packed for a return to Ohio when he got a call to understudy in a Neil Simon play, *Biloxi Blues*, on Broadway. While Woody was working for Neil, he was dating Simon's daughter, Nancy, and in 1985, they took a long weekend in Tijuana, Mexico, deciding it would be a hoot to get married on Saturday and grab a quickie divorce the next day. They didn't know the chapels were closed on Sundays, and both had to be back at work on different coasts the next day. It was ten months later before they got their official divorce.

Despite his tumultuous private life, Woody's work on Broadway earned him great notices, a part in *Wildcats* with Goldie Hawn, and then his Emmy-winning role as Woody the bartender on *Cheers*. During its nine-year run, he has found time to act in the films *Doc Hollywood*, *White Men Can't Jump* and, most recently, *Indecent Proposal*. Lately, he's also been gaining recognition in San Francisco and New York as lead singer with his rock group, Manly Moondog & the Three Kool Kats. He's even taming the shrew in himself, settling down with girlfriend Laura Louie and their newborn daughter. The real Woody may even become as docile as the TV Woody but with one big exception: Woody Harrelson only acts dumb when it's smart to. "In Hollywood," he says, "the best time to play dumb is when it's time to negotiate."

MARY HART

REAL NAME: Mary Hart
DATE OF BIRTH: November 8, 1950
PLACE OF BIRTH: Sioux Falls, South Dakota

EYE COLOR: Blue   HAIR COLOR: Blond
HEIGHT: 5'5"   WEIGHT: 115

One could describe Mary Hart as a bottle of Perrier, wholesome and effervescent. When asked if she ever tires of her bubbly image, Mary says, "Obviously, not everything I do is for public consumption. But if the overall impression is that I'm a pleasant person—whether that means perky, smily or whatever—then I'm perfectly satisfied with the description, because I am a highly enthusiastic individual."

Mary's father was an executive with International Harvester, so she found herself uprooted from Sioux Falls at age eight and relocated in Denmark for the next eleven years. Until then, she had lived a little girl's perfect childhood and had trouble with the transition. Looking back, Mary says, "It was hard. I not only couldn't speak the language, but I didn't dress like the other kids. So it was like, 'Look at that funny American girl,' and it took a while before I fit in." After several more moves, Mary found herself growing more resilient and now considers the experience invaluable. Finally stateside again at eighteen, she entered a Lutheran college back in Sioux Falls and earned an English degree. When she was asked to enter the Miss South Dakota contest in 1970, she was undecided until her father forbade her to even consider the notion. "I'll be darned if my family tells me what I can do!" said Mary. "So I entered the pageant and ultimately won, and eventually I became a runner-up for Miss America."

Completing her tenure as Miss South Dakota, Mary turned to teaching high school English but found it unrewarding. On the side, she started doing some community theater and eventually found a slot hosting a local cable show. By now, she had a thirst for show

business and followed radio and TV-hostess gigs in Cedar Rapids and Oklahoma City before joining *PM Magazine*. A brief co-hosting stint on *The Regis Philbin Show* captured enough recognition to become the choice as *Entertainment Tonight*'s new anchorperson in 1981. She's been there ever since.

But Mary has a burning desire to stretch herself and pursue a more serious acting career, and toward that end, has retained superagent Jay Bernstein, who designed Farrah Fawcett's aura. He began by creating a flap over Mary's legs when he had them insured by Lloyds of London for $2 million. Meanwhile, Mary and producer/businessman Burt Sugarman tied the knot in 1989 and had a child in 1993.

GOLDIE HAWN

REAL NAME: Goldie Jeanne Hawn
DATE OF BIRTH: November 21, 1945
PLACE OF BIRTH: Washington, D.C.

EYE COLOR: Blue   HAIR COLOR: Blond
HEIGHT: 5'6"   WEIGHT: 119

The ditzy, ding-dong blonde who giggled her way through dialogue twenty years ago on *Laugh-In* has proven to be a fine dramatic actress and a savvy producer. But there's still a piece of that girl in Goldie's spirit: "I've possessed a certain joy all my life. I had that before anyone ever knew my name." Her mother adds that Goldie "at any function would always put on her tutu and dance, whether you wanted her to or not."

The second daughter of a Jewish mom and a Presbyterian dad who performed as a musician at White House functions, Goldie got her show-business training early. Dance lessons began at age three, and her father gave her voice lessons that continued throughout childhood, culminating with performances in high school plays and community theater productions in her hometown of Washington, D.C. After graduation from high school, she taught dance while studying drama at American University, dropping out after a year. Dying to cut loose, she became a go-go dancer, shaking it up in the Manhattan disco Dudes 'n' Dolls and at the Desert Inn in Las Vegas. Goldie calls that period "the saddest part of my life." She says, "I got to see the world from the bottom. Dancers are the low end of show business, and we saw all kinds of behavior down there—stars who came in and acted like jerks, people who were disrespectful and thought they were just the biggest things. It became very distasteful. Since then, my feet have always been pretty much on the ground."

She was discovered by Hollywood agent Art Simon while dancing in the chorus of an Andy Griffith TV special in 1967. After a short run on a failed sitcom for CBS, she became a regular on *Laugh-In*, and she took that image to the big screen with a best supporting actress Oscar for her role as Walter Matthau's mistress in *Cactus Flower*. After she left *Laugh-In* during the 1969-70 season, she began easing into dramatic roles in films such as *Shampoo* and *The Sugarland Express*. But it's still as the adorable fluff in comedies like *Private Benjamin*, *Foul Play*, *Overboard* and *Protocol* that Hawn has become a household name. In recent years, she vacillates between giving the public the zany comedies they still love, such as *Housesitter* and *Death Becomes Her*, and heavily dramatic films like *Deceived* and *Crisscross*. With her own production company and the backing of Disney, Goldie is currently considered one of the most powerful women in Hollywood and has the reputation of an actress with a slick mind for business.

The girl who declared years ago that "I'm old-fashioned. I just want desperately to get married" did just that—twice, to director Gus Trikonis and singer Bill Hudson (to whom she had to pay alimony). In 1984, she and Kurt Russell, five years her junior, met on the set of *Swing Shift* and have been inseparable ever since. Goldie's two children by Hudson and her son by Kurt complete the Hawn/Russell household. "Maybe later on in life we'll get married," she says, "But right now, we're so close to these ex-spouses who keep knocking on the door. And we look at each other and I think, Gee, I just love you too much to put that ring on your finger."

KATHARINE HEPBURN

REAL NAME: Katharine Hepburn
DATE OF BIRTH: November 8, 1907
PLACE OF BIRTH: Hartford, Connecticut

EYE COLOR: Blue   HAIR COLOR: Reddish brown
HEIGHT: 5'4"   WEIGHT: 110

The reserved facade of Katharine Hepburn is no acting feat. She and her two younger brothers and sisters were raised in a strict, no-nonsense Yankee home that insisted on, among other things, cold showers every morning. Her father was a doctor and a pioneer in personal hygiene; her mother was a militant suffragette and birth

control advocate. In spite of her staunch home life, Katharine was still considered a tomboy and so was educated at home by private tutors. Once tamed, she entered the Hartford School for Girls and Bryn Mawr College. As a young girl, Hepburn had wanted to be a doctor like her father, but she realized that few women entered medicine in those days and turned her attention to dramatics. She began participating in student plays and, upon graduation, did summer stock on the East Coast.

She eventually made it to Broadway in 1928 and four years later had her first hit there with *The Warrior's Husband*. When this brought Hollywood offers, she signed with RKO Pictures and began her long sojourn into films. For the next six years she gave RKO their money's worth with a score of movies. Her very first best actress Oscar was won in 1933 playing an actress in *Morning Glory*. While at RKO, she rebelliously refused to accept roles she didn't like and would not go along with the expected practice of fawning for the press, so she was considered an ornery and snobbish oddity. Katharine returned to critical praise on the stage in 1939 as the luminous star of *The Philadelphia Story*. In 1942, she began her long romantic association with Spencer Tracy, playing opposite him in *Woman of the Year*.

In 1952, after a string of classic films with Tracy, she made one of her most famous films, *The African Queen*, and received her fifth Academy Award nomination. In 1967, she starred opposite Tracy one last time—and won a best actress Oscar for her role as the mother of a feisty, independent daughter who marries a black man in *Guess Who's Coming to Dinner*. Her subsequent films, including her fourth Oscar-winning performance in *On Golden Pond*, have made her a legend as well as an icon of iron femininity.

In 1992, Katharine released her long-awaited autobiography, *Me*, in which she discusses not only her 27-year love affair with Spencer Tracy, but the story of her only marriage, to a man named Ludlow Smith in 1928. After two weeks of trying to be a "proper wife," she left him and turned to her career. Claiming that her long life holds no regrets, she says, "I'm an atheist, and that's it. I believe there's nothing we can know except that we should be kind to each other and do what we can for other people."

BARBARA HERSHEY

REAL NAME: Barbara Herzstein
DATE OF BIRTH: February 5, 1948
PLACE OF BIRTH: Hollywood, California

EYE COLOR: Brown   HAIR COLOR: Brown
HEIGHT: 5'4"   WEIGHT: 105

Explaining her childhood, Barbara Hershey has said, "Whenever anyone asked, 'What do you want to do?' I would say, 'I'm an actress.' I didn't say I wanted to be an actress. So I always felt very blessed. It was a comfort to know that sort of passion so young." Indeed, she was so precocious that her family nicknamed her Sarah Bernhardt.

The youngest of three children and a native of Hollywood, where her father was a bookie and wrote for the *Daily Racing Form*, Barbara was a pom-pom girl and a member of the drill team at

Hollywood High School. Before graduation, which she accomplished in two and a half years, she had been active in the theater and was discovered by an agent during a student production.

Her first professional acting job was in the '60s on an episode of *Gidget* with Sally Field. Soon after, at only seventeen, she was given the lead in the TV series *The Monroes*, which lasted one season. She made her first movie, in *With Six You Get Eggroll*, in 1968 and the next year starred in *Last Summer*. An incident during that filming sparked a life and career change that would last a decade. She explains: "There was a scene where I had to throw a trained bird up in the air, trying to make it fly. This bird was very special. I felt her spirit. But we had to reshoot the scene over and over. I knew she was exhausted, and I told the director that I couldn't throw her again; and he told me on the last throw she had broken her neck. At that moment I felt her soul enter me. I didn't tell anybody for a long time. I just realized, finally, that the only honest, moral thing would be to change my name." And she became Barbara Seagull. Shortly thereafter, she began living in a log cabin in the hills with David Carradine, and their hippie-ish lifestyle—during which she touted smoking peyote—earned her a kooky image with the Hollywood establishment. Although she worked fairly regularly, the parts diminished in substance, falling into the B-grade category.

In 1978, director Frank Rush went to bat for Barbara and cast her as the lead in *The Stunt Man*, her first notable screen appearance in many years. Since then, she has played perhaps more different types of roles than any of her peers—among them, the seductress who tried to kill Robert Redford in *The Natural*, the youngest of the three siblings in *Hannah and Her Sisters*, Mary Magdalene in *The Last Temptation of Christ*, and Ruth the Louisiana Bayou recluse in *Shy People*. Further solidifying her reputation as a respected artist were her performances in *The Right Stuff* and *Beaches*.

Since her relationship with Carradine ended in 1975, she has not married. Their son, Free, changed his name to Tom when he was nine. And Barbara changed her name back to Hershey in 1976, perhaps confirming her return to "the Establishment." Her renegade days behind her, Barbara leads a quiet life—far from the dazzle that surrounds the business—either at her home in Santa Monica, or at her 300-year-old farmhouse in Connecticut, where she enjoys gardening, dancing and playing the flute.

CHARLTON HESTON

REAL NAME: Charles Carter
DATE OF BIRTH: October 4, 1924
PLACE OF BIRTH: Evanston, Illinois

EYE COLOR: Blue-gray   HAIR COLOR: Brown
HEIGHT: 6'3"   WEIGHT: 200

With a successful 50-year career and more than 60 films, Charlton Heston is entitled to an ego. But playing Ben-Hur, Moses and Michelangelo, he says, has been humbling for him: "When you're playing Moses, you go to your hotel and try to part the water in the bathtub. When it doesn't part, you feel pretty humble."

One of America's living legends, Charlton Heston spent his early years in the backwoods of Michigan where his father worked in a lumber mill. There were only thirteen students in the one-room schoolhouse he attended, and the absence of nearby friends turned him into an avid reader. To further his enjoyment of books, Charlton acted out the stories he read. "More than most kids, I suppose, I played games—imaginary, pretend games—living in a madeup world," he remembers. Then, when he was twelve, his mother divorced and moved with him to Wilmette, a suburb of Chicago, where she married Chester Heston and enrolled Charlton in New Trier High School, one of the best in the country. Like the country mouse in the city, he felt awkward and inferior, so he avoided the abundance of extracurricular opportunities and joined the school's theatrical program. "What acting offered me," he says, "was the chance to be many other people. In those days, I wasn't satisfied with being me." He also began acting in the Winnetka Community Theater, winning a scholarship with which he attended Northwestern University. While there, he met actress Lydia Clarke, and they married in 1944. After his sophomore year, he interrupted his education to serve three years in the Air Force as a B-52 radio gunner. After graduation, he and Lydia moved to New York, where Heston hoped to become an actor. Living in Hell's Kitchen, they paid their dues for a while, living off his military pay and odd jobs, including nude modeling for him at the art students' league. He got his break on Broadway in 1947, landing a role as Caeser's lieutenant in *Antony and Cleopatra*. From there, he found steady work in theater and television and in 1950 made his screen debut in the film *Dark City*. Though it failed, reviews for Heston were good and they jump-started his career. Dozens of movie roles followed, the most notable among them Cecil B. DeMille's *The Ten Commandments* in 1956. Winning the title role in *Ben-Hur* over Marlon Brando, Rock Hudson and Burt Lancaster, Charlton went on to win a best actor Oscar.

Charlton is still married to Lydia, and they have two grown children; their son Fraser is a screenwriter and producer, in several of whose films Charlton has appeared as a star. Still in possession of a remarkable physique, he whips it daily playing tennis, swimming or jogging. Many of his own sketches have been exhibited in art galleries around the world. After serving from 1965 to 1971 as the president of the Screen Actors' Guild, he was publicly critical of ex-president Ed Asner's use of SAG as a forum for political issues, though he himself has been an outspoken supporter of President Ronald Reagan. But Heston says he entertains absolutely no political designs for himself: "I've played three presidents, three saints, two geniuses. That should satisfy any man."

DUSTIN HOFFMAN

REAL NAME: Dustin Hoffman
DATE OF BIRTH: August 8, 1937
PLACE OF BIRTH: Los Angeles, California

EYE COLOR: Brown   HAIR COLOR: Brown
HEIGHT: 5'6"   WEIGHT:135

He was once described by columnist Lloyd Shearer as "the anti-star hero, the one actor who looks least like such Establishment heroes as Gregory Peck, John Wayne and William Holden." But after thirty years as a star, Dustin Hoffman is still one of the hottest actors working today.

Short, with braces, plagued by acne as a child, Hoffman was not athletic and did not do particularly well in school. One of two boys born to a furniture designer and a prop man at Columbia Pictures, he took advantage of his diminutive size to gain attention as well as a part playing Tiny Tim in junior high school. Once at Los Angeles High, though, he became the proverbial little fish in a big pond. "I was an outsider, an observer," he remembers. "That's the way I'll probably always see life." Too small for contact sports, he turned to weightlifting, tennis and piano. While attending Santa Monica City College as a music major, Hoffman became interested in acting and, after a year, left to study drama at the Pasadena Playhouse.

Two years later, he moved to New York and proceeded to struggle for seven years, winning primarily bit parts on television and doing most of his acting in summer stock while he studied at Lonnie Chapman's acting studio. Dustin proved his perseverance during those years, living in a cold-water railroad flat—when he could afford it—or sleeping on Gene Hackman's kitchen floor. His meager income came from washing dishes, checking coats, waiting tables, cleaning a dance studio and selling toys at Macy's. At the latter, he demonstrated the ultimate acting feat: persuading a customer to "buy" Gene Hackman's eighteen-month-old baby in the belief that he was a life-size doll.

In 1961, he made his Broadway debut with a walk-on part in the play *A Cook for Mr. General*. He continued to act on the stage until his breakthrough role in the 1967 hit film *The Graduate*. His performance as the innocent, idealistic Benjamin Braddock brought Hoffman an Academy Award nomination and made him an overnight sensation. But it was his roles as Ratso Rizzo in *Midnight Cowboy* and the 121-year-old man raised by Indians in *Little Big Man* that cemented his reputation. Hoffman went on to star in many films, including *Lenny* and *Tootsie*, and won Oscars for *Kramer vs. Kramer* and *Rain Man*. After appearing in the film *Hook* as the nefarious Captain Hook opposite Robin Williams' Peter Pan, he returned to his origins on the stage in the Broadway play *Death of a Salesman*.

After a first marriage and two daughters, he married attorney Lisa Gottsegen in 1980, and they have three children of their own.

BOB HOPE

REAL NAME: Leslie Townes Hope
DATE OF BIRTH: May 29, 1903
PLACE OF BIRTH: Eltham, England

EYE COLOR: Brown   HAIR COLOR: Brown
HEIGHT: 5'10"   WEIGHT: 170

During a long and illustrious career, Bob Hope has starred in more than 55 films, entertained millions all over the world, received nineteen honorary degrees and collected more than 1,000 awards, among them five special Oscars and the Congressional Gold Medal for outstanding service to the cause of democracy throughout the world. But one of his brightest memories has to be when he had the opportunity to banter with Edward VII of England: "The only time I ever had a king for a straight man."

Hope was born in England but moved to Cleveland, Ohio, with his mother and his father, a stonemason, when he was four. The fifth of six sons, he ran with the neighborhood toughs, changing his name from Les to Bob early in school because the kids started calling him Hopeless. His mother, a former concert singer, gave him voice lessons, but while singing at a family gathering, his voice cracked, and the resulting laughter so delighted him that he resolved to become a comedian. During high school, in addition to taking tap dancing lessons and running track, he earned money working in a drugstore, selling papers and golf caddying. When his tap dance instructor left to seek his fortune in Hollywood, Hope took over his classes. After high school, he even had a short run as an amateur boxer (using the name Packy East) before becoming an entertainer.

Hearing that a road show featuring Fatty Arbuckle was in need of additional talent, Hope and partner George Byrne put together an act and won a place in the show. From that point until 1928, they traveled the vaudeville circuit doing blackface, dancing and moving the scenery between acts while Bob sang and played the saxophone. During the late '20s, Hope split from Byrne, began performing as a stand-up comic in small Ohio clubs and eventually headed for the big time in Chicago. But for a time he was unable to find steady work

and was $4,000 in debt.

Finally, however, a friend helped him land a gig as the emcee at a small nightclub, and he was so popular that he won a six-month run at the Stratford Theater. In 1938, Hope made his first movie, The *Big Broadcast of 1938*, and went on to star in a string of films, many of them with longtime co-star Bing Crosby. When World War II broke out, Hope tried to enlist but was told he would be more valuable to the war effort as an entertainer. By the end of the war, he had appeared at virtually every camp, naval base and hospital in the country and had made six trips to entertain the troops overseas. When the Vietnam War came along, Bob picked right up where he had left off.

An avid golfer, he hosts the annual Bob Hope Desert Classic golf tournament in Palm Springs, California, which has raised nearly $10 million for charities. Married since 1934, he and Dolores have four adopted children who are grown. At 90, Bob is semiretired and spends most of his time at home in Palm Springs where, he once said, "George Burns and I, for excitement on Saturday night, sit around and see whose leg falls asleep faster."

ANTHONY HOPKINS

REAL NAME: Anthony Hopkins
DATE OF BIRTH: December 31, 1937
PLACE OF BIRTH: Port Talbot, South Wales

EYE COLOR: Blue   HAIR COLOR: Brown
HEIGHT: 5'10"   WEIGHT: 155

The object of newfound celebrity in the wake of his Oscar-winning role as Hannibal Lecter in the hit film *The Silence of the Lambs*, Anthony Hopkins has also won both the Actor of the Year Award from Great Britain's Academy of Film and Television Arts and an Emmy Award for his role in the TV movie *The Lindbergh Kidnapping Case*.

Hopkins had an unhappy childhood. Big and awkward for his age, he recalls that his father was "a man of little tolerance who was always putting me down." Although his parents worked in a bakery, they managed to earn enough money to send their only child to the Cowbridge boarding school to save him the harassment of his peers. It didn't work. Not only was he snubbed by his wealthy classmates, but he says, "Academically, I was an idiot. I wouldn't learn math. I didn't know what I was going to do. The only talent I had was for playing the piano and impersonating the schoolmasters."

After leaving Cowbridge, he worked for a time as a steelworker and began taking acting classes at the Cardiff College of Drama. At twenty, he was called to military service and turned in the required two years, then joined the Manchester Library Theatre where he served as stage manager between small parts in the company's plays. Unfortunately, he had trouble remembering his lines and was fired. On the suggestion of his director, he ended up at the Royal Academy of Dramatic Arts and studied there for two years. So enthusiastic was he over his craft that he took outside classes in the Stanislavsky "Method," from which he feels any actor can learn to achieve "a kind of fluid, total, immediate reality." With the ultimate goal of becoming a member of the National Theatre, he spent the next three years with various repertory companies, and finally gained an audition for Sir Laurence Olivier. When Anthony had finished reading a speech from

Othello, Olivier said, "I don't think I'm going to lose any sleep tonight, but would you like to join us?"

In 1969, he made his American film debut as Richard the Lionhearted in *The Lion in Winter*. Among his many films, in addition to his chilling portrayal of Hannibal the Cannibal, his most notable are *Magic, The Bounty, 84 Charing Cross Road, Young Winston, A Bridge Too Far, The Elephant Man, Great Expectations* and *Howards End*.

Anthony's first marriage ended in 1972, with one daughter. He and his present wife have no children, and he devotes his leisure time to astronomy and playing the piano.

RON HOWARD

REAL NAME: Ron Howard
DATE OF BIRTH: March 1, 1954
PLACE OF BIRTH: Duncan, Oklahoma

EYE COLOR: Hazel   HAIR COLOR: Red
HEIGHT: 5'10"   WEIGHT: 145

Ron Howard made his debut as an actor when he was eighteen
months old. His dialogue needed work, but other than that, he had
the makings of a star.

Ron and his brother, also an actor, had an actress and an
actor/director/writer for parents. In his second acting job, at age two,
he was directed by his father in a stage production of *The Seven-Year
Itch*. From toddlerhood on, Ron enjoyed being on the set or stage
watching his father direct and trading lines with him. "But acting
was never pressed on me," says Ron. "It was something I did with my
dad, so when I started doing it with other people it was just something I did for fun. The fun has remained, because otherwise I would
have gotten out." By the time he was five, Howard was a full-fledged
actor, appearing on *Playhouse Theater* and *The General Electric
Theater*, among other shows. In 1960, at six, he was cast as Opie on
The Andy Griffith Show, and for eight years America watched him
grow up under Andy's watchful eye.

His next big break came when George Lucas gave him the lead in
his surprise hit *American Graffiti*. That led to the role of Richie
Cunningham on the *Graffiti* clone *Happy Days*, and Howard, who
had once been America's favorite kid, became America's favorite teen.
Meanwhile, he wasn't sitting on his laurels. While he was still at
Burroughs High School, he won a national Kodak film contest for a
Super 8 short, then studied cinema arts at the University of Southern

California. In exchange for his acting services in a B-movie, *Eat My Dust*, Roger Corman gave Howard his directorial debut in *Grand Theft Auto*, a car-chase movie that Howard co-wrote with his father. From there, he went to the big time as the director of *Splash*, *Cocoon*, *Backdraft* and *Far and Away*, achieving even more status as a director than he had enjoyed as an actor.

Still married to his high school girlfriend, he and his wife have four children. They live a very Mayberryish, homespun life in which Ron says his favorite pastime is watching the Dodgers and washing down junk food with a beer. The opposite of his artsy colleagues, Ron considers what he does just a job. "I have a lot of patience," he says, describing himself. "I rarely feel betrayed or disgruntled. I don't get revved up."

WILLIAM HURT

REAL NAME: William Hurt
DATE OF BIRTH: March 20, 1950
PLACE OF BIRTH: Washington, D.C.

EYE COLOR: Blue   HAIR COLOR: Blond
HEIGHT: 6'2"   WEIGHT: 180

As a child, William Hurt grew up island-hopping in the South Pacific: His father was a director of trust territories for the State Department. When his parents divorced in the late '50s, he moved with his mother and two brothers to New York City. They lived in a small, depressing apartment until 1960, when his mother married

Time magazine's Henry Luce III, and Hurt's life changed dramatically. "I had been a street fighter, a little punk kid, and suddenly I was in an eastern-establishment-type school, wearing Bass Weejuns, white socks, herringbone jackets, and ties," he says. It was at Middlesex prep school in Connecticut that he started developing a taste for acting in student plays. At Tufts University, he majored in theology, but he soon became more interested in acting and spent his senior year in England studying theater. Upon graduation from Tufts with honors in 1972, he enrolled at Juilliard to further his thespian studies.

During his third year at Juilliard, Hurt's marriage to actress Mary Beth Hurt broke up and, distraught, he climbed on his motorcycle and took off. He ended up in Oregon, where he won the role of Edmund in the Oregon Shakespeare Festival's production of *Long Day's Journey Into Night*, then returned to New York, where he worked both on and off Broadway until his film debut in the 1980 film *Altered States*. After a quick return to the stage, Hurt appeared in the romantic thriller *Eyewitness* in 1981, and that same year as the womanizing attorney Ned Racine in the soon-to-be-classic *Body Heat*, which made him a star. From there on, he divided his time between plays such as David Rabe's *Hurly Burly* and movies such as *The Big Chill* and *Kiss of the Spider Woman*. His portrayal of the homosexual Luis Molina in *Spider Woman* earned him a best actor Oscar in 1985. To prepare for his complicated character, William searched for "the line between the female and masculine parts of ourselves—a line that moves around all the time." He has begun filming his latest role in *Trial by Jury*.

William has a son from his common-law marriage to dancer Sandra Jennings, which ended in divorce, then culminated in a bitter and widely publicized child support battle in court. Since ending his live-in relationship with actress Marlee Matlin, there seems to be no current serious flame. His reputation among peers is one of intensity and unpredictability. Preferring to keep his private life to himself, Hurt says, "I don't want to be known as an actor. I want to be known for my acting, and there is a difference."

ANJELICA HUSTON

REAL NAME: Anjelica Huston
DATE OF BIRTH: July 8, 1951
PLACE OF BIRTH: Los Angeles, California

EYE COLOR: Brown   HAIR COLOR: Brown
HEIGHT: 5'8"   WEIGHT: 118

Many actresses would feel intimidated by the legacy left by their male forebears. Anjelica Huston's grandfather, Walter Huston, was a famous character actor, and her father was the gifted director John, who left behind such films as *The Maltese Falcon* and *The Asphalt Jungle*. But Angelica's philosophy on carrying the family torch is: "I feel very much backed by my ancestors."

Anjelica was born during the filming of one of her father's all-time classics, *The African Queen*. Five months later, she, her brother and her mother moved to the 110-acre estate St. Clerans in Ireland, where she attended an Irish convent school. She spent what she calls a "fairy-tale childhood" there, especially when John would return home from location with gifts for all. "The house would come alive," she says. "He always had a taste for adventure, a taste for the good things. That included other women. Eventually my father had a son with another woman, and my mother had a daughter with another man. It was evident that things were never going to go back to where they had been." When they finally separated, she was eleven, and she moved to England.

After a series of unhappy experiences at various London educational institutions, Huston quit school and worked as a model before her father gave her the lead in his film *A Walk With Love and Death* in 1969. Just when the film was ready for release, Anjelica's mother was killed in a car accident, and Anjelica says, "It was like losing my best friend, my mother and my sister all in one. Nothing has happened to me before or since to equal the impact of that shock." On top of that, Huston's performance was universally panned, and she went to New York to understudy the role of Ophelia in Tony Richardson's production of *Hamlet*. She stayed in New York and worked as a model until 1973, when she moved to Los Angeles,

where her father was living with his fifth wife. There, she continued to model while taking acting classes with drama coach Peggy Feury.

Through her stepmother, Anjelica met Jack Nicholson at a party. Jack recalls their first star-crossed encounter: "What can I say? I can't come up with words poetic enough to describe her. She has a very strong aura. She struck me as being stunning. Not pretty, but very beautiful in a powerful way. Deep class." It didn't take long for Anjelica to move in with Jack, whose star was rising. Still reeling from her mother's death and career knocks, Anjelica wanted to take a year's sabbatical and rest, but it turned into five years.

When she finally went back to work, Anjelica began with small parts in such movies as *The Last Tycoon*, *The Swashbuckler* and *The Postman Always Rings Twice*. She didn't work with her father again until he cast her as a Mafia princess—opposite Nicholson—in *Prizzi's Honor*. She won a best supporting actress Oscar, and the role became the turning point of her acting career. She has since been nominated for two more Oscars for her roles in *Enemies, A Love Story* and *The Grifters*, and in 1989, she was awarded an Emmy for her performance in the miniseries *Lonesome Dove*. Anjelica is reprising her role as the Addams Family matriarch, Morticia, in *Addams Family Values*.

After seventeen years of a complicated up-and-down relationship with Nicholson, Anjelica finally called it off when he sired a child by another actress, Rebecca Broussard, and in 1992, she married artist/sculptor Robert Graham.

JEREMY IRONS

REAL NAME: Jeremy Irons
DATE OF BIRTH: September 19, 1948
PLACE OF BIRTH: Cowes, Isle of Wight, Great Britain

EYE COLOR: Brown   HAIR COLOR: Brown
HEIGHT: 6'2"   WEIGHT: 175

"I've always rather regretted that I've never had a gay experience," says Jeremy Irons, "It's not too late, and maybe I will one day." Coming from an enigmatic actor prized for his portrayal of complicated characters, this statement doesn't seem that surprising.

The son of an accountant, Irons, along with his brother and sister, enjoyed a serene, middle-class English upbringing. At Sherbourne, one of London's best private schools, he excelled at rugby, the fiddle and the clarinet, and headed the cadet corps. "The way to enjoy yourself," he decided, "was to get to the top so you could tell other people what to do." While attending the Bristol Old Vic School, he joined that school's repertory company, then moved to London in 1971, supporting himself as a housecleaner and a gardener and acting when he could. Eight years later, after versatile roles on stage and British television, he hit his mark in *Brideshead Revisited*, which is still frequently aired in this country.

Jeremy came to America's attention when he appeared opposite Meryl Streep in *The French Lieutenant's Woman*. Never seeking films with commercial success in mind, he explains that "I was educated to be this English held-back, held-in, don't-show-emotion chap. Since drama school I've tried to dig deep and let it all out—to get away from the fear of nakedness." He has accomplished this in roles such as a Polish carpenter in *Betrayal*, a Jesuit priest in *The Mission*, the Oscar-winning, nebulous wife murderer in *Reversal of Fortune*, and dual roles as the bizarre twins in *Dead Ringers*, which he considers his best work ever. His latest film, *Damage*, in which he plays the ardent pursuer of his son's fiancee, stirred up the critics and the media because of its initial NC-17 rating.

In real life, Jeremy plays the proper English gentleman on his comfortable but unpretentious estate between London and Oxford. His wife of twenty years, Sinéad Cusack, is a stage actress, and they have two sons. Refusing to live in Los Angeles as many other British actors have, he says, "I've always felt that would be a bit like living over the shop."

PETER JENNINGS

REAL NAME: Peter Charles Jennings
DATE OF BIRTH: July 29, 1938
PLACE OF BIRTH: Toronto, Canada

EYE COLOR: Brown   HAIR COLOR: Brown
HEIGHT: 6'2"   WEIGHT: 180

ABC news anchor Peter Jennings began his broadcasting career at age nine when he hosted *Peter's People*, a Canadian Broadcasting Corporation radio show for children. The older of two children, he had the perfect role model in his father for his own life's work. Charles Jennings was a broadcast journalist for the CBC and eventu-

ally its vice president of programming. Peter says his father was considered "roughly the equivalent on Canadian television of Edward R. Murrow."

At Trinity College School prep school, Peter was a star athlete but a poor student who was "bored" by academics. After leaving high school without graduating, he worked his way up through the CBC as an interviewer, hosting several public affairs and talk shows and, finally, working on the documentary series *Close-Up*. By 1962, he was hosting the *CTV National News*. After seeing his coverage of the Democratic National Convention in 1964, ABC News hired him as a correspondent in New York, then shocked everybody, including Jennings, by making him the anchor of their nightly national newscast only a few months later. At 26 the youngest network anchor ever, he was forced to go up against media giants Walter Cronkite and David Brinkley. "It's like being nominated for president. You can't turn it down," advised Howard K. Smith. Reaction was mixed, with many critics labeling him a "glamorcaster," and after three years, Jennings was removed. Looking back on that period as almost an apprenticeship, he says, "It was a little ridiculous when you think about it. I was simply unqualified."

He spent the last part of the '60s traveling around the world as a foreign correspondent until returning to the United States in 1975 as Washington correspondent and news reader for *A.M. America*. After that show ended a year later, ABC put Jennings on a plane with the title of Chief Foreign Correspondent and Foreign News Desk for *World News Tonight*. By the time he took over as permanent anchor in 1983, Jennings had become the world-class journalist that position demanded. His straight arrow, just-the-facts delivery style is, for many, a welcome relief from the contrived buddy system reporting found on many news reports.

Once divorced, Peter is married to former ABC News Bonn bureau chief and author Kati Marton; they have two children. Mindful of the never-ending newscast ratings race, Peter tries to stay arm's length from that aspect of the business. "It's a very big job," he says. "But it is a job. It's not being anointed. You sit down and ask yourself: Can I do it, with all its components? Am I emotionally ready? Am I qualified? I think I am. But a year from now if they don't like me doing it, I'll still have a job."

DON JOHNSON

REAL NAME: Don Wayne Johnson
DATE OF BIRTH: December 15, 1950
PLACE OF BIRTH: Flat Creek, Missouri

EYE COLOR: Blue   HAIR COLOR: Blond
HEIGHT: 5'11"   Weight: 170

"What strikes me about fame is that once you achieve it, there's nothing left but to become infamous," says Don Johnson.

The first of four children, Don was born in his grandmother's house on a Missouri farm. His mother was a beautician and his father a farmer until 1955 when his dad moved the family to Wichita, Kansas, to work for an aircraft manufacturer. When Don was eleven, his parents divorced, and Don was devastated. "In one instant, life changed," he says. "Suddenly there were major choices I had to make that you shouldn't have to make when you're eleven years old. I realized then it was dog eat dog, every man for himself." Johnson started hanging out with thugs, got caught stealing a car when he was twelve and spent several weeks in a juvenile detention home. Hoping for a fresh start when he was released, he went to live with his father and stepmother in Wichita. But all he and his dad did was fight, so he

struck out on his own at sixteen. Moving in with a 26-year-old cocktail waitress, he supported himself with a part-time job in a meat-packing plant. During his senior year of high school, he enrolled in a drama class and was almost immediately cast in the lead of *West Side Story*. "Acting struck something in me that was true and honest," Don remembers. "It was like having lost one's mother and all of a sudden being reunited. For the first time in my life, I felt that I belonged to something." Don eagerly auditioned for and earned a drama scholarship to Kansas University, where he became romantically involved with one of his drama professors. When she left for San Francisco to study acting at the American Conservatory Theater, Johnson followed, landing his first professional role in the ACT's production of *Your Own Thing*.

During the next fifteen years or so, Johnson acted in forgettable movies, did guest spots on TV shows and filmed five TV pilots, all of which failed. The frustration of seeing his contemporaries sail past him into success spiraled him downward into drugs and alcohol. "Stardom takes maturity," he says, "and I wasn't ready to deal with it. So drugs were a convenient way to put that off." His reputation made NBC skeptical about casting Johnson as Sonny Crockett in the new show *Miami Vice* in 1984, but when he read with Philip Michael Thomas, who would later play Tubbs, the energy between the two actors was so electric that Johnson got the job. After the demise of *Miami Vice* in 1989, Don appeared in the TV remake of *The Long Hot Summer*. He also chose two films that would keep him close to his wife, Melanie Griffith, *Paradise* and *Born Yesterday*.

Don's reputation as a Don Juan is no fable; when he was twelve he seduced his baby-sitter, and he had two youthful annulled marriages before tapping Hollywood's bounty. He had affairs with enough of the top glamorous stars to give Warren Beatty a run for his money as THE bachelor about town. As if this weren't enough to keep a man busy, his personal itinerary also included a brief marriage to the youthful Melanie Griffith, ending in divorce in 1976, and then a six-year live-in relationship with actress Patti D'Arbanville, which produced a son. He and Melanie reignited their flame when she finished rehab, and they wed again in 1989. With a child of their own, they also house her son and occasionally his. During the five years he spent in Miami, Don acquired a love for speedboat racing; he is also an avid skier which he enjoys on his frequent visits to his home in Aspen.

JAMES EARL JONES

REAL NAME: James Earl Jones
DATE OF BIRTH: January 17, 1931
PLACE OF BIRTH: Arkabutla, Mississippi

EYE COLOR: Brown   HAIR COLOR: Black
HEIGHT: 6'1 1/2"   WEIGHT: 210

Belying his benign demeanor, James Earl Jones is actually an outspoken activist who cites Malcolm X and Muhammad Ali among his heroes. "A lot of actors would prefer to ignore their Negroness," he said many years ago, "as if it were a limp that you hope people won't notice onstage. I don't want the audience to forget I'm a Negro. Acting is a visual art, and you want everything to count.... I ask an aesthetic response to my color."

Jones' father, boxer and actor Robert Earl Jones, left home before he was born. His mother remarried and Jones grew up with his grandparents, who soon adopted him. As a child, he developed a severe stammer and at times was able to communicate only by writing. In order to overcome his impediment, Jones joined the debate team at Norman Dickson High School, and by the time he got out of school, the stutter was gone. James is in touch with the hurt and pain inflicted on him by parental abandonment but blames the hard times of the Depression, not his mother and father. "No matter how old the character I play, even if I'm playing Lear," he says, "those deep childhood memories, those furies will come out. I understand this." An excellent student, he enrolled at the University of Michigan on scholarship with hopes of a career in medicine. Searching for something to like within himself, he joined the school's drama club. Finding it more rewarding than he had dreamed, he changed his major to drama during his senior year and graduated cum laude with a drama degree in 1953.

After a two-year stint in the Army, Jones moved to New York and lived briefly with his father. He studied acting at the American Theater Wing and with famed acting coach Lee Strasberg, making his New York stage debut off-Broadway in 1957's *Wedding in Japan*. Throughout the following years, while supplementing his income

refinishing floors and making sandwiches, Jones made a name for himself on the New York stage by taking on a variety of demanding parts. Chief among them were the title role in *Othello* and his electrifying performance as the first black heavyweight boxing champion in *The Great White Hope*, which made him a star and earned him a 1969 Tony Award for best dramatic actor. "No other play," he says, "has drawn as much out of me. It's like a birthing." With Broadway success came Hollywood, and since 1963 he has hit the big screen in dozens of films, including the *Star Wars* series, in which he was the voice of Darth Vader. More recently, he appeared as Admiral James Greer in *The Hunt for Red October* and author Terence Mann in *Field of Dreams*.

Previously married to actress Julienne Marie, he now lives with second wife, Cecelia, and a collection of animals in Pawling, New York, and spends his time reading.

RAUL JULIA

REAL NAME: Raul Rafael Carlos Julia y Arcelay
DATE OF BIRTH: March 9, 1940
PLACE OF BIRTH: San Juan, Puerto Rico

EYE COLOR: Gray   HAIR COLOR: Black
HEIGHT: 6'2"   WEIGHT: 190

Most recognizable to movie audiences as the campy Gomez in *The Addams Family* movie, Raul Julia is actually a distinguished stage actor with a penchant for Shakespeare. "I revere Shakespeare," he says. "I love the rhythm, the music, the poetry. I make it my own.... I become a poet."

The oldest of four children, Raul grew up in Puerto Rico, the son of a successful restaurant owner. He enjoyed a life in the countryside outside San Juan and received his primary education from American nuns. A shy child by nature, he began acting during his youth, performing in school plays and at local parties. "It was a marvelous experience in which I entered and let go of myself," he explains. "I became sort of like possessed or something." Graduating from San Ignacio de Loyola High School, he went on to earn a degree in liberal arts at the University of Puerto Rico with little desire or intention to do anything but act. After graduation, he continued acting in local amateur productions until Orson Bean saw him in a San Juan nightclub and suggested that he go to New York and study acting. Raul did so and in 1964 made his New York debut in a Spanish-language production of *Life Is a Dream* at the Astor Place Playhouse. Determined to shake Latino typecasting, he bravely pursued more and more unusual roles and, two years later, performed as Macduff in the New York Shakespeare Festival's production of *Macbeth*. Throughout the next decade and a half, Raul established himself as one of the finest actors on Broadway, taking on a number of diverse parts including

Proteus in *Two Gentlemen From Verona* and the title role in *Dracula*. During 1972, he even held his own in two entirely different plays at once. Although his credits include more than a dozen films, his first outright hit on the big screen came in 1985 with *Kiss of the Spider Woman*. Further demonstrating his diversity, he appeared in the comedy *Moon Over Parador* and will soon bring back Gomez in *Addams Family Values*.

When he's not working, Raul keeps fit by playing tennis and relies on the practice of EST to sustain his energy. He also works diligently as a spokesperson and fund-raiser for The Hunger Project. Making his home in New York, he is married to dancer/actress Merel Poloway, and they have two children.

DIANE KEATON

REAL NAME: Diane Hall
DATE OF BIRTH: January 5, 1946
PLACE OF BIRTH: Santa Ana, California

EYE COLOR: Green   HAIR COLOR: Brown
HEIGHT: 5'7"   WEIGHT: 118

A talented dramatic actress, Diane Keaton may be destined to be remembered primarily as Woody Allen's goofy leading lady.

Growing up in Santa Ana, California, as the eldest of four children, Diane grew up singing in the church choir and performing for the family at every opportunity. Her father was a civil engineer, and her mother was once crowned Mrs. Los Angeles. It was her mother's

maiden name, Keaton, which she adopted when she started performing professionally. All along, she acted in high school and local theater but says, "I wanted to be more than a nice girl. I felt I wasn't really interesting enough. I think that's one of the reasons I went into acting."

She attended Santa Ana College and Orange Coast College before accepting, at the age of nineteen, a scholarship to the Neighborhood Playhouse School of the Theater in New York. In her off hours, she sang and danced with a rock band called The Roadrunners, playing for ten dollars a night in out-of-the-way clubs. It was good training, because a year after graduation, she was given the role as understudy to the female lead in a Broadway production of *Hair*. When the star left the production, Keaton stepped in and took over (even though she was the only cast member who refused to take off her clothes for the final act). After *Hair*, she began her long association with Woody Allen, trying out for and getting the part of Allen's best friend's wife in his first play, *Play It Again, Sam*. It was there that she first began developing her screen persona as a woman who seems chronically at a loss for words. For the next few years, she supplemented her infrequent acting checks with TV commercials and guest shots on TV shows.

It was during the production of *Play It Again, Sam*, that Allen and Keaton became lovers, a relationship Allen fictionalized in the film that made her a star, *Annie Hall*. Anxious to be recognized on her acting merits and not just as Woody's "straight man," she hit pay dirt as Al Pacino's wife in *The Godfather* and won a best actress Oscar for her interpretation of Woody Allen's love interest in *Annie Hall*. Although their intimate relationship ended years ago, she has continued to collaborate with Woody on his films while interspersing them with heavyweight roles such as a journalist opposite Warren Beatty in *Reds*. After Woody Allen's legal and child custody scuffles with Mia Farrow flared up, Diane replaced her in *Manhattan Murder Mystery*, which was in early production at the time. Since then, Diane has been concentrating her talents on directing a new film, *Pet People* and the TV movie *Wildflower*.

Never married, Diane had a lengthy liaison with Beatty in the '80s and refused his marriage proposal. An avid photographer, she has her own darkroom and has published books on the subject, including her own works.

MICHAEL KEATON

REAL NAME: Michael Douglas
DATE OF BIRTH: September 9, 1951
PLACE OF BIRTH: Pittsburgh, Pennsylvania

EYE COLOR: Blue   HAIR COLOR: Brown
HEIGHT: 5'11"   WEIGHT: 155

Michael Keaton spent his childhood as the youngest of seven children in a town just outside Pittsburgh. Educated in a strict Catholic school, he describes it as "unusual. Remember when girls were told never to wear patent-leather shoes, because boys could see the reflection of their underwear in them? Well, in my school, the girls couldn't wear patent-leather underwear for fear that boys would look up their skirts and see their shoes." Michael was a good student until, he says, "I got into the ninth grade and discovered girls would pay attention to me. I was a very weird combination of shy and crazy—but when I committed to being crazy, I'd usually get real crazy." The attention from girls and the dating that followed inspired him to develop the "credit confession" system—confessing in church that he had scored just in case he ever got lucky. Michael says, "I have so much credit, I may never have to go to confession again."

After graduation from high school, he spent two years at Kent State University studying speech. But once he became active in plays and writing comedy ideas, he lost interest in an academic future and dropped out of college. Returning home, he drove an ice cream truck and a taxi before taking a job at the Pittsburgh PBS station, WQED, as a part of their technical staff. In 1972, he went to Los Angeles, where he slept in his car while doing gigs as a stand-up comic until joining the Los Angeles branch of the Second City comedy troupe. In 1979, he got a break and was cast along with Jim Belushi in the sitcom *Working Stiffs*, one of four failed TV series in which he had a part. His first film, *Night Shift*, was more of a critical success for Keaton than a box office hit, but his next film, *Mr. Mom*, was a blockbuster. Although he gained fame as a comedian, Michael Keaton seems unwilling to be just funny, stretching himself into dramatic roles during the prime of his career. Keaton was the surprise choice for the title role in the smash hit *Batman*, but more than $200 million in box office grosses quieted his detractors. His roles—in everything from *Beetlejuice* to *Gung Ho*—have run the gamut from hit to flop and comedy to drama.

It's always difficult to get a straight answer to a straight question from him: Michael says that for exercise he does "basketball and bondage." He was married in 1982 and has a ten-year-old son.

GENE KELLY

REAL NAME: Eugene Curran Kelly
DATE OF BIRTH: August 23, 1912
PLACE OF BIRTH: Pittsburgh, Pennsylvania

EYE COLOR: Brown   HAIR COLOR: Dark Brown
HEIGHT: 5'10"   WEIGHT: 143

Along with Fred Astaire, Gene Kelly is considered the top male dancer of all time. He explains how he and Fred shared that turf: "If they wanted someone to play Prince Charming or to wear evening clothes, they got Fred. I was always the blue-collar dancer, the guy with the rolled-up sleeves and the white socks."

Kelly took his first dance lesson when he was eight years old. His Irish mother believed it was important that he and his two brothers and sisters better themselves, and so all were enrolled in a dance academy. He hated dance lessons, of course, and spent most of his time at St. Raphael's grammar school playing football, baseball and ice hockey. While attending Peabody High School, in addition to continuing sports, Kelly was social chairman of his class, edited the school newspaper and, to impress girls, took part in campus theater productions. He majored in law at Penn State University and supported himself by working as an apprentice bricklayer and mixing sodas in a drugstore. During the Depression, he and his brother Fred put together an act and earned money performing at amateur nights and local nightclubs. Kelly eventually graduated from the University of Pittsburgh and spent a short time in law school before dropping out to become a dance instructor, operating from a basement while he supplemented his income by digging ditches.

Making up his mind to look for real success on Broadway, Kelly left his brother in charge of running the dance studio and moved to New York, where he was able to land small parts in several shows. In 1942, established on Broadway, he made his film debut opposite Judy Garland in *For Me and My Gal*. "I got started dancing because I knew that was one way to meet girls," says Gene. "Then I found out that it was good for a hell of a lot more—like being a movie star." He went on to dance in dozens of MGM musicals, such as the Oscar-winning film *An American in Paris*, eventually moving on to choreography and a fair share of dramatic roles, most notably in *Pal Joey*. His classic dancing-in-the-rain number in *Singin' in the Rain*—considered the most famous dance number ever filmed—not only featured Gene but was choreographed by him. His attempts at directing were equally impressive in *Flower Drum Song* and *Hello, Dolly!* His last starring role was in the 1980 film *Xanadu*, but—still spry and dapper—he served as both choreographer and narrator for *That's Entertainment, Part II*.

After a divorce from his first wife, Gene married Jeanne Coyne in 1960. She died of leukemia in the mid-'70s, leaving him with a son and a second daughter. Gene is modest about his legendary status as a dancer in Hollywood musicals: "It was just luck to be around when the public wanted it. If the public doesn't want it, the studios won't give you money. They're not dancers, they're bankers."

LARRY KING

REAL NAME: Lawrence Harvey Zeiger
DATE OF BIRTH: November 19, 1933
PLACE OF BIRTH: Brooklyn, New York

EYE COLOR: Brown   HAIR COLOR: Brown
HEIGHT: 5'8"   WEIGHT: 165

According to Larry King, "The thing in my makeup that makes me so very good and also makes me so harmful to myself is an incredible impetuosity, which I bring to the air and to my personal life."

The elder of two sons, Larry was a good student, skipping the third grade, but after being emotionally crushed by the death of his father at age ten, he abandoned his studies and barely graduated from high school. His mother, a Russian Jewish immigrant, supported him and his brother on relief payments until she found a job in the garment district. Thinking that his father had abandoned him, Larry recalls his torment: "If he left me, who would leave me next? And so nothing else was worth it but the things I liked—and the things I liked were broadcasting and sports." Determined to break into broadcasting, but not sure how to do it, King spent the next four years working at odd jobs such as delivery boy and mail clerk. He saved all his money and finally made his play at age 23, moving to Miami and taking a job as a floor sweeper at radio station WAHR.

He got his break in 1957 when one of the station's disc jockeys quit. Left in the lurch, the manager had Larry replace him—changing his name from Zeiger to King. Sitting in front of a microphone for the first time in his life, realizing his dream was coming true, Larry says, "The theme music was supposed to fade, and I was supposed to do a voice-over. But every time the music faded, I'd turn it back up again. Finally the station manager stuck his head into the studio and said, 'Remember, this is a communicating business.' I let the music go down and told the audience what had just happened. Those were my first words on radio." And that launched his career.

Throughout the '60s, King became a dominant force in the Miami media, hosting his own radio shows and writing columns for several Miami papers. In 1971, however, he was involved in a finan-

cial debacle that resulted in his arrest and forced him to declare bankruptcy. As Larry's career and income soared, his spending had far outpaced them. Deeply in debt, he took a $5,000 check given to him by financier Louis Wolfson with the intention of passing it on to New Orleans D.A. Jim Garrison to assist in his investigation of JFK's murder, and used it to pay his own overdue taxes. That indiscretion called attention to other nefarious Wolfson deals, which landed the financier in prison. In retaliation, Wolfson had King arrested for grand larceny, and his career blew up. For the next seven years, Larry struggled to re-establish himself by working as a free-lance writer and doing public relations for a race track in Louisiana. He eventually noodled his way back behind a mike in 1978 with a five-hour talk show, *The Larry King Show*, for the Mutual Broadcasting System. The show proved so popular that in 1985, CNN signed King to do a similar but shorter version of the show called *Larry King Live*.

His marital record should be so successful: After an annulled teenage marriage, four more followed, twice to the same woman, by whom Larry has a 26-year-old daughter. Probably the only interviewer who does no advance preparation for quizzing guests, Larry says, "The key to my success as an interviewer is in the fact that I am truly interested in a person's craft. And when you sincerely want to find out how and why people do what they do, you are going to learn a lot. The less I know in advance, the more curious I am on the air."

KEVIN KLINE

REAL NAME: Kevin Delaney Kline
DATE OF BIRTH: October 24, 1947
PLACE OF BIRTH: St. Louis, Missouri

EYE COLOR: Blue   HAIR COLOR: Brown
HEIGHT: 6'   WEIGHT: 160

Gorgeous, sexy and quirky, Kevin Kline is a truly talented singer as well as a dramatic and comic actor.

With an agnostic Jewish father and an Irish Catholic mother, Kline grew up in St. Louis attending a Catholic school run by Benedictine monks. Influenced by his father's passion for opera and piano, Kevin was playing at an early age while performing on the football and soccer fields as well. He says, "I grew up with music always in the house. I didn't really discover theater until I was in college. I was interested in composing and conducting." Originally intending to become a concert pianist, he entered Indiana University as a music major. But while he was there, he began taking acting classes and before long switched his major to drama.

After college, he moved to New York to attend the drama branch of Juilliard and ended up a founding member of John Houseman's Acting Company. Like most actors, Kline paid his dues, working on soap operas and commercials and doing a number of off-off-Broadway plays. He made his debut on Broadway with a Tony-winning performance in *On the Twentieth Century*, following it with a second Tony in *The Pirates of Penzance*. The progression to film was natural, and in 1982 he made his film debut, wowing audiences with his portrayal of schizophrenic Nathan Landan opposite Meryl Streep in *Sophie's Choice*. He then established himself as a solid male lead with dramatic roles in *The Big Chill* and *Silverado* and broke out as a comic actor as the neurotic villain, Otto, in *A Fish Called Wanda*, for which he received an Oscar for best supporting actor. And he's the main reason for the success of Ivan Reitman's latest film, *Dave*.

Kevin keeps trim by working out daily. He married actress Phoebe Cates in 1989. Outraged by the tabloids, Kevin feels an actor's mystique can be preserved only with a shroud of privacy. "I think it's important for the public not to know that an actor's favorite food is fish and that he likes to go skin diving," he says. "The less they know about you, the more likely they are to accept the roles you play. When you lose your anonymity, you lose a valuable tool for an actor—to be able to observe without people acting funny."

JACK KLUGMAN

REAL NAME: Jack Klugman
DATE OF BIRTH: April 27, 1922
PLACE OF BIRTH: Philadelphia, Pennsylvania

EYE COLOR: Brown   HAIR COLOR: Brown
HEIGHT: 5'10"   WEIGHT: 180

"I'm a loner. I like a good meal, a good script and a good BM. That to me is a great life." What else would you expect from *Odd Couple* slob Oscar Madison?

The sixth child born to Russian immigrants, Jack was raised in the poor section of South Philly, fully aware that he didn't possess the looks he would need to become a movie star. Being neither academically nor athletically inclined, he roamed the streets when he wasn't shooting pool or rolling dice in the alley. Searching for approval among the other streetwise guys, he adjusted his personality to whomever he was with at the moment. A gambling junkie by fifteen, Jack started facing the dim future he was carving out for himself. Realizing he had become a "pleaser," Jack remembers himself as "always doing things for other people so I'd be a part of things but never feeling like a champion, you know?" After serving in the Army during World War II, he enrolled at Carnegie Tech and studied acting for two years on the GI Bill. Moving to New York, he auditioned for roles and supported himself by working at the post office and painting houses on weekends with his brother.

Ten years of summer stock and off-Broadway later, Klugman got his big break on Broadway, appearing as Dowdy in *Mister Roberts* with Henry Fonda. When the show went on tour, he went along in the role of Doc. Returning to New York, he found work on television and eventually ended up starring in the short-lived series *Harris Against the World*. By this time, Jack's gambling on the horses was so heavy that he was taking cash—virtually every penny earned each week—in suitcases to the track. In 1966, he appeared as Oscar Madison in the London production of *The Odd Couple*, and when the play was adapted for television in 1970, he got the chance to reprise his role, opposite Tony Randall. By the time it went off the air five years later, Klugman had won two Emmys and become a star. He then spent the late '70s and early '80s as a crime-solving coroner in the unlikely hit *Quincy*. In 1991, in an attempt to help Randall raise funds for a national theater company, Klugman reprised Oscar opposite Randall's Felix in a New York Belasco Theater production of *The Odd Couple*.

In 1989, Jack submitted to radiation therapy and had his right vocal cord removed in a fight against throat cancer. He is currently in remission, although his naturally raspy voice is now even rougher. Divorced from actress Brett Somers, he has two grown children and lives with a girlfriend on his horse ranch.

BURT LANCASTER

REAL NAME: Burton Stephen Lancaster
DATE OF BIRTH: November 2, 1913
PLACE OF BIRTH: East Harlem, New York

EYE COLOR: Blue   HAIR COLOR: Brown
HEIGHT: 6'   WEIGHT: 200

Burt Lancaster grew up as the fourth of five children in a tough section of New York, but "it was very happy," he recalls. "Cold-water flats, gas, toilets in the hall didn't mean a thing. We were healthy. There was love in the family." But he might have been tempted to join the gangs that roamed the streets if he hadn't spent his spare time in the library and playing basketball at the Union Settlement House, where he began acting as well. He entered New York University at the age of seventeen on an athletic scholarship. As a physical education major, he ran the gamut of baseball, track and gymnastics before dropping out after two years to perform as an acrobat in the circus. He spent the next seven years traveling the country and eventually made it to the Ringling Bros. and Barnum & Bailey Circus as a performer on the horizontal bars. When a hand injury forced him to retire in 1939, he spent several years working odd jobs in Chicago as a singing waiter, hat salesman, and floor walker, but all that ended when he was drafted into the Army in 1942.

After serving for three years, he returned to New York and soon won a part in the Broadway play *A Sound of Hunting*. Well received, it landed him a film contract with Hal Wallis, who promptly cast him in a demanding role for his dark film *The Killers*. It was successful, and Lancaster became a star overnight. In the more than 45 years since, he's made dozens of great films: *Gunfight at the OK Corral*, *The Birdman of Alcatraz*, *From Here to Eternity*, *The Rainmaker* and *Seven Days in May*, among many others. Determined to avoid being pigeonholed, he has deliberately balanced the action/adventure films that fed the studio's coffers with soul-searching, artistic roles that satisfied his own creative cravings.

With the title role in *Elmer Gantry*, he finally took home an Oscar in 1960. "Swaying people's emotions excited me," he said about it. "It was the easiest role I was ever given to play because I was, in essence, playing myself." But many critics think that his finest performance ever was in 1981 as a small-time, has-been gangster in *Atlantic City*. Most recently, Lancaster appeared as "Doc" Graham in the 1989 smash hit *Field of Dreams*.

Lancaster had a brief marriage to an acrobat in the '30s and a twenty-year marriage that ended, five children later, in 1969. His son Bill is a screenwriter, and his daughter Joanna is a producer. His famous mouthful of teeth, which has immortalized his grin, is the result of custom dental surgery. A passionate art collector and opera devotee, he has also served as president of the American Civil Liberties Union.

JESSICA LANGE

REAL NAME: Jessica Lange
DATE OF BIRTH: April 20, 1949
PLACE OF BIRTH: Cloquet, Minnesota

EYE COLOR: Hazel   HAIR COLOR: Blond
HEIGHT: 5'7 1/2"   WEIGHT: 124

Nominated for five Academy Awards, Jessica Lange is also the first actress to be nominated for two films during the same year. Although she didn't win for her role as Frances Farmer in *Frances* in 1983, she won as supporting actress for her part in the hit comedy *Tootsie*.

Lange moved eighteen times throughout rural Minnesota while she was growing up with her traveling salesman father, mother and three siblings. Surviving her mobile childhood by retreating into movies, she formed an obsession for *Gone With the Wind*, rereading the book and watching the movie often enough to play Melanie's death scene from memory and move herself to real tears. A straight-A student and a member of the National Honor Society at Cloquet High School in Cloquet, Minnesota, she originally intended to become a painter and enrolled at the University of Minnesota on an art scholarship. But before her freshman year was over, she forfeited

her education to travel across the country in a truck with Spanish photographer Paco Grande. They ended up in New York, and when Lange separated from him in 1971, she moved to Paris to study mime with famed instructor Etienne Decroix.

After two years, she returned to New York, took a job as a waitress at a Greenwich Village restaurant and began modeling and taking acting classes. A friend at the Wilhelmina modeling agency sent her photograph to Dino DeLaurentiis, who gave her a screen test and then awarded her the role of Dawn in his $24 million remake of *King Kong*. But she resisted his attempt to capitalize on his discovery of an unknown model whom he made into a star. "There was a myth generated that I was this high-paid, top cover girl," she recalls. "But that was bull. There were no covers. And I hated it, being lumped into that category of model-turned-actress." Although she won some good notices for that part, Lange was unemployed for the next two years while she pursued more acting classes. During this time she found herself in a romantic liaison with director/choreographer Bob Fosse, who proceeded to cast her as the Angel of Death in his film *All That Jazz*. Then came her breakthrough part opposite Jack Nicholson in the 1981 version of *The Postman Always Rings Twice*.

Eager to maintain her momentum, Lange campaigned one director after another to star her in a film on the life of Frances Farmer, the tragic '30s actress who went mad. She finally made the film, but then found herself teetering on the brink of an emotional breakdown from dredging up the old childhood anger with which she'd fueled the character's neuroses. "I was really hell to be around," said Jessica.

She regained her equilibrium by going straight into the comedy *Tootsie* and captured even more accolades. Since then, Jessica's career has blossomed into roles in *Country*, *Sweet Dreams*, *Music Box* (all of which earned her best actress Oscar nominations), *Everybody's All-American* and most recently *Cape Fear*.

Although monogamous by nature, Jessica has refused to marry either of the two men who have fathered her children. After living with Mikhail Baryshnikov, by whom she had a daughter in 1981, she has gone on to have two more children with her longtime lover, playwright/actor Sam Shepard. When she's not working, she spends most of her time living on one of the many plots of land that she's acquired around the country. But her favorite spot is a cabin just a few miles from her childhood home in Minnesota.

ANGELA LANSBURY

REAL NAME: Angela Brigid Lansbury
DATE OF BIRTH: October 16, 1925
PLACE OF BIRTH: London, England

EYE COLOR: Blue   HAIR COLOR: Blond
HEIGHT: 5'11"   WEIGHT: 135

Even though she had two twin brothers and a half sister, Angela admits that she grew up a lonely and morose child—a "skirt hider-behinder" as she puts it. Her father, a lumber merchant, had died when she was nine, and when she turned fourteen, she chose to stay home and study acting when her mother offered to send her off to boarding school. Angela studied voice and dancing under a private tutor for six months before enrolling in the Webber-Douglas School of Singing and Dramatic Arts. When the Germans started bombing London during World War II, Angela and her family escaped to the United States, and she enrolled in New York City's Feagin School of Drama and Radio. Realizing that she needed to find her own niche in such a competitive business, Angela found it as a comedienne. She said, "I was never the ingenue type—luckily, since there were too many girls who looked like ingenues. But I would have been a character actress in any case. It was my bent from the beginning."

When her mother, an actress herself, moved to Los Angeles to act, Angela joined her, working first as the ticket taker in her mother's theater and then as a clerk in Bullock's department store. In 1943, she went to MGM to audition for *The Picture of Dorian Gray* and was told the studio was looking for someone to play the part of the maid in *Gaslight*. She auditioned, got the role and signed a seven-year contract with the studio. She could sing and dance as well as act, and she wasn't too vain to play the kind of unsympathetic roles that most stars shunned. In seven years, she appeared in 70 films.

Lansbury achieved stardom with her showcase portrayal of *Mame* in the 1966 Broadway version of the play. *Time* magazine called her "the liveliest dame to kick up her heels since Carol Channing opened in *Hello, Dolly!*" And Angela has four Tony awards to prove it.

However, it still wasn't until she began solving crimes as Jessica Fletcher on the TV series *Murder She Wrote* that Angela truly became a household name. Between syndicated reruns and the first-run episodes, which still pull down solid ratings on Sunday nights after nine years on the air, Lansbury has become one of the most recognizable personalities on television.

Angela remains married (since 1949) to Peter Shaw, who manages her career. They have two grown children, a stepson from Peter's previous marriage, and several grandchildren. Vowing that she could never retire from acting, she has even taken over the reins as executive producer on her own show.

SPIKE LEE

REAL NAME: Shelton Jackson Lee
DATE OF BIRTH: March 20, 1957
PLACE OF BIRTH: Atlanta, Georgia

EYE COLOR: Brown   HAIR COLOR: Black
HEIGHT: 5'6"   WEIGHT: 125

"Movies are the most powerful medium in the world, and we just can't sit back and let other people define our existence, especially when they're putting lies out there on the screen...." says Spike Lee, about the fantasy version of black culture dished up by Hollywood.

Spike and his four younger siblings moved to Chicago soon after his birth before settling in the Fort Green section of Brooklyn and then Brooklyn Heights. His father, a noted jazz musician and composer, and his mother, an art and literature teacher, graduated from Morehouse and Spelman colleges, respectively. Educated in a string of Brooklyn public schools, young Spike attended John Dewey High School in Coney Island, while his mother nurtured his artistic

propensities with trips to museums, plays and galleries; his father allowed him to sit in on his performances in jazz clubs. Set on attending a black college, he enrolled at Morehouse in Atlanta. The atmosphere there planted in Spike the notion that blacks were in their own particular time warp. He recalls that it was "like Richard Pryor talked about in his concert film of his experience going to Africa, and the wonderful feeling he had being in a place where everybody is black. Black professors, black doctors; it was a great experience," he recalls.

After graduation with a degree in mass communications, Lee spent the summer interning at Columbia Pictures in Los Angeles, and it was during this time that he decided to become a filmmaker. Returning to New York, he enrolled at New York University's Tisch School of the Arts, and his 1980 thesis film, *Joe's Bed-Stuy Barbershop: We Cut Heads*, won the Student Academy Award from the Academy of Motion Picture Arts and Sciences and earned him a master's degree from NYU. Six years later, after living on $200 a week shipping film for a distribution house, Lee wrote, directed, produced and acted in his first feature, *She's Gotta Have It*. Begging and borrowing money to meet production costs from everyone he'd ever known, Spike recalls, "Each day while we were shooting, someone would go back to my house to see if any checks had come and then rush them to the bank, and we'd just hope they'd clear in time." The film, which finally cost $175,000 to make, earned $8 million. It also brought Lee the 1986 Los Angeles Film Critics Best New Director Award and the Best New Film award at the Cannes Film Festival.

Spike's next films continued to earn praise and awards: *School Daze*, a dizzy hip-hop college comedy with a virtually all-black cast; *Do the Right Thing*, a powderkeg drama of black-white hatred and violence; *Jungle Fever*, a steamy interracial romance; and his magnum opus, the powerful three-hour epic *Malcolm X*, which won an Oscar nomination. His next film, *Crooklyn*, based on his family's Brooklyn neighborhood, is currently being shot.

Preferring to remain on his old stomping grounds in New York, Spike has avoided the usual trappings of success and fame. The only perk he has allowed himself is a choice seat at his beloved Knicks games and introductions to star players. Says Lee, "I'm doing this because I want to make films and love filmmaking, not to have ten million women dangling on my arm ... or to make tons of money."

JENNIFER JASON LEIGH

REAL NAME: Jennifer Lee Morrow
DATE OF BIRTH: February 6, 1962
PLACE OF BIRTH: Los Angeles, California

EYE COLOR: Brown   HAIR COLOR: Blond
HEIGHT: 5'3"   WEIGHT: 104

Known for her ability to carry off the grittiest parts, Jennifer Jason Leigh has said, "I always pursue roles that are very challenging and mysterious and disturbing and exciting to me. I could never play the ingenue, the girl next door or the very successful young doctor. That would be a bore." In order to prepare for her performances, she writes a complete diary that her character would have kept since she was a little girl, describing everything from her favorite foods to her first sexual experience.

The older daughter of the late film actor Vic Morrow and screenwriter Barbara Turner, Leigh was born Jennifer Lee Morrow and took the name Jason as an homage to Jason Robards, an old friend of her family's. She grew up in beautiful Pacific Palisades, California, until her parents divorced when she was two. She was nine when her stepfather, Reza Badiyi, gave her a nonspeaking role in *Death of a Stranger*. At Pacific Palisades High School, she wrote and directed plays but dropped out six weeks before graduation to become an actress.

Her first film roles included that of a blind girl stalked by a rapist in *Eyes of a Stranger* and an anorexic teenager in *The Best Little Girl in the World*, for which she lost thirteen pounds and learned to eat without her lips touching the fork. Her breakthrough role was as a California teenager eager to experience sex in the smash cult comedy *Fast Times at Ridgemont High*. She prepared for that film by spending three weeks behind the counter at a local pizza restaurant. Since then, she has taken on widely diverse roles including the hooker Tralala in *Last Exit to Brooklyn* and undercover narc Kristen Cates

in *Rush*. Before playing the pathetic bimbo in *Miami Blues*, she spent three weeks in rural Florida among the teens there, picking up the hopeless mentality and local lingo. Her most recent "crazy" role was as the psychotic roommate in *Single White Female*.

Jennifer is currently working on developing a new film with her mom. In between projects, she devotes time to decompressing from the last character that possessed her. For Jennifer, "a character can invade your body and take over like a virus," she explains. And when the film is finished, "it's like getting over a sickness: You slowly but surely get well and come back to yourself."

JACK LEMMON

REAL NAME: John Uhler Lemmon III
DATE OF BIRTH: February 8, 1925
PLACE OF BIRTH: Newton, Massachusetts

EYE COLOR: Blue   HAIR COLOR: Gray
HEIGHT: 5'10"   WEIGHT: 160

Jack Lemmon couldn't wait to be born. Interrupting his mother's bridge game in the seventh month of her pregnancy, he made his dramatic entrance into the world in the elevator of the hospital. He's been in a hurry ever since. Playing lovable, fidgety, slightly neurotic characters, he used to call himself a "clown for the age of anxiety."

Although he was a sickly child, Jack still managed to excel in track and football at Rivers Country Day School and Philips Andover. From the time he made his stage debut at four with his father (a vice president of the Doughnut Corporation of America who was also an amateur dancer) in a play called *Gold in Them Thar Hills*, he knew he would become an actor. Troubled by his parents' rocky marriage,

Jack developed a facade of joviality and started creating comedy routines to convince everyone he was happy. They separated when he was eighteen. "While my parents were great when they were apart," he recalls, "they were terrible together." Upon graduation from prep school, he enrolled at Harvard and eventually became the president of the drama department's Hasty Pudding Club. When World War II broke out, he left to join the U.S. Navy and served as a communications officer on an aircraft carrier, returning after the war to earn his B.A. and B.S. degrees from Harvard.

In 1946, Jack moved to New York with a $300 loan from his father. Paying the rent by waiting tables, serving as a music hall bouncer and playing piano in movie houses, he struggled to make it on Broadway. "Fortunately, I was too stupid to give up," he remembers. "If I'd been bright, I'd have realized that I was horribly uncomfortable, amazingly frustrated and, like any sensible person, I'd have quit. But it never occurred to me that I wouldn't be successful eventually."

Although he managed to find work on radio and in TV soap operas, Lemmon didn't make his Broadway debut until 1953 in a revival of *Room Service*. It led to his first film role, in the romantic comedy *It Could Happen to You*. Just three pictures later, he won an Academy Award for best supporting actor for his portrayal of Ensign Pulver in *Mister Roberts*. Throughout the '50s and '60s Lemmon was known primarily as a comic in such hits as *Some Like it Hot, The Apartment, The Fortune Cookie* and *The Odd Couple*. But he proved that he was also capable of spectacular dramatic performances in such films as *Days of Wine and Roses, The China Syndrome* and *Glengarry Glen Ross*. A veteran of more than 50 films in the past four decades, he has been nominated for eight Academy Awards, receiving a best actor Oscar for *Save the Tiger*, and was the first actor to win an Oscar for both best actor and best supporting actor. In 1988, in honor of his long and distinguished career, he received the Life Achievement Award from the American Film Institute.

Lemmon relies on the piano, composing and playing, to relax and pass the time on sets; it's even a stipulation that he have one handy during any film he is making. At home with his second wife, actress Felicia Farr, he plays tennis and swims for recreation. By his first wife, he has a son, Chris, who is an actor, and his daughter with Felicia is a journalist.

JAY LENO

REAL NAME: James Douglas Muir Leno
DATE OF BIRTH: April 28, 1950
PLACE OF BIRTH: New Rochelle, New York

EYE COLOR: Blue   HAIR COLOR: Black
HEIGHT: 6'   WEIGHT: 180

Once turned down for a film role because the casting director thought he might be "frightening" to children, Jay Leno has risen chin first to become one of the most popular entertainers in America.

Jay's Scottish mom and Italian father, who was an insurance salesman, gave him and his older brother a comfortable middle-class home, which he still cherishes. "I come from the kind of family where my mom ironed my socks," says Jay. "In case my shoe ever fell off, people would know I came from a good family." On his report

card, his fifth-grade teacher noted: "If Jay spent as much time studying as he does trying to be a comedian, he'd be a big star." Compelled to further his education, Jay enrolled in Emerson College, where he established himself as the emcee of student talent shows and, before long, found himself with a real comedy routine. Soon he was earning extra tuition money by appearing in local comedy clubs at which he often had to bribe the bartender to let him on the stage.

Before long, Jay had run out of comedy clubs and was working bar mitzvahs and strip joints. "I was 22 years old, I had six nude girls in my dressing room, I was a college student and I was making thirty, forty bucks a night," he recalls. "It was great!"

With his degree in speech therapy from Emerson, Jay took a day job as a mechanic and deliveryman for an exotic auto shop while honing his comedy around town. He soon struck out for New York at Catch a Rising Star and other Manhattan venues. Ironically, it was after seeing an unfunny episode of *The Tonight Show* in 1975 that Leno decided to move to the West Coast and break into television. Along with friends David Letterman and Elayne Boosler, he began auditioning for the comedy clubs in Los Angeles and got his first break when comedian Jimmie Walker hired him to write gags. At Jay's suggestion, Walker went on to hire Letterman, too. Years later, Letterman would return the favor, giving Leno much needed exposure with guest appearances on *Late Night*. Leno finally made his first appearance on *The Tonight Show* in 1977, and with each appearance increased his following. A sold-out appearance at Carnegie Hall in 1986 led to a one-hour special on Showtime, and the next year, Johnny Carson made him a permanent guest host on his show. In 1992, following Johnny's retirement, Leno was given the ultimate honor when he was chosen to take the reins as host of *The Tonight Show*. After an unsteady beginning—and in the face of mounting late-night talk show competition—he has solidified his ratings and made the show his own.

With all this success, Jay has increased his collection of vintage cars and motorcycles, which he tends with powder-puff care. Since 1980, he's been married to scriptwriter Mavis Nicholson. Even his new rival, David Letterman, considers him the same nice guy in person as he is on stage. "The only difference between Leno the man and Leno the performer," says Dave, "is that Jay wears less makeup offstage."

DAVID LETTERMAN

REAL NAME: David Letterman
DATE OF BIRTH: April 12, 1947
PLACE OF BIRTH: Indianapolis, Indiana

EYE COLOR: Blue   HAIR COLOR: Brown
HEIGHT: 6'2"   WEIGHT: 180

Ever wonder what it'd be like to put on a Velcro suit and stick yourself to a wall? David Letterman's done it. In fact, if he thinks it might be funny, Dave might do just about anything. He's already jumped into a tub of water wearing a suit covered with Alka-Seltzer, pioneered Stupid Pet Tricks and the Monkey Cam, and given his dog, Bob, the opportunity to show several of his own films on television.

The second of three kids born to a florist dad and church secretary mom, David derives his preppy persona from a "solid Father Knows Best or Leave It to Beaver type of lower middle-class family." As David explains it, he's able to get away with barbs and stunts that would come off as sleazy from your average shiny-suited lounge lizard. With a degree in radio and TV broadcasting from Ball State University in Muncie, Indiana, he started out as a broadcaster, spending five years as an announcer and fill-in weatherman at an ABC affiliate in his hometown of Indianapolis. But "you can only announce the weather, the highs and the lows, so many times before you go insane," says David. "In my case, it took two weeks. I started clowning. I'd draw peculiar objects on the cloud maps and invent disasters in fictitious cities. I made up my own measurements for hail, and said hailstones the size of canned hams were falling."

Longing to go where he would be appreciated, Letterman packed up and moved to Los Angeles. After failed attempts to sell some comedy scripts he'd written, he began doing stand-up along with other young comics, including Jay Leno, on the L.A. comedy scene. His first gag-writing gig for comedian Jimmie Walker led to other writing jobs and a stint on Mary Tyler Moore's short-lived variety show, *Mary*, which gave Letterman enough exposure to get him on *The Tonight Show* in 1978. After he had appeared several times as a guest, Carson asked him to fill in as host, and he did so well that

NBC gave him his own daytime show, *The David Letterman Show*. It lasted four months before it was canceled because of low ratings, but his next show, *Late Night With David Letterman*, debuted later that year and soon became a staple for the hip late-night crowd. David explained his theory on humor when he said, "What I look for are the setups in life, and then I fill in the punch lines. One of my favorite jokes came right out of the *National Enquirer*, which every week gives you a million setups. I'm standing there buying cantaloupes, and there's this headline in the *Enquirer* that says 'How to Lose

Weight Without Diet or Exercise.' So I think to myself, 'That leaves disease.' I've been doing that word for word for years, and it never fails to get a laugh.... They're not so much jokes as they are sarcastic comments." Letterman was considered as a replacement for Carson until Leno was given the job in 1992. The next year Letterman left NBC to join CBS as their answer to Leno's competition.

His first marriage ended in divorce in 1977 with no children, and he had a lengthy live-in relationship with Merrill Markoe, who was the writing supervisor for his show. Several years ago his home was terrorized by a female fan calling herself Mrs. Letterman, who would appear on his property at odd hours of the night. She was finally forced into treatment after being apprehended.

SOPHIA LOREN

REAL NAME: Sophia Villani Scicolone
DATE OF BIRTH: September 20, 1934
PLACE OF BIRTH: Rome, Italy

EYE COLOR: Brown   HAIR COLOR: Brown
HEIGHT: 5'8 1/2"   WEIGHT: 125

"To have perfect beauty is not so special," Sophia Loren says. "To have a special look, one must have irregularities. Otherwise you look like everyone else. My nose is too long, my chin too short, my hips too broad. But together, all these irregularities seem to work." You could say that again: Sophia Loren is considered one of the world's most legendary beauties.

She grew up during World War II in the town of Pozzuoli, where her family was so poor that all eight family members slept in one bedroom of her grandmother's house. Her last name of Loren is a version of Scicolone, the surname of her father, who never married her mother. Sophia had only one dress, and because there was never enough food to eat, she subsisted entirely on goat's milk for most of her early childhood. As a child, she was so thin and plain that classmates at her Catholic school called her "the stick." She left school at age twelve with hopes of becoming a teacher and studied for three years at the local Teachers' Institute. With puberty, however, Loren's body bloomed, and she soon grew into a beautiful young woman. When she was fourteen, her mother entered her in the Queen of the Sea beauty contest, the prizes for which were 23,000 lire, a tablecloth with twelve napkins, several rolls of wallpaper and a train ticket to Rome. Wearing a dress made from window curtains, Loren came in second. Encouraged, she decided to drop out of school and attempt to become an actress.

Using the train ticket, she moved to Rome with her mother and started out as a film extra and model for fumetti comic strips. After two and a half years of struggle, she met producer Carlo Ponti, who helped her get her first big role in the film *Africa Under the Sea*. It launched her European film career, and during the next three years, she made more than twenty films. In 1955 came her American debut

opposite Frank Sinatra and Cary Grant in *The Pride and the Passion*. Her robust sexiness, along with her acting skills, won her an Academy Award in 1961 for her performance in the film *Two Women*. Among her many other credits include *El Cid*, *The Fall of the Roman Empire* and *Marriage Italian Style*.

A collector of art and jewelry, Loren has written an autobiography and a cookbook, *In the Kitchen, With Love*. She married the captain of her destiny, Carlo Ponti, in 1966 after he acquired French citizenship to avoid a bigamy suit against him in Italy. They have two grown sons. In 1982, Sophia served seventeen days of a 30-day sentence in prison for tax evasion. A true Italian, she still spends her happiest hours in the kitchen preparing pasta.

ROB LOWE

REAL NAME: Rob Lowe
DATE OF BIRTH: March 17, 1964
PLACE OF BIRTH: Charlottesville, Virginia

EYE COLOR: Blue   HAIR COLOR: Brown
HEIGHT: 5'10"   WEIGHT: 155

Growing up in Dayton, Ohio, Rob Lowe remembers watching a lot of television and memorizing all the lines in *The Wizard of Oz*. One of his favorite pastimes, like many kids, was dressing up as characters such as Batman and acting out their superhero deeds. He went on to recording radio dramas on his tape recorder and making his own Super 8 films, then persuaded his mom to ferry him to auditions. He made his stage debut at eight and was soon acting regularly in summer stock and commercials. By the age of twelve, he had done more than 30 plays. "A lot of kids gave me a hard time about it," he remembers. "They wondered why I'd rather go into a dark, dank theater than be out playing ball on a Saturday." After his parents' separation that same year, he and his brother, Chad, moved to Malibu and attended Santa Monica High School, where he joined a class that included Sean Penn and Emilio Estevez.

While in high school, Rob resumed going on auditions and soon afterward appeared in two *Afterschool Specials*. Lowe was even nominated for a Hollywood Foreign Press Association Golden Globe award for his role in the TV movie *Thursday's Child*. Reflecting on his rather tumultuous childhood, Rob says, "In my last year of high school, I missed a lot. I missed the senior prom and graduation—all of the things that are such an important part of people's lives. But on the other hand, I got to play in the celebrity all-star game at Dodger Stadium—and I'm the ultimate baseball fan. Not everybody gets a chance to do that sort of thing, and I wouldn't trade it for the world."

In 1981, anxious to move on to meatier roles on the big screen, he got his chance as part of the talented ensemble cast in *The Outsiders*. A classic story of teenage rebellion and friendship, this movie launched several careers, Lowe's among them. Sexy lead roles in such movies as *Class*, *Youngblood* and *Oxford Blues* cemented his status as a certified heartthrob, a label that strong dramatic performances in such movies as *The Hotel New Hampshire* have done little to dispel. In 1992, he took a character departure when he appeared in the zany cult film *Wayne's World*.

A dark smudge on his career came several years ago when he was accused of videotaping a sexual encounter with an underage girl while he was doing volunteer campaign work for the Democratic presidential campaign. In his own defense, Lowe summed up the sordid experience: "There was never anything wrong with my ethics, there were things wrong with my judgment."

A former charter member of the Hollywood Brat Pack, he is now married to makeup artist Sheryl Berkoff.

SHIRLEY MACLAINE

REAL NAME: Shirley MacLean Beaty
DATE OF BIRTH: April 24, 1934
PLACE OF BIRTH: Richmond, Virginia

EYE COLOR: Blue   HAIR COLOR: Auburn
HEIGHT: 5'6"   WEIGHT: 118

Many years ago, when Shirley MacLaine was on the launch pad of stardom, she said, "I want to be hungry sometimes. I want to be thirsty. I want the struggle, I want the pain, I want the rain so I can enjoy the sunshine." Reviewing her full-to-the-brim personal life and her multifaceted career, she has surely satisfied everything on her "want" list.

She was born into what she affectionately calls a "cliche-loving, middle-class family" composed of her high school principal father (a former bandleader), her drama coach mother and her younger brother, Warren Beatty. "We were all Baptists," she has said. "We were taught to respect all material possessions. We lived according to what our neighbors thought." After she started dance lessons at age three, the family moved to Arlington, Virginia, where Shirley went on to attend the Washington School of Ballet. Aspiring to a serious career in dance, she worked hard enough to be performing with that school's company at the Washington Constitutional Hall by the age of twelve. By that time, unfortunately, she had grown too tall to be accepted as a ballerina and turned her sights toward musical theater. At sixteen, after spending the summer in New York dancing in the chorus of *Oklahoma!*, she returned home to finish high school at Washington and Lee High School and then headed back to New York. One of her first jobs there was dancing in a traveling show that promoted refrigerators until a spot in the chorus of *The Pajama Game* came her way in 1954.

In addition to appearing in the chorus line, MacLaine also understudied that show's lead dancer and got her first big break when the lead injured her ankle. Taking over the role, she was so successful that producer Hal Wallis signed her to a long-term movie contract. By 1964, she was earning $800,000 a pop in such films as *Gambit*

and *Sweet Charity*. She went on to become a major star in *Irma La Douce* and has remained one ever since, most recently winning an Oscar for her co-starring role in *Terms of Endearment* and rave reviews for her featured performances in the ensemble hits *Steel Magnolias* and *Used People*.

In addition to her appearances on screen and on stage—as a star of her own one-woman show—her quest for personal enlightenment has led her into a career as a writer. In the first of several best-selling books about her spiritual journey, she wrote about her existence in previous lifetimes. In this life, she has been married only once, in 1954. For most of their marriage, she and her husband lived on separate continents—he in Japan and she in the United States—but they have one daughter, Sachi Parker, born in 1956, who grew up with her father but has recently moved to Los Angeles. Still very active, MacLaine stays in shape by running, lifting weights, doing yoga and, most of all, by dancing.

JOHN MALKOVICH

REAL NAME: John Malkovich
DATE OF BIRTH: December 9, 1953
PLACE OF BIRTH: Christopher, Illinois

EYE COLOR: Brown   HAIR COLOR: Brown
HEIGHT: 6'2"   WEIGHT:185

As a child, John Malkovich was a class clown at school, shy but volatile at home. "We had a lot of freedom, too much freedom," he has said of himself and his four rowdy siblings. "It was always chaos." They would lock him out of the house when his moodiness and tantrums got out of control. His sensitivity ran so deep that he suffered for months after seeing his first play, *Our Town*. "It was such a

morbid play, really, and so sad," he recalls. By the time he entered high school, he tipped the scales at 230 pounds. He played football and tuba in the band but was a mostly haphazard student, preferring to read novels.

After graduation, he enrolled in Eastern Illinois University with the intention of pursuing environmental studies; his father had been an environmentalist. But after falling for a female drama student, he developed an interest in theater work. The romance didn't pan out, but he transferred to Eastern Illinois State to study drama. There he acted in school productions, performed at local coffeehouses and became known as a flamboyant man about campus, dressing in capes, platform shoes and outlandish paraphernalia. "He was always a great poseur," recalls a fellow student. "And he had this huge head. We used to call him Tweetybird. He was sort of like the hippie actor. You weren't really sure what he was doing there."

He left school without matriculating to become a founding member of the Steppenwolf Theater Ensemble in Chicago's Highland Park and stayed with the group for six years, directing as well as acting. In 1982, he won the Joseph Jefferson Award for his work in a local production of *True West*, then went on to earn an Obie Award in the New York version of that show. After his film debut as news photographer Al Rockoff in *The Killing Fields*, he received an Academy Award nomination for his performance as a blind boarder in *Places in the Heart*. Though his movie career was well-established, he didn't abandon the theater, and in 1982-83 won raves for his portrayal of Biff in *Death of a Salesman* with Dustin Hoffman. But it's for his movie work that Malkovich is best known and most widely admired for such films as *Empire of the Sun, Dangerous Liaisons, The Object of Beauty, Of Mice and Men* and the 1993 hit *In the Line of Fire*. Describing his own approach to getting into character, he says, "The more I think about it, the more complicated it gets and the more it shuts me off emotionally. Good technique should be like the motor in a Rolls-Royce. You shouldn't hear it running."

Formerly married to actress Glenne Headly, John has settled in Los Angeles with Nicole Peyran and their two children. He says he prefers the quiet, small-town life to the big cities and explains the lifestyle discrepancy by saying, "I'm still really a small-town person. I've never used drugs. I don't even drink. My idea of fun is to stay home and stain a piece of furniture."

PENNY MARSHALL

REAL NAME: Carole Penny Marshall
DATE OF BIRTH: October 15, 1942
PLACE OF BIRTH: New York, New York

EYE COLOR: Green   HAIR COLOR: Brown
HEIGHT: 5'6"   WEIGHT: 123

Coming from a show-business family, one would think Penny Marshall had been groomed to follow in their footsteps. Not true. Penny's father was a producer and her mother a dance instructor, her older brother, Garry, a writer-producer and her sister, Ronny, an associate producer. But Penny's mother had a different goal in mind for her: "She wanted me to meet and marry a Jewish fellow." Even though they were Congregationalists, her mother was convinced that Jewish men make the best husbands, so she sent Penny to a Jewish summer camp each year as a teenager. When that didn't pan out, Penny's father enrolled her at the University of New Mexico in Albuquerque to study math and psychology. But, in her sophomore year, Penny dropped out of school to marry a fellow student and quickly had a baby, with a divorce not far behind. While supporting herself and the child by teaching dance—which she'd learned from the age of three in her mother's studio—she dabbled in some local theatrics just to make friends but found herself ostracized as a divorced woman with a child. Penny found herself undatable, and the future looked bleak. "I didn't know what to do. I had no future in New Mexico, and if I went back to New York, my family would have treated me like a child. So I picked up a phone and called my brother in Hollywood."

By this time—in 1967—Garry Marshall was a successful writer-producer, and he advised her to study acting. She did, taking courses at night and paying the bills by working as a secretary. The training paid off. In 1970, she and fellow classmate Rob Reiner—with whom she had grown up in Brooklyn and whom she would eventually marry—auditioned for the sitcom *All in the Family*. Reiner landed

the part of Mike, but Penny lost the part of Gloria to Sally Struthers. One year later, though, Garry became executive producer for *The Odd Couple* and got Penny her first big job as Myrna, Oscar Madison's secretary. It was also Garry who talked ABC into making the comedy series *Laverne and Shirley*, on which his sister would gain stardom as Laverne. When the show went off the air after seven years, she went on to become even more successful as a director, at first on television and then in the movies with such hits as *Big* with Tom Hanks, *Awakenings* with Robin Williams and Robert De Niro and *A League of Their Own* with Hanks and Madonna.

Divorced from Reiner since 1979, Penny lives in Los Angeles with her daughter, Tracy.

STEVE MARTIN

REAL NAME: Steve Martin
DATE OF BIRTH: August 14, 1945
PLACE OF BIRTH: Waco, Texas

EYE COLOR: Blue   HAIR COLOR: White
HEIGHT: 5'10"   WEIGHT: 150

It's been a long, strange road for Steve Martin. Growing up in the shadow of the Matterhorn at Disneyland in Garden Grove, California, he started his show-business career performing magic tricks and playing the banjo at the Magic Kingdom. It was there that he acquired his penchant for arrow-through-the-head humor, a combination of slapstick, observational and physical comedy, that would eventually make him famous.

When Steve was five, he and his sister moved with their parents to Inglewood, California, where his real estate father acted in local stage productions. This was the age at which Steve became enamored with comedy: "I'd watch skits on the Red Skelton show, memorize 'em and then go to school and perform during 'Show and Tell.' " Five years later, when the Martin family relocated to Garden Grove, Steve wasted no time grabbing an after-school job selling guidebooks at Disneyland. For the next eight years, he was a fixture around the Disneyland shows, developing a two-man comedy act that he and his partner performed in a local coffeehouse.

Three years into studying philosophy at Cal State Long Beach, Steve was earning straight A's when he became disillusioned with "the whole philosophy of philosophy" and dropped out. Yearning for the performing arts, he reasoned, "It was the only thing that had real meaning because it had no meaning. It can't be measured. You don't have to explain why, or justify anything. If it works, it works. As a performer, non sequiturs make sense, nonsense is real." With that in mind, he enrolled in a comedy writing class at UCLA and began doing stand-up at comedy clubs around town. A job writing for *The Smothers Brothers Comedy Hour* led to other jobs writing material for performers such as Sonny and Cher and Glen Campbell.

Not satisfied with providing jokes for others, Martin eventually returned to stand-up, opening for rock acts and playing the club scene. Soon he adopted his trademark white suit and was one of comedy's fastest rising stars. His *Let's Get Small* album was a smash, and "Excuuuse me!" was a catchphrase for teenage boys nationwide. Appearances on *The Tonight Show* and *Saturday Night Live*, as well as a second comedy album, *Wild and Crazy Guy*, made him a celebrity. Since then, he has appeared in many movies, including *The Jerk, All of Me, Little Shop of Horrors, Roxanne* and *Housesitter*. With films such as *Parenthood, Grand Canyon* and *L. A. Story* (which he also wrote and produced), Martin has proven himself an actor and writer of both comic and dramatic depth.

When he's just being Steve Martin, he's known to be very serious, quiet and retiring. And along with his wife, British actress Victoria Tennant, he is a dedicated art collector.

MARLEE MATLIN

REAL NAME: Marlee Matlin
DATE OF BIRTH: August 24, 1965
PLACE OF BIRTH: Morton Grove, Illinois

EYE COLOR: Blue   HAIR COLOR: Brown
HEIGHT: 5'4"   WEIGHT: 111

When Marlee Matlin was born, not only was she a perfect baby girl, but she rounded out a family with two older boys and a happily married mother and father. Eighteen months later, she came down with roseola virus, and it was a severe case that went into her ears. It took a while for people to notice she wasn't responding to noises, and then she was diagnosed as completely deaf in her right ear, with only 20 percent hearing in her left. She began to learn sign language at five, as did the rest of the family. A sprightly little girl, she started asking for acting parts after a few years at the Children's Theater for the Deaf, and at eight, landed the lead in her first play, going on to star in Children's Theater productions of *The Wizard of Oz* and *Mary Poppins*. But as she got older, she began to tire of the competitiveness of acting and gave it up when she started high school.

Harboring a secret desire to be a policewoman, she went on to study criminal justice for two years at William Rainey Harper College in Palatine, Illinois. But when she learned that being able to hear was required for police work, she began acting again and was discovered while playing the role of Lydia in a Chicago revival of *Children of a Lesser God*. Her first film role, as Sarah in the film version, resulted in a best actress Oscar. Matlin then appeared in the TV movie *Bridge to Silence* and the feature *The Man in the Golden Mask*. In her latest role, she portrays a deaf attorney in the TV drama *Reasonable Doubts*.

As spokesperson for the National Captioning Institute, Marlee is able to relate, with a personal perspective, how painful it is to be shut out of the joys of television, especially as a child. Remembering how her family would sign the TV dialogue for her, Marlee remembers, "Only through my mother could I understand the antics of *The*

Electric Company. Only through my dad could I understand what Mannix said to his Girl Friday, and only through my brother could I understand the laughter on *All in the Family*." Although closed captioning became available a few years later, it required a special box and about $200 for the service. Thanks to Marlee's testimony at a Capitol Hill hearing, a law was passed that requires all television sets of thirteen inches and larger to be manufactured with built-in chips that allow viewers to flip a switch and receive captioning on their screens.

After a stormy two-year relationship with William Hurt, her co-star in *Children of a Lesser God*, Marlee is engaged to a policeman (surprise!) who happens to be proficient in sign language, which was a required course in his college language arts. A devout baseball fan, Marlee takes her own glove to baseball games.

ED MCMAHON

REAL NAME: Edward Leo Peter McMahon Jr.
DATE OF BIRTH: March 6, 1923
PLACE OF BIRTH: Detroit, Michigan

EYE COLOR: Hazel   HAIR COLOR: Brown/gray
HEIGHT: 6'2"   WEIGHT: 210

The son of a traveling bingo operator at carnivals, Ed McMahon grew up idolizing his father. "He really set a fine example of what not to do, but he did it with such class, was such a strong character, that I guess I'd have tried to follow in his footsteps if he'd been Jack the Ripper," Ed recalls. Listening to his father call bingo, Ed learned the power and authority that one's voice can command, and during summers at his grandmother's house in Lowell, Massachusetts, he delighted in listening to a radio his grandfather had built and idolized personalities such as Fred Waring's golden-voiced announcer, Paul Douglas. During his high school years in Lowell, he sold bingo cards after school for his father and spent three summers working the northeastern carnival circuit while he cultivated his "mike voice" calling bingo games. His carny career, along with part-time construction work, gave him enough cash to enroll at Boston College, where he majored in electrical engineering and worked nights at radio station WLLH.

In 1944, McMahon joined the Marines, serving as an instructor and test pilot during World War II. Before his discharge, he had flown 85 combat missions and risen to the rank of full colonel. Upon leaving the service, he studied speech and drama at Catholic University of America and supported himself by selling stainless-steel cookware door to door. He also worked as a pitchman for vegetable slicers during the summer on the boardwalk in Atlantic City. After earning his degree in 1949, he moved to Philadelphia, where he worked first in radio and then as the producer of thirteen separate TV shows before landing a job as Johnny Carson's announcer on

Carson's show, *Who Do You Trust?* Four years later, in 1962, he went along when Carson took over as host of *The Tonight Show*. Johnny may have been the king of late-night television, but Ed became America's favorite sidekick, and his hearty, nonstop laughter became widely imitated. Before Johnny's retirement in 1992, Ed found time to co-host the Jerry Lewis Muscular Dystrophy Telethon and partici- pate in many charitable causes. Besides making McMahon a rich man, *Tonight* led to other jobs as host of *Star Search* and *TV's Bloopers and Practical Jokes*.

Previously married with four children, Ed wedded Victoria Valentine, with whom he adopted a daughter, but they too divorced. In 1992, Ed was married once again to Pamela Hurn. In 1986, he was given a star on Hollywood Boulevard next to that of W.C. Fields.

BETTE MIDLER

REAL NAME: Bette Midler
DATE OF BIRTH: December 1, 1945
PLACE OF BIRTH: Honolulu, Hawaii

EYE COLOR: Blue   HAIR COLOR: Auburn
HEIGHT: 5'1"   WEIGHT: 110

One of the many qualities that makes Bette Midler such a unique entertainer is her absolute self-assurance: "I don't have any heroes. I don't lionize anyone. To my credit, I think. I am my own person and I'm centered in myself. I know that I'm unique, and I know that I'm different and special, and I am thrilled to death to be this person."

Midler, who is named after actress Bette Davis, is a native of Hawaii. She and her three siblings grew up in a mostly Samoan community near Honolulu's U.S. naval base, where her father worked as a house painter for the Navy. Being an overweight and unattractive Jewish girl in a non-Jewish neighborhood did not make her a particularly happy child. But as the years rolled by, she decided that her escape from this unhappy existence would be to become an actress. She appeared in every speech, singing or acting festival available, and after graduation from high school as the class valedictorian, she studied drama for a year at the University of Hawaii before dropping out to concentrate on acting.

After a year of odd jobs, including separating pineapple for canning at a pineapple factory and being a secretary, she won her first professional movie role as the seasick wife of a missionary in the movie *Hawaii*. When the movie completed filming in 1965, she flew to New York, still determined to become an actress. Paying her rent by working as a saleswoman in a department store, a hatcheck girl and a typist, she performed in Greenwich Village coffeehouses with the La Mama acting troupe. In 1966 she answered an open audition and won a role in the chorus of *Fiddler on the Roof*, eventually working her way up to the role of Tevye's oldest daughter, Tzeitel. When that role didn't lead to other Broadway parts, Bette spent a year in depression and analysis before reviving herself with daily voice and acting lessons.

In the meantime, she was barely earning a living as a go-go girl in a Manhattan bar. When she heard that a gay Turkish bath club had just opened, she jumped at the opportunity to sing for $50 a night at New York's Continental Baths. Belting out hits from the '40s, '50s and '60s for an audience of homosexuals in towels, Bette formulated the campy, sleazy/breezy style that made her famous. Her funky delivery and stunning talent spread around town, and soon the Baths were forced to open their doors to everyone. Now that her career had been jump-started, offers from record companies and nightclubs flooded in, including an appearance on *The Tonight Show*. She began touring and performed at several major venues including Carnegie Hall. In 1972, her first album, *The Divine Miss M*, went gold and won her a Grammy award as Best New Artist. She went on to set box office records for her Clams on the Half Shell tour, record a platinum record and win an Oscar nomination for her movie-debut role in *The Rose*. In the years since then, she has appeared in a great number of movies—among them *Down and Out in Beverly Hills*, *Ruthless People*, *Beaches* and *For the Boys*—and never fails to give her audiences their money's worth.

Bette married ex-commodities broker and performance artist/filmmaker Martin von Haselberg in 1984, and they have one daughter.

ROBERT MITCHUM

REAL NAME: Robert Charles Duran Mitchum
DATE OF BIRTH: August 6, 1917
PLACE OF BIRTH: Bridgeport, Connecticut

EYE COLOR: Blue   HAIR COLOR: Brown
HEIGHT: 6'   WEIGHT: 200

Robert Mitchum did not have an easy childhood. One of three children of an Irish railroad worker who died when Robert was eighteen months old, he and his siblings were raised by their Norwegian mother, who worked as a teletype operator until she remarried. Withdrawn and lonely, he was talented enough to write several poems for the local newspaper. But he became a disciplinary problem as he grew older and was sent to live with his grandmother in Delaware. Expelled from school, he joined his older sister Julie in New York, where she was a struggling actress. The atmosphere at Haaren High in Hell's Kitchen did nothing to improve his temperament, so he dropped out at fourteen.

Feeling the urge to move to California, he set out on foot—hitchhiking, stowing away on freight trains and taking odd jobs to pay his way. At one low point on the journey, he was arrested for vagrancy in Savannah, Georgia, and spent six days on a chain gang until he escaped. Before he finally settled in Long Beach, California, Mitchum had worked as a coal miner and even taken a shot at boxing. For a time after arriving on the West Coast, he was a ghost writer for the astrologer Carroll Righter, but he returned to Delaware in 1940 and married his childhood sweetheart, Dorothy, bringing her back to Long Beach on a bus.

When World War II broke out, Mitchum joined the war effort and took a job working a drop hammer at Lockheed until the deafening noise ruined his hearing and a doctor ordered him to find other work. His theatrical career began in 1943 when he ran into his sister's old agent, who began booking him as an extra and eventually as a cowboy in a series of *Hopalong Cassidy* movies. He signed a contract with RKO in 1944 but didn't become a star until United Artists cast him in *The Story of G.I. Joe,* a role for which he received a best supporting actor Oscar nomination.

Over the next decade, Mitchum worked nonstop, turning out an average of two movies per year, mostly portraying thugs and cowboys, though always with an undercurrent of softness and sensitivity. He was a bit of a rogue off screen as well, serving 60 days in jail for possession of marijuana in 1948. Asked what jail was like, he said, "It's just like Palm Springs without the riffraff." In the '50s, the audiences saw Mitchum in more and more dramatic and versatile roles, and his reviews got better and better. Some favorites are *Heaven Knows, Mr. Allison*, *The Enemy Below*, *Home From the Hill*, *Thunder Road* and *Cape Fear*. A true Hollywood legend, Mitchum starred in more than 45 films before making his only appearance on television as star of the epic miniseries *The Winds of War*.

Mitchum and his wife have three children, two of whom—Jim and Christopher—embarked on acting careers of their own. Never one to mingle in Hollywood's social swirl, Mitchum stays at arm's length from the press as well: "I never take any notice of reviews— unless a critic has thought up some new way of describing me. That old one about my lizard eyes and anteater nose and the way I sleep my way through pictures is so hackneyed now."

DEMI MOORE

REAL NAME: Demetria Guynes
DATE OF BIRTH: November 11, 1962
PLACE OF BIRTH: Roswell, New Mexico

EYE COLOR: Blue   HAIR COLOR: Brown
HEIGHT: 5'7"   WEIGHT: 110

One of *People* magazine's 50 Most Beautiful People in 1993, Demi Moore was cross-eyed as a child and underwent an eye operation to correct it, followed by another when she became walleyed. Of this awkward period, she says, "I must have been so pitiful looking, a patch over one eye, blue cat-eye glasses, and I was so skinny. Pathetic." Not anymore. She is proud of her body, which she works hard to maintain, and has displayed it on two controversial *Vanity Fair* covers, in one of which she was eight months pregnant.

Raised by her mother and stepfather, who were married and divorced twice, Demi met her biological father only once at age thirteen, after confronting her mother with her suspicions regarding her parentage. Because her stepfather, Danny Guynes, was an ad man for Scripps Howard and went where he could get work, she and her mother and her younger brother, Morgan, moved frequently, often every six months. Throughout her childhood, she attended two schools a year, more than twenty in all. Her mother left Guynes for the second time when Demi was fifteen—he committed suicide two years later—and the three of them moved to West Hollywood.

It was while she was attending Fairfax High School that Demi met a seventeen-year-old German actress, Nastassia Kinski, who lived in the same apartment building. So greatly did she admire Kinski's beauty and self-assurance that Demi used her as a role model and decided to become an actress herself. In pursuit of her newfound ambition, she left school and moved to Europe, where she modeled for magazines. After returning to the States, Demi enrolled in acting classes, but it took four years for her to break in with bit parts in such films as *Choices* and *Young Doctors in Love*. Then came a recurring role on *General Hospital*, favorable notices in *Blame It on Rio*, and her breakthrough film, *St. Elmo's Fire*. Ironically, before

Demi could play the part of the coked-out Jules in that picture, she had to sign a contract that required her to stop her own drug and alcohol abuse. Within 24 hours of signing, she cleaned herself up and turned her life around. During that production, she was dating co-star Emilio Estevez, and the two maintained a three-year relationship that included co-starring roles in Emilio's writing and directing debut, *Wisdom*. The relationship ended when Demi left after wedding invitations had already been sent out.

Her role as Molly in 1990's highest grossing film, *Ghost*, revived her slumping career and made her one of the most sought-after and highest paid actresses in Hollywood. She set up her own production company, Rufglen Films, and began developing her own projects, including the less than well-received *Mortal Thoughts*, co-starring her husband, Bruce Willis. Her latest effort, *Indecent Proposal*, had every couple in America asking the question, "Would you sleep with someone other than your spouse for money, and how much?"

Demi was married by Little Richard to Bruce Willis in 1987, and they have two daughters, Rumer and Scout.

DUDLEY MOORE

REAL NAME: Dudley Stuart John Moore
DATE OF BIRTH: April 19, 1935
PLACE OF BIRTH: Dagenham, Essex, England

EYE COLOR: Blue   HAIR COLOR: Black
HEIGHT: 5'2"   WEIGHT: 136

"I think most comedians start off defending themselves with comedy," Dudley Moore says. "They feel inferior in some way. I certainly did feel inferior. Because of class. Because of strength. Because

of height.... I guess if I'd been able to hit somebody in the nose, I wouldn't have been a comic." Few would have predicted a comedy career for Dudley. As a child, he was shorter than most of his classmates and self-conscious due to a club foot. He developed into what he called "an overserious, pompous boy," and in addition to being a choirboy he took music lessons throughout his youth. By age twelve he was studying violin at London's Guildhall School of Music and was soon playing the organ for $15 at weddings. On a music scholarship to Magdalen College at Oxford, he began writing music for plays and was given the chance to act in some of them as well. The applause and attention he received were so rewarding that he stayed on another year after graduation and earned an advanced degree while developing his stage presence.

After leaving Oxford, he spent several years working as a jazz musician before joining the satirical review *Beyond the Fringe*, which ran for two years in London and then became a smash hit on Broadway, where it ran for another two. When it closed in 1964, Moore played jazz piano for a while before returning to England to star with Peter Cook in the BBC television series *Not Only...But Also*. During the rest of the '60s and throughout the '70s, Moore led a varied professional life, appearing in films, writing movie scores and touring with his jazz group, the Dudley Moore Trio. During the mid-'70s, after meeting Moore in a psychotherapy group, director Blake Edwards tapped him to replace George Segal as the lead in his new film, *10*. It was a smash, and so was the megahit *Arthur*, which took him to the pinnacle of his acting career. With the exception of *Six Weeks*, a potboiler about a girl dying of leukemia, Dudley has wisely stayed with comedy. Many critics have compared his flawless timing, elfin appeal and bad luck with women to Chaplin and Keaton.

Success at the box office has not distracted him from his medium of choice—music. He's cut more than a half dozen records and performed at the Hollywood Bowl and the Metropolitan Opera House, among other prestigious venues. Dudley has two ex-wives: actresses Suzy Kendall and Tuesday Weld, by whom he has a son. In 1988, he married Brogan Lane.

MARY TYLER MOORE

REAL NAME: Mary Moore
DATE OF BIRTH: December 29, 1937
PLACE OF BIRTH: Brooklyn, New York

EYE COLOR: Brown   HAIR COLOR: Brown
HEIGHT: 5'7"   WEIGHT: 118

The first of three children, Mary Tyler Moore was raised a strict
Roman Catholic and attended parochial schools when she was growing up in Brooklyn. Moving to Los Angeles with her family, she
joined the local USO troop at twelve and began entertaining on L.A.
area military bases. In 1955, when she was seventeen, she married
for the first time and had her first child, a son named Ritchie, in
1957. The marriage soon ended, and Mary struck out for a career in
show business, first using the dance skills she'd acquired through
years of childhood training, then turning to acting. When she auditioned for the role of the oldest daughter on *Make Room for Daddy*,
star Danny Thomas passed her up because he knew no one would
believe they were related. But when Carl Reiner was casting for *The
Dick Van Dyke Show*, Thomas suggested a young woman he remembered to play the wife.

Mary won two Emmys and the heart of America as Laura Petrie,
the role that became the cornerstone of her career. But she topped it
with her second series, *The Mary Tyler Moore Show*, which won her
three more Emmys and countless other awards for what most people
still consider the best sitcom ever on television. Since the show's tri-
umphant farewell, Mary went on to a movie career, most notably as
the mother in the acclaimed *Ordinary People*, for which she won an
Oscar nomination. Although her professional life has known great
success, her personal life, in contrast, has seen much upheaval.

In 1978, her sister died of a drug overdose at the young age of 21.
Two years later, her son accidentally shot himself to death. And then
her seventeen-year marriage to TV executive Grant Tinker ended in
1981. "I've been through some devastating moments in my life," she
says of this tragic period. "I think that helps you put things in perspective. It makes me a little less afraid of life because I know I have

withstood some pretty awful things. So I'm not so fearful any more. I've already seen the darkness." Then she met cardiologist Robert Levine, a man fifteen years her junior, and married him in 1983. "I felt no trepidation about marrying Robert," she says. "It started as a strong attraction for a wonderful guy, and before I knew it I was a little in love, and then I was a lot in love. Then I was devoted, and then I was married!" Her new husband helped her not only to come to terms with the events that preceded their relationship, but to confront another demon as well: alcoholism. In 1984, Mary gave up cigarettes and alcohol on the advice of her doctor and checked herself into the Betty Ford Center. Although she believes her alcoholism was never out of control, it was too much a part of her life, and drinking threatened her health because of her diabetes.

She lives in New York with her husband and commutes to Los Angeles only when she's working. "The problem with Hollywood," she says, "is that it's a fancy ghetto—everybody's driving around in a silver Mercedes with no place to go at night."

EDDIE MURPHY

REAL NAME: Eddie Murphy
DATE OF BIRTH: April 3, 1961
PLACE OF BIRTH: Brooklyn, New York

EYE COLOR: Brown   HAIR COLOR: Black
HEIGHT: 5'10"   WEIGHT: 155

Even before graduation from high school, Eddie Murphy had begun carving out a comedy career and decided he would become a star. Next to his picture in the class yearbook, he had an inscription that summed him up at the time: "In reality, all men are sculptors, constantly chipping away the unwanted parts of their lives, trying to

create a masterpiece."

Eddie's father, a policeman and part-time comedian, and his mother, a telephone operator, divorced when he was three years old. Following his father's death two years later, when his mother became ill and was hospitalized for a long period of time, he and his brother were forced into the care of a woman whom he remembers as "a kind of black Nazi." To camouflage his unhappiness, he turned to imitating cartoon characters and doing impressions of stars like Elvis Presley. Eddie's mom remarried when he was nine, and his stepfather moved everyone to a middle-class suburb on Long Island. By the time he entered Roosevelt Junior High, Eddie says he regarded school as "a never-ending party" where he was on stage creating laughter all around. Making a half-hearted attempt at athletics and working part-time in a shoe store, he decided he was "going to be bigger than Bob Hope," and started focusing on that goal.

Finding a talent agent who landed him gigs in stand-up clubs around Long Island, Eddie graduated from pilfered comedy material to writing his own and was soon booked into clubs in Manhattan, making $300 a week at the age of seventeen. With little time or interest for schoolwork, he had to repeat the tenth grade, an experience he still remembers as his greatest humiliation. After finishing high school, he enrolled at Nassau Community College but dropped out during his first year to join the cast of *Saturday Night Live*. When the show was overhauled after the 1980-81 season, only he and Joe Piscopo were kept on board, and over the next few years, Eddie proceeded to steal the show with his wicked send-ups and satires.

In 1982, he made his movie debut in *48 Hrs.* and followed it up with *Trading Places*, both hits. Teamed with established stars in both films, Murphy stole the show again. In his next film, *Beverly Hills Cop*, he carried the movie by himself and became one of America's top-ranking box office stars. In *Coming to America*, he began a transition from straight comic to more serious leading-man roles, most recently in *The Distinguished Gentleman*. In addition, Eddie has cut several albums, both comedic and pop.

In 1993, he married the mother of his two children, bringing to fruition his statement five years ago: "I don't care who you are, what you have or what you did, there's always a woman out there who can bring you down to one knee. I can be brought to one knee, but the woman would have to have a helluva punch."

BILL MURRAY

REAL NAME: Bill Murray
DATE OF BIRTH: September 21, 1950
PLACE OF BIRTH: Wilmette, Illinois

EYE COLOR: Brown   HAIR COLOR: Brown
HEIGHT: 5'11"   WEIGHT: 180

Like so many popular comedians, Bill Murray is a product of the
Second City to *Saturday Night Live* pipeline. When he first turned
up on prime-time television, neither critics nor audiences could de-
cide what to make of his deadpan delivery and sardonic personality.

Growing up in the suburbs of Chicago, Bill was the fifth of nine
children in a raucous household. He says that his late father, a lumber salesman, was quite a comedian himself and that getting him to
laugh was almost an honor. Bill explains, "He was very dry. But my
father's father was the real nut ... the kind of guy who had the light-
up bow tie." Bill attended parochial schools and was an admittedly
lame student: "Studying was boring. I was lazy. I'm still lazy. And I
had no interest in getting good grades."

Unlike his brother, actor Brian Doyle Murray, Bill wasn't initially
interested in show business. Instead, he flirted with a professional
baseball career and eventually enrolled in medical school at the
Jesuit-run Regis College in Denver, Colorado. Med school, however,
didn't take, and he dropped out, moving to Chicago where brother
Brian was a member of the Second City comedy troupe. Bill soon
became friends with cast members John Belushi and Harold Ramis
as well as with Bernie Sahlins, who ran Second City, and before long,
he had joined the troupe himself. In 1974, Belushi brought both Bill
and Brian with him to New York to work on *The National Lampoon
Radio Show*, which he was helping to produce. Howard Cosell
caught the act and recruited Bill for his show, *Saturday Night Live
With Howard Cosell*. It was canceled after just half a season, but
when Chevy Chase decided to leave *SNL* in 1977, the show's produc-

er, Lorne Michaels, picked Murray as his replacement. In 1979, Bill's star surge began with the screwball comedy *Meatballs* and has continued to ascend with such films as *Caddyshack, Stripes, Tootsie* and *Scrooged*. With 1993's *Groundhog Day* and *Mad Dog and Glory*, Bill's career took a quantum leap into the superstar realm. Bill's wife, Mickey Kelley, was a fellow high school student who wound up in show business herself as the talent coordinator for the *Tonight* and *Dick Cavett* shows. She has given that up, however, in favor of raising their son, Homer Banks, named after Chicago Cubs player Ernie Banks.

MIKE MYERS

REAL NAME: Michael Myers
DATE OF BIRTH: 1964
PLACE OF BIRTH: Scarborough, Ontario, Canada

EYE COLOR: Brown   HAIR Color: Brown
HEIGHT: 5'8"   WEIGHT: 158

Getting onto *Saturday Night Live*, the show that finally made him famous, was a dream for comedian Mike Myers from the time he was eleven years old.

Born to a Better Business Bureau staffer father and office supervisor mother, Mike grew up in the Toronto suburb of Scarborough with his two older brothers, Peter and Paul. He had what he described as a typical "suburban heavy-metal youth," hanging out at the local doughnut shop with his metalhead friends. As the social conscience of his peer group, Mike made sure they didn't do too much harm: "If we were whipping snowballs at cars, I would be, like, 'No whipping snowballs at old ladies,' 'Don't put any rocks in the snowballs, it could crack a windshield and cause an accident.' "

At age eight, Mike made his acting debut in a TV commercial with, ironically, Gilda Radner playing his mother. Like so many other successful comedians, he got his break with the Second City comedy troupe in Toronto. He tried out on his high school graduation day, and he says of his audition, "My last exam was at nine a.m. My audition for Second City was at twelve, and I was hired at three p.m." From there, he moved on to an all-night Canadian music video show in 1987, then graduated to the Chicago branch of Second City in 1988.

With his addition to the cast of *Saturday Night Live* in 1989 as its youngest cast member, Mike brought to the screen a number of original characters, including Dieter Gruber, the kinky host of "Germany's Most Disturbing Home Videos," and the irrepressible Wayne Campbell of "Wayne's World" fame. With his partner in crime, Garth Algar, played by Dana Carvey, Wayne hosts his own version of a

talk show from his basement in Aurora, Illinois, on the local cable access channel. Since the skit's premiere during the 1989 season, it has spawned a hit movie, creating catchphrases like "NOT!" and "Schwing!" Mike had been doing the character of Wayne since his teenage years in Ontario, modeling Wayne on himself and his metal-head friends. "I did him in kitchens at parties to make girls laugh," says Mike.

The success of the film *Wayne's World* has launched Mike into a new movie career that continued in the summer of 1993 with his starring role in *So I Married An Axe Murderer*. And Mike's life seems to be coming together in more ways than one: he and aspiring actress Robin Ruzan, whom he met at a hockey game, were married in May 1993.

BOB NEWHART

REAL NAME: George Robert Newhart
DATE OF BIRTH: September 5, 1929
PLACE OF BIRTH: Chicago, Illinois

EYE COLOR: Blue   HAIR COLOR: Sandy brown
HEIGHT: 5'8"   WEIGHT: 148

Bob Newhart enjoys the distinction of being the only person to have had two hit TV shows. Both *The Bob Newhart Show* and *Newhart* were consistently at the top of the ratings, and this unprecedented success has not been duplicated by any other actor.

Bob, whose father was a plumbing and heating contractor and whose mother was a homemaker, grew up in a quiet suburb of Chicago. Raised a strict Roman Catholic, he and his three boisterous sisters attended parochial schools; one of whom eventually became a

nun. He was shy and introspective as a teenager except when he was among friends and family. At St. Ignatius High School in Chicago, he quietly demonstrated his sense of humor: "I kind of sat back on the edge of the crowd and whispered funny things to the guy next to me, who'd break up," he recalls. "To me, comedy became a peculiar way of looking at life." He studied business at Loyola University in Chicago and, after graduation in 1952, spent two boring years in the Army as a clerk. He then flunked out of law school and turned back toward business by becoming an accountant.

His career in comedy began over the telephone. He and friend Ed Gallagher often had long, hilarious phone conversations to kill time while working. They moved this exchange to parties, and friends encouraged them to go pro. Their act was too low-key for the comedy circuit, though, and when Ed went back to his advertising job, Bob tried his luck by making the conversations one-sided. These early classic routines are the template for his comedic style. Bob recorded his first album, *The Button-Down Mind of Bob Newhart*, in 1959 and leapt to national fame as it went to number one.

He followed this success with TV appearances and, briefly, in 1961, his own one-hour variety show, which was critically acclaimed but seldom watched. In 1972, he hit it big with *The Bob Newhart Show*, which ran until 1978, when he retired it voluntarily despite its continued ratings success. He hit again in 1982 with *Newhart* and again ended it, in 1990, while it was in its prime. He knows when it's time to quit the grind of series television. "After I've been in a series for about six years, when I get in the car in the morning to drive to work in the Valley, I have a big fight with the automobile," he quips. "It wants to drive to Santa Barbara and I insist I have to go to work. We have the same conversation several times a week, but the car always loses. It's one of the small victories I look forward to." Post-*Newhart*, Bob went back to stand-up, performing in larger-sized arenas with both classic and new material, including a stint as headliner at the Montreal Comedy Festival. His latest TV effort, *Bob*, debuted in 1992 and has been picked up for the 1993-94 season.

Newhart met Ginnie, his wife since 1963, on a blind date arranged by friend Buddy Hackett, and they have four children. They are also close friends with Don Rickles and his wife, and the couples still see each other almost every day. When Bob is between shows, he concentrates heavily on his family and his golf game.

PAUL NEWMAN

REAL NAME: Paul Leonard Newman
DATE OF BIRTH: January 29, 1925
PLACE OF BIRTH: Cleveland, Ohio

EYE COLOR: Blue   HAIR COLOR: Light brown/gray
HEIGHT: 5'9"   WEIGHT: 150

The second son of the owner of a sporting-goods store, Paul Newman was quite an athlete in his youth. Excelling at both football and baseball, he won an athletic scholarship to Kenyon College, but during his three years with the Navy in World War II, he suffered a knee injury that dashed all hopes of a career in pro sports. After returning to school, he realized that his interests were changing and switched his course of study from economics to English, then to drama. Something of a roustabout in college, he spent a night in jail after a barroom brawl during his junior year.

Two hours after graduation in 1949, with degrees in economics and drama, he headed for Wisconsin and summer-stock work. When his father died, he had to return to Ohio to take over the family store, but after only eighteen months, he discovered his aversion to business, handed the reins over to his brother and left for the Yale School of Drama. "I wasn't driven to acting by any inner compulsion," Paul says. "I was running away from the sporting-goods business." From Yale, he moved on to New York and the Actor's Studio. His first movie role, as a Greek slave in *The Silver Chalice*, was disappointing, but he worked at his craft and has won impressive reviews with almost every film he's starred in ever since. They've ranged from huge popular successes in such classics as *The Sting* and *Butch Cassidy and the Sundance Kid*, to Oscar-nominated performances in *Cat on a Hot Tin Roof, The Hustler, Hud, Cool Hand Luke* and *Absence of Malice*. Though he won in 1986 for reprising his role as Fast Eddie Felson in *The Color of Money*, many felt he had given the performance of his life in 1980's *The Verdict*. Not content to remain in front of the camera, Newman has also produced, written and directed in such films as *Rachel, Rachel* and *The Effect of Gamma Rays on Man-in-the-Moon Marigolds*.

His role in the movie *Winning* required him to race cars, and he was hooked. Since then, he has won a number of races and has even set a track record on the Grand Prix circuit. "On the racetrack, the guy that crosses the finish line is the winner, and there's no further discussion about that," he says. "It's hard to be competitive about acting, and I'm a very competitive person. So I like to race cars."

Newman's first marriage produced three children, and he has three more from his marriage since 1958 to Joanne Woodward, to whom he is still devoted after more than 35 years. "I feel privileged to love that woman," he says. "That I am married to her is the joy of my life." After the death of his son Scott in 1978, he set up the Scott Newman Foundation, which provides antidrug education, and proceeds from his Newman's Own products go to the Foundation. Also, he and Joanne run the Hole-in-the-Wall Camp in Connecticut for terminally ill children. Charity work fills his time between roles, which are increasingly rare. He finds his decreased screen presence indicative of the diminishing quality of films these days. "It used to be that if you read ten scripts you could find something that you really wanted to do," he says. "Today, if you read 150 scripts, you can maybe be talked into something you'll regret."

JACK NICHOLSON

REAL NAME: Jack Nicholson
DATE OF BIRTH: April 22, 1937
PLACE OF BIRTH: Neptune, New Jersey

EYE COLOR: Brown   HAIR COLOR: Brown
HEIGHT: 5'9"   WEIGHT: 170

The arched eyebrows and demonic grin seem to say it all. But his friend for the last 30 years, writer-producer Don Devlin, offers a deeper insight: "Jack's career was based on being a puncturer of the balloons of pomposity. He was the anti-Establishment guy, which is why young people always loved him so much. Well, the irony now is, because of the length of his career and how successful he's become, Jack is the Establishment."

Jack Nicholson and his two sisters were raised in an apartment above a beauty shop run by his mother, Ethel May. Believing that his father had abandoned the family, Jack flourished as the only male in the household and the center of attention. In 1975, when he was 38, Ethel died, and a long-held family secret was revealed: Jack had been born illegitimately to June, one of the women he had believed was his sister, and Ethel was actually his grandmother. The identity of his father remains a mystery to him. Even without a father, his childhood was fairly happy, though, and he enjoyed sports, clowning and girls, not necessarily in that order, throughout high school. Nicholson first became interested in acting as a way to meet the opposite sex in student theater productions, but instead of continuing his dramatic training in college, he moved at the age of seventeen to Los Angeles, where June worked as a showgirl.

Landing a job as a messenger in MGM's cartoon department, he began taking acting classes at the urging of producer Joe Pasternak and soon became associated with the Player's Ring Theater in Hollywood. After making his first stage appearance in a production of *Tea and Sympathy*, Jack waded into television as a regular on such shows as *Divorce Court* and *Matinee Theater*. In 1958, after making his film debut as a teenager who believes himself to be a murderer in *Cry-Baby Killer*, he went on to pay his dues in almost twenty B-

movies, but he was actually considering giving up acting in favor of directing when he was tabbed to replace Rip Torn as the alcoholic attorney who trades booze for grass and drops out in *Easy Rider* in 1969. The role earned him his first Academy Award nomination. Over the ensuing years, he went on to become Hollywood's most popular bad boy, cracking wise in films like *One Flew Over the Cuckoo's Nest, Terms of Endearment* (both of which earned him Oscars), *Chinatown, The Shining* and his tour de force as the Joker in *Batman*. In the course of his long career, Nicholson has been nominated nine times for Academy Awards in his more than 40 films—the latest of which, *Hoffa* and *A Few Good Men*—were released simultaneously last year.

Married once in the early '60s to actress Sandra Knight, he has a grown daughter, Jennifer. Since his divorce nearly 30 years ago, his reputation as a Casanova has been brought to the public's attention, but his former lovers seem to be his biggest fans. One exception, however, might be Anjelica Huston, with whom he had a seventeen-year relationship, much of it in cohabitation, which came to an end in 1990 when he revealed that actress Rebecca Broussard, his daughter's best friend, would bear his child. Although they maintain separate households, Jack and Rebecca had a second child in 1992.

LESLIE NIELSEN

REAL NAME: Leslie Nielsen
DATE OF BIRTH: February 11, 1922
PLACE OF BIRTH: Regina, Saskatchewan, Canada

EYE COLOR: Gray   HAIR COLOR: White
HEIGHT: 6'1"   WEIGHT: 170

It could be said that Leslie Nielsen has had two acting careers. The first, spanning almost 40 years as a dramatic actor, and the second as the zany star of such slapstick films as *Airplane!* and *The Naked Gun*. Leslie feels that he is finally playing the roles that reflect his real personality.

The son of a Canadian Mountie, Nielsen grew up with two brothers in a log cabin 200 miles south of the Arctic Circle, a harsh childhood he regards as "character building." He recalls, "You didn't have radio. You had no modern appliances. You didn't have electricity. My mother had to do all the things you see pioneer women do in films: hunting, fishing, skinning, tanning." As a result of their limited diet and lack of sunshine, he suffered a case of childhood rickets, which left his legs bowed at the ankles. Nevertheless, he chose acting as his career. "The tragic disappointment," he deadpans, "was that I couldn't fulfill my wish to play Tarzan's son." When he couldn't find acting jobs after moving to Los Angeles in 1945, he went home to Canada and worked as a nighttime disc jockey in Calgary. After studying acting at Lorne Greene's Academy of Radio Arts in Toronto, he went to New York City on a theater scholarship.

New York jump-started his career, and Nielsen began acting regularly, both in B-movies and on television, graduating to serious roles in major films such as the sci-fi classic *Forbidden Planet* and the smash disaster film *The Poseidon Adventure*. It was in 1980 that Nielsen read the script of a disaster parody that changed his career forever: *Airplane!* Playing off his strait-laced, self-important screen image, Nielsen won big laughs and great reviews, soon becoming the favorite of the film's creators. They cast him in 1982 as the star of their TV comedy *Police Squad*. It didn't last long, but the subsequent movie versions—*The Naked Gun* and *The Naked Gun 2 1/12: The Smell of Fear*—were smash hits, with Nielsen as the idiotic police detective Frank Drebin.

Leslie has been married three times, with two grown daughters from his second marriage. One of his brothers, Eric, served 31 years in the Canadian Parliament, part of it as deputy prime minister of Canada, until three years ago. In his free time, Leslie does "absolutely nothing. I am into loafing. You never know when you're finished. And the moment you get up in the morning, you're on the job."

LEONARD NIMOY

REAL NAME: Leonard Nimoy
DATE OF BIRTH: March 26, 1931
PLACE OF BIRTH: Boston, Massachusetts

EYE COLOR: Brown   HAIR COLOR: Black
HEIGHT: 6'2"   WEIGHT: 175

Perhaps no other actor has been as closely associated with a single role as Leonard Nimoy. Although he played Mr. Spock on *Star Trek* for only three years, Nimoy will always be Spock to many of his fans, no matter what other roles he performs.

The son of Russian immigrants, he began acting with juvenile roles in productions at Boston's Elizabeth Peabody Playhouse and earned a drama scholarship to Boston University, but dropped out during his first year and moved to California to study acting at the Pasadena Playhouse.

For the next seventeen years, Nimoy worked on his craft and appeared both on television and in the movies, but never really made his mark on the profession. He was teaching drama at his own studio in 1965 when producer Gene Roddenberry starred him in a TV show called *The Lieutenant*. At the time, Roddenberry was working on the pilot film of a new series called *Star Trek* and became convinced that Nimoy was just the man he needed for the role of Spock, the half-human, half-Vulcan first officer of the starship Enterprise. The series lasted just three seasons on NBC, but it became a favorite in syndication and was soon being rerun on stations all over the world. Nimoy went on acting, most notably as host of the show *In Search Of...*, but was never able to shake the image of Spock. When Paramount reunited the cast of the Enterprise in the first *Star Trek* movie,

Trekkies surfaced from nowhere and showed up in droves. It was followed by five money-making sequels, several of them directed by Nimoy, and spawned a spin-off TV series, *Star Trek: The Next Generation*, which has become an even bigger hit than the first one. And Nimoy himself has gone on to direct other films, most notably 1988's *The Good Mother* starring Diane Keaton.

In addition to an autobiography, *I Am Not Spock*, he has written three books of poetry and even recorded two albums of romantic ballads. He has two grown children from a previous marriage and was remarried in 1989.

NICK NOLTE

REAL NAME: Nick Nolte
DATE OF BIRTH: February 8, 1941
PLACE OF BIRTH: Omaha, Nebraska

EYE COLOR: Blue   HAIR COLOR: Blond
HEIGHT: 6'2"   WEIGHT: 190

"The stories are notorious," says Nick Nolte about his early image as a bad boy. "I helped perpetuate those stories. I used to do every interview with a six-pack of beer. But I never missed a day's work, I never was fired, and I never was down in that metaphorical gutter writers so often put me in."

When Nick was born, his father was serving in World War II, and Nick didn't see him until the age of three. After the war, his father resumed his job as an irrigation pump salesman and began moving Nick and his older sister, Nancy, around the Midwest. An active, athletic child, he ran around the neighborhood so much that once, at age ten, he was impaled on a neighbor's picket fence while trying to leap over it, leaving a serious scar in his groin. Nick soon turned to sports to channel his energy and talent in a more productive direction. In high school, he lettered in five sports: track, wrestling, basketball, baseball and football. He played the last so well that he was offered a football scholarship to Arizona State University. While there, he ran into a bit of trouble for selling draft cards to minors, receiving a $75,000 fine, a suspended sentence and five years' probation. The incident provided time for some needed personal reflection. He locked himself in the back room of his parents' home in Phoenix "for most of a year and disintegrated. I saw how I had spent nearly all my life contriving this athletic dream, and when I came out of it I realized I had been acting the part of a football star." Over the next few years he transferred to four different colleges. Finally, at Pasadena City College, a drama coach talked him into reading for a play, and he was hooked: "The competition was just as keen in acting as in football, and I guess that's what appealed to me."

Beginning in 1962, Nolte traveled the country doing regional theater, mostly drama, including extended stays at the Old Log Theater

in Minneapolis and the Actor's Inner Circle Theater in Phoenix. He won favorable notices for his performances in a New York workshop production for Cafe LaMama and a regional presentation of William Inge's *The Last Pa,* which caught the attention of the playwright, who delayed its Los Angeles opening so that Nolte could star. Two nights before its opening, Inge committed suicide, and the play went on with a pall hanging over it. It proved to be Nolte's breakthrough as an actor, and he began winning TV and film roles, including the 1976 ABC miniseries *Rich Man, Poor Man* and 1977's *The Deep,* which made him a star.

Since then, Nolte has starred in numerous films—including *Cannery Row, 48 Hrs., Q & A* and *The Prince of Tides,* for which he received an Oscar nomination in 1992. That year was filled with several high points for Nick: In addition to being selected as *People* magazine's Sexiest Man Alive, he reconciled with his wife, Rebecca. Married twice before, he also had a long-term, live-in relationship that ended with a $5 million palimony suit that was finally dropped after six years. With Rebecca he has one son, Brawley King, born in 1986. Sadly, the couple lost their first and third children.

In his spare time, Nick is a tinkerer and enjoys working on trucks and cars and with electrical stuff around the house. He maintains his athletic physique by swimming, jogging and lifting weights. He has been sober since 1990, when Rebecca walked out on him.

CARROLL O'CONNOR

REAL NAME: Carroll O'Connor
DATE OF BIRTH: August 2, 1924
PLACE OF BIRTH: New York, New York

EYE COLOR: Blue   HAIR COLOR: White
HEIGHT: 5'10"   WEIGHT: 210

Though he became famous as the loud-mouthed but lovable bigot Archie Bunker, Carroll O'Connor grew up in a tolerant home filled with a diverse group of friends. He describes the prejudice he so accurately portrayed for seven seasons on *All in the Family* as "the hallmark of ignorance."

The oldest of three sons, Carroll was born into a family of teachers on the Grand Concourse in the Bronx, New York. After graduation from high school, he joined the Merchant Marines and at the end of World War II decided to go back to school, enrolling at the University of Montana. After taking a trip to Ireland with his brother Hugh, he became interested in his heritage and moved to Ireland, transferring to the National University of Ireland with girlfriend and future wife Nancy Fields. It was in Ireland that he discovered his calling as an actor. While pursuing a history degree, he began performing in student productions before turning professional. After repertory work with prominent British actors, he became a member of the internationally known Dublin Gate Theater while directing on a freelance basis, and as he became known, did stage and TV work in Edinburgh, London, Paris and Amsterdam.

After returning to the States, he found roles elusive and so returned to school, earning master's degrees in English and speech from the University of Montana in 1956, then moving back to New York to teach high school English for two years. Teaching didn't bring him the same satisfaction as acting, so Nancy prodded him to start going out on auditions. "She'd listen to me shouting, 'That's it!' " he recalls, "and she'd say, very calmly, 'No, you're going to keep at this.' Having her was fortunate, critical. She's the diplomat, the smart and strong one. I was lucky." Eventually, he started to get roles in such films as *Lonely Are the Brave*, *Cleopatra* and *What Did You*

Do in the War, Daddy? Producer Norman Lear saw him in the latter during a flight, recognized his talent and decided to cast him in a new series he was producing, *All in the Family*. During its seven-season run on CBS, O'Connor earned three Emmys, then continued the part for several more years on *Archie Bunker's Place*.

After taking a respite from series work, he came back to star in *In the Heat of the Night*. The first couple of seasons were hard on him, though, as he was unhappy with the producers. In 1989, he underwent a six-vessel coronary bypass operation. Recovery required him to reduce his stress level, so upon returning to the show he took almost complete creative control with a new group of producers.

Throughout his life, O'Connor has been politically active, supporting various liberal causes, although he calls himself a true conservative. He enjoys traveling immensely and considers Rome his second home. While there during the filming of *Cleopatra*, he and Nancy adopted their son, Hugh. He also enjoys spending time at his Beverly Hills restaurant, Carroll O'Connor's Place.

AL PACINO

REAL NAME: Alberto James Pacino
DATE OF BIRTH: April 25, 1939
PLACE OF BIRTH: New York, New York

EYE COLOR: Brown   HAIR COLOR: Brown
HEIGHT: 5'7"   WEIGHT: 140

Al Pacino has been taking acting seriously ever since he faked a death scene in front of his grandmother when he was just a kid.

An only child born in East Harlem, New York, Al accompanied his mother when she went to live with her parents in the Bronx after divorcing Al's father when Al was two. The grandparents did their best to protect him from the dangers of the neighborhood, and for much of his early childhood, Pacino led a sheltered existence. "My mother and grandmother never let me out of the house until I was seven," Al remembers. Except when his mother took him to the movies. The next day, he would re-enact for his grandmother the film he had seen the night before, impersonating all the characters. Even after he was old enough to be allowed outside by himself, movies continued to be one of his favorite pursuits, and he spent every Saturday afternoon at the local theater. But at school each weekday, he was unable to leave behind his imaginary world of exciting characters and fascinated the other children with wild tales about himself. "I'd tell the kids stories, that I was from Texas, that I had ten dogs," he recalls. It was during elementary school that he began to channel his creative energies into school plays and decided to become an actor. He enrolled at the High School of the Performing Arts but became frustrated and dropped out when he was seventeen.

Taking odd jobs—including movie theater usher and mail boy for *Commentary Magazine*—he pursued his interest in acting, joining the Herbert Berghof Studio and finally gaining admission to the Actor's Studio in 1966. His first success came two years later when he won an Obie for his portrayal of a savage thug in an off-Broadway production of *The Indian Wants the Bronx*. In 1969, Pacino made his Broadway debut in *Does a Tiger Wear a Necktie?* and his film debut

with a small role in the movie *Me, Natalie*. But his first starring role didn't come until 1971, when he scored big as a drug addict in *Panic in Needle Park*. It was his success in that role that led to his breakthrough as Michael Corleone in *The Godfather*, for which he received an Oscar nomination in 1972. With his emergence as a major star, he was able to garner even more demanding dramatic roles in such films as *Dog Day Afternoon, Scarface* and *...And Justice for All*. After a long hiatus from the screen, Pacino returned triumphantly in *Sea of Love* and finally won an Oscar for his portrayal of a blind, belligerent ex-soldier in 1992's *Scent of a Woman*.

Al has been called the male Greta Garbo because of his fierce protection of his privacy, but we know he is presently single.

GREGORY PECK

REAL NAME: Eldred Gregory Peck
DATE OF BIRTH: April 5, 1916
PLACE OF BIRTH: La Jolla, California

EYE COLOR: Brown   HAIR COLOR: Dark brown/gray
HEIGHT: 6'4"   WEIGHT: 180

As a young boy, Gregory Peck wanted most to be a boat builder. He built his first vessel, The Daisy, from the ground up, at age nine. After two days of sailing and bailing, the boat sank. When he took his blistered hands to the doctor, he became fascinated with medicine and leaned toward a medical career, which pleased his father, who operated a local drugstore. Excelling at both academics and athletics at San Diego High, he played baseball and swam, and after graduation joined the San Diego rowing team, of which his father had been captain. He spent one year at San Diego State College, then moved on to UC Berkeley as a pre-med major. He joined the university crew, but on a trip to New York in 1938 for the Poughkeepsie Regatta, he suffered a spinal injury that permanently sidelined him.

Gregory soon decided that medicine wasn't for him and changed his major to English. He also took up theater and began acting in a school production of *Anna Christie*. After graduation in 1939, he moved to New York in search of a career as an actor. With help from one of his father's friends, he got a job as barker at the World's Fair, but after several days of yelling for eight hours straight, his voice was strained and he decided to move on to Radio City Music Hall, where he worked as a guide until he had to give that up for fear of fallen arches from walking all day. Resuming his pursuit of acting, he won a scholarship at the Neighborhood Playhouse School of Dramatics, and after his two-year stint there, moved on to the Barter Theater in Abingdon, Virginia, where the local farmers bartered for admission with produce such as eggs, chickens and spinach. Peck soon began getting parts on Broadway and delivered well-received performances in a series of flops. It wasn't until he moved to Hollywood—during World War II, when many of the major stars were away fighting in the armed services—that he began to achieve quick success. Tall, dark and handsome, he was admired by women and men for his strong physical presence and the intelligence and morality that came across the screen so sincerely. After four nominations, for *The Keys of the Kingdom*, *The Yearling*, *Gentleman's Agreement* and *Twelve O'Clock High*, he finally won an Oscar in 1962 for his heroic portrayal of Atticus in *To Kill a Mockingbird*.

Aside from his extensive acting career, which has spanned over five decades and included such classics as *Roman Holiday*, *Spellbound* and *The Guns of Navarone*, Peck has been active in the film community as well as with various charitable and political causes. He was appointed by President Johnson to the National Council on the Arts and has served on the boards of the American Cancer Society, the American Film Institute, the Academy of Motion Picture Arts and Sciences, the Salk Institute and theater support groups in Los Angeles and San Diego. He helped found the La Jolla Playhouse, which has become a rich source of culture for Peck's hometown. In addition, he formed and headed two production companies, Anthony Productions and Brentwood Productions, for which he produced such films as *Cape Fear*, *The Big Country* and *Pork Chop Hill*.

Peck has four surviving children; one of his three sons from his first marriage committed suicide in 1975, and he has a son and daughter from his second marriage since 1955 to French journalist Veronique Pasani. An ardent student of Lincoln, he describes himself as a "poor man's Carl Sandburg" and keeps at his Brentwood home his 1,000-plus volume collection of Lincolniana. He also breeds racehorses and is an expert amateur photographer.

LUKE PERRY

REAL NAME: Coy Luther Perry III
DATE OF BIRTH: October 11, 1965
PLACE OF BIRTH: Fredericktown, Ohio

EYE COLOR: Brown   HAIR COLOR: Brown
HEIGHT: 5'10"   WEIGHT: 165

He was five years old when he saw Paul Newman's film *Cool
Hand Luke* and decided, "From that point on, I was very proud that
my name was Luke."

Luke Perry's early childhood was marred by the turbulent marriage of his parents, who divorced when he was six. His brother and
sister remember a sour relationship between Luke and his father,
which endured until Coy Jr.'s death in 1980. His mother remarried
six years later—to a construction worker—and her children enjoyed
a close and loving bond with him. But at Fredericktown High
School, where Perry played on the baseball team and was the school's
mascot, his teachers remember him as "mischievous, a thrill-seeker,"
and a mediocre student. During one junior high math class, when
Luke was caught daydreaming, he announced to the class that he
was going to be an actor.

After graduation in 1984, Perry moved to Los Angeles, where he
took acting classes and supported himself by working in a factory
and laying asphalt, a trade he'd learned from his stepfather. After
hundreds of rejections, Perry landed the part of Ned Bates on the
soap opera *Loving* and spent a year on that show before moving on to
commercial work in New York. Moving back to Los Angeles in 1990,
Perry again worked in construction until he landed the part of Dylan
on *Beverly Hills 90210*. Soon afterward on the set of the show, which
is filmed at Torrance High School, Luke pointed to a speed bump in
the parking lot and said to the producer, "See that speed bump? I

made it. I was laying asphalt the week before I got *Beverly Hills, 90210*. I'll do whatever it takes to pay the rent." The part catapulted him to stardom—and a constant presence in the teeny-bopper fan magazines. In addition to his TV work, Perry has appeared in several films, among them *Buffy the Vampire Slayer*. Luke is teaming up with Jason Priestley and Vegas veteran Tom Jones to cut an album this year.

When he is not acting or answering the thousands of fan letters he receives each week, Perry says he likes to relax by bungee jumping and playing with his pet pig, Jerry Lee.

JOE PESCI

REAL NAME: Joe Pesci
DATE OF BIRTH: February 9, 1943
PLACE OF BIRTH: Newark, New Jersey

EYE COLOR: Brown   HAIR COLOR: Brown
HEIGHT: 5'6"   WEIGHT: 155

Small in stature but towering in talent, Joe Pesci has consistently delivered unforgettable performances in a variety of roles.

Raised in the Bronx, New York, Pesci started out as a child actor on the *Star Time Kids* radio show at age four. He continued to perform on stage, appearing in dramas, musicals and stand-up comedy acts in New Jersey and New York. His father, Angelo, was a songwriter and encouraged a show-business career for his three children, especially for little Joe, who had perfected his Jimmy Durante impression at age five. Angelo worked three jobs—as a forklift driver for Anheuser-Busch and General Motors and as a bartender—to pay for his son's various lessons, and he oversaw Joe's studies in acting, tap dancing, singing and guitar.

Pesci dropped out of high school and turned to music in his late teens, singing in nightclubs and playing guitar for Joey Dee and the Starliters. He recorded an album of jazz-blues songs as Little Joe Ritchie in the '60s and then, with friend Frank Costello, toured the nightclubs with a musical-comedy act. After making a low-budget film, *The Death Collector*, he moved to Hollywood but couldn't get work or an agent. Discouraged, he gave up acting and show business entirely, but his work in that film came to the attention of Robert De Niro. Joe was managing a restaurant to make ends meet when De Niro asked him to read for the part of Jake LaMotta's brother Joey in *Raging Bull*. Pesci refused, but De Niro persisted and introduced him to the director, Martin Scorsese. Still reluctant, Joe told them to "give it to some working actor, because I know what these kids go through, and they'll appreciate it more than I will at this point." He soon realized, though, that this was more than "just a role in a film" and accepted. His performance earned him a slew of best supporting actor nominations, including one for an Oscar. His reunion with De Niro and Scorsese in *Goodfellas* earned him another nomination and eventually the coveted statuette.

Although most of Pesci's roles have been heavy and dramatic, he has also proved to be an equally talented comedic actor as the bumbling burglar in the *Home Alone* movies, the thrill-seeking accountant in the *Lethal Weapon* movies and the inexperienced attorney in *My Cousin Vinny*.

Pesci has been married three times, splitting recently from his third wife, 24-year-old Marti, and he has a 26-year-old daughter from his first marriage.

MICHELLE PFEIFFER

REAL NAME: Michelle Pfeiffer
DATE OF BIRTH: April 29, 1957
PLACE OF BIRTH: Santa Ana, California

EYE COLOR: Blue   HAIR COLOR: Blond
HEIGHT: 5'5"   WEIGHT: 110

For most of her youth, Michelle Pfieffer was an avowed tomboy who didn't take guff from anybody and was even known to beat up on boys. Her father, the owner of a heating and air-conditioning business, believed in teaching the value of the work ethic to his four children at an early age, and Michelle had her first job at fourteen, selling clothes after school. In her free time, she hung out at the beach with the other beach bunnies and experimented with drugs. She got her first taste of drama when she began attending acting classes as a way to avoid taking English at Fountain Valley High School. Discovering that she had a talent for it, Pfeiffer enrolled in professional drama classes and was soon commuting to Los Angeles to study. After high school, while attending Golden West Junior College—ostensibly to study psychology—she continued to take acting lessons, paying for them by working as a checkout clerk at Vons. When a friend entered her in the Miss Orange County beauty pageant, Michelle played along and ended up winning. That led to an agent and, before long, she began appearing in commercials.

Her first role on television was a one-liner on the series *Fantasy Island*. After playing a bombshell in *Delta House*, she made her motion picture debut in the 1980 film *Falling in Love Again*. By the mid-'80s she had played starring roles in such films as *Ladyhawke*, *Married to the Mob* and *Dangerous Liaisons*, which won her an Oscar nomination. Most recently, she camped it up as Catwoman in *Batman Returns* and turned in a critically acclaimed and Oscar-nominated dramatic performance in *Love Field*.

During her early years in Hollywood, Michelle became a member

of an extreme vegetarian cult and even became ensnared in mind control. She says, "I stopped seeing them just two weeks after meeting my husband. I'd wanted to stop months before but found it difficult; they get you to believe you won't be able to survive without them." She was married to actor Peter Horton, who starred in *thirtysomething*, but they divorced in 1989. In 1993, she opted for single parenthood and adopted a baby girl.

REGIS PHILBIN

REAL NAME: Regis Philbin
DATE OF BIRTH: August 25, 1934
PLACE OF BIRTH: New York, New York

EYE COLOR: Brown   HAIR COLOR: Brown
HEIGHT: 5'8"   WEIGHT: 145

Bearing the name of your father's alma mater—Regis High School—is enough to put a chip on anyone's shoulder, but even after Johnny Carson razzed him in a monologue—"Regis is an English cigarette or a hotel"—he's as good-natured and unflappable as he appears on television.

The eldest son born into a strict Catholic family, Regis Philbin attended parochial schools in Manhattan. Introverted at home and school, he turned into Mr. Entertainment when he had an audience of street buddies. After taking a degree in sociology from Notre Dame in 1953, Regis spent two years in the Navy and conquered his shyness sufficiently to work as a stagehand in Hollywood. Thus began his bicoastal, pingpong path to stardom.

Leaving Hollywood, he served as a page for *The Tonight Show* in New York for a short time. Coming back to Los Angeles, he drove a truck and wrote news copy for KCOP-TV, where he sat in one night for a sportscaster and got his foot in the door as a broadcaster. Moving on to newscasting, he was picked as Steve Allen's replacement on Westinghouse's late-night show in 1964. From 1967 to 1969, he sat in the sidekick seat beside Joey Bishop on that late-night show, but it was dropped when it failed to compete with Johnny Carson. Regis finally found his niche as a host of the *A.M. Los Angeles* show for seven years, then took himself and his format to New York on the local *Morning Show* in 1983. Kathie Lee Gifford joined him after he watched her fill in for Joan Lunden on *Good*

Morning America in 1985. The two schmoozed their way into syndication as *Live With Regis and Kathie Lee* in 1988. It's a combination that works, with a daily audience of twenty million tuned in to their breezy banter and intimate revelations.

Regis' wife, Joy, who sits in for Kathie Lee when she's on vacation, seems to hold her own on the show as well as she does at home, where they're raising two teenage daughters. He has two other grown children from a previous marriage that ended in 1968.

SIDNEY POITIER

REAL NAME: Sidney Poitier
DATE OF BIRTH: February 20, 1927
PLACE OF BIRTH: Miami, Florida

EYE COLOR: Brown   HAIR COLOR: Black
HEIGHT: 6'2"   WEIGHT: 180

When Sidney Poitier was an infant, his parents took him and his seven older siblings from their home in Miami to live on their tomato farm in the Bahamas. Until the Depression destroyed the market for fresh tomatoes, he was educated by private tutors and at Governor's High School in Nassau. But his father's arthritis and lack of business forced Sidney to leave school at fifteen and work to help support the family. That same year, he returned to Miami to live with a married brother and look for a better paying job. The only work he could find was as a delivery boy for a drugstore, but he found something else he had never encountered before: racial prejudice. Sidney recalls the white world being surrounded by "barbed wire" and says, "My life was full of frustration and confusion. I experienced tremendous loneliness as a result of realizing for the first time that I couldn't trust adults."

From Miami, he hitched a ride on a freight train to New York and arrived in Harlem with one dollar and fifty cents. Sleeping on a rooftop, he washed dishes and worked at other menial jobs. When the Japanese bombed Pearl Harbor, he enlisted in the Army and served as a physiotherapist until 1945. Back in New York after the war, he was accepted into the American Negro Theater, which at the time was home to Harry Belafonte. So determined was Sidney to become an actor that he did backstage chores in exchange for acting lessons from the director. His experience with ANT led to a breakthrough role in his first hit film, *No Way Out*, in 1950. In less than a year, he became a box office attraction and went on to star in such

American classics as *In the Heat of the Night, They call Me Mr. Tibbs* and *Guess Who's Coming to Dinner*. He's accomplished about all there is to do in the world of film, including directing and producing, and has penned an autobiography entitled *My Life*. After starring in *A Piece of the Action* in 1977, Poitier took a ten-year break from acting, returning to the screen in the modestly successful *Shoot to Kill*.

Off-screen, he campaigns vigorously for equal opportunity for blacks in Hollywood. An avid fitness devotee, he took up tennis at 46 and skiing at 50. Married with two daughters, he has four daughters from his first marriage.

JASON PRIESTLEY

REAL NAME: Jason Priestley
DATE OF BIRTH: August 28, 1969
PLACE OF BIRTH: Vancouver, British Columbia

EYE COLOR: Blue   HAIR COLOR: Sandy brown
HEIGHT: 5'7"   WEIGHT: 145

Jason Priestley isn't much like his *Beverly Hills, 90210* character, Brandon Walsh. He plays an all-American kid, but Jason was born

and raised in Vancouver, and unlike Brandon—who remains unaffected by his move from Minnesota to the glamorous Beverly Hills—Jason has taken full advantage of his newfound stardom. He and *90210* co-star and fellow heartthrob Luke Perry have often been seen about town in the company of beautiful women, seldom with the same one twice.

Jason's mother was an actress in Canada, so he was exposed to the profession early. A successful child actor, he did commercial and modeling work and appeared on television, dropping out in his teens to concentrate on school and hockey. At sixteen he rejoined the ranks of actors, participating in workshops and doing TV movies and guest spots on series, including one on *21 Jump Street* with teen idol Johnny Depp. With his numerous appearances, he became one of the hottest local actors in Vancouver, narrowly missing a role in the Canadian series *Danger Bay*.

Shortly thereafter he moved to Los Angeles and made the rounds of auditions, winning his first role as one of a group of orphans raised by a strict but hip nun in the series *Sister Kate*. Tori Spelling, daughter of *90210* producer Aaron Spelling and now starring on the show with Jason, saw him on *Sister Kate* and told her dad that Jason had a great look and lots of potential. She was right. Since the debut season of *90210*, Jason has achieved national stardom. During the show's first two seasons, the cast did promotional appearances, which drew so many screaming fans that the local police would often have to shut them down. Since achieving TV success, Jason has branched out to star in his first feature film, director Penny Marshall's *Calendar Girl*.

A self-confessed adrenaline junkie, he pursues sports with a passion. Like a true Canadian, he loves ice hockey, watching it whenever he can and now playing regularly on a celebrity team. The thirteen scars on his face, one of which he got in a hockey game and all of which he is very proud of, attest to his addiction.

In February 1993, Jason took on the additional task of directing a *90210* episode. The experience was better than he had hoped. He says, "It's breathed new life into the show for me. Being the social consciousness of America can become a bit tedious."

RICHARD PRYOR

REAL NAME: Richard Pryor
DATE OF BIRTH: December 1, 1940
PLACE OF BIRTH: Peoria, Illinois

EYE COLOR: Brown   HAIR COLOR: Black
HEIGHT: 6'   WEIGHT: 160

Any comedy hall of fame would be incomplete without the inclusion of this multitalented performer. Box office giants such as Eddie Murphy credit Richard Pryor with influencing their styles as well as opening doors for them.

The only child of a broken home, Pryor has never discussed the marital status or whereabouts of his father, only that he died in 1970. Regarding his mother, he will say only that he was born in Peoria's St. Francis Hospital. About his family life while growing up, he says, "We were very affluent—had the biggest whorehouse in the neighborhood. My grandmother, she was the madam. We had three on one block."

After dropping out of school at fourteen, Pryor had plenty of time on his hands to develop his street-corner comedy act and managed to get by on jobs like janitor and packing-house worker. Once he was old enough to enlist, he did a tour of duty in the Army in Germany, where he performed in amateur shows. After discharge, he started landing gigs in small comedy clubs in Peoria, moving on to other cities like St. Louis and Buffalo, then on to New York in 1963. Richard finally graduated from his nightclub act to appearances on top TV shows like *The Tonight Show with Johnny Carson*, and by 1966, he was a $3,000 a week performer in Las Vegas. When the Establishment pressured him to tone down the earthy profanity in his act, he refused and was finally fired.

Seeking his fortune in Hollywood, he landed a part in *Busy Body*, a crime spoof with Sid Caesar, in 1967. For the next few years, Richard's career started taking off with comedy albums and movies. But his personal life went into a tailspin. Calling it his "super-nigger rich phase," he seemed determined to find out how much cocaine and booze he could pump into his system, and ended up with a record of arrests for possession of drugs, assault charges and tax evasion. Somehow, from this maelstrom of pain, he managed to extract more material with which to entertain audiences, and through it all, he even managed to achieve big-time movie stardom with such hits as *Uptown Saturday Night, Silver Streak, Stir Crazy* and *Harlem Nights*. His "syndrome of irresponsibility" culminated in 1980 when the comedian lit himself on fire while attempting to freebase cocaine. After recovering, with a new perspective on life, Pryor was still able to laugh at the tragedy and work it into his act for a number of years.

Nearly immobilized today with multiple sclerosis, Pryor has four children by his five wives and one by a mistress. In spite of his self-destructive lifestyle, he has always considered himself a religious man. Believing that "the elements take care of me," he says, "I see God in the streets. He's in me and around me."

TONY RANDALL

REAL NAME: Anthony Leonard Rosenberg
DATE OF BIRTH: February 26, 1920
PLACE OF BIRTH: Tulsa, Oklahoma

EYE COLOR: Brown   HAIR COLOR: Brown
HEIGHT: 5'8"   WEIGHT: 150

The other half of the *Odd Couple* tries desperately to convince people that he's not the same fuss-budget, opera-loving, highbrow neatnik in real life as he is on screen and stage. But he just can't help himself. During one appearance on *The Tonight Show*, he threatened

to grab a cigarette out of Johnny's hand and shred it in front of the audience if Johnny didn't put it out.

The son of a traveling art and antique dealer who had to follow his rich clientele from coast to coast, Tony Randall attended 24 different schools while he was growing up. He knew from the age of twelve that he wanted to become an actor, but his father's frequent trips made it difficult for him to land roles in any school plays. He was thirteen when his dad left home for good, but Tony wasn't sorry to see him go: He had considered his father a rival for his mother's heart. She was "the great love of my life," says Tony. Finally able to put down some roots in Oklahoma, he attended a play and says he instantly "knew exactly what I was going to do in life. It was acting or die." After graduation, he enrolled in speech and drama at Northwestern University.

His postcollege career began in New York City, where he studied with Sanford Meisner at the Neighborhood Playhouse. But much of Randall's early work came in radio, where he appeared regularly on such soap operas as *I Love a Mystery* and *Life's True Story*. After his Broadway debut in 1941 in the play *Circle of Chalk*, Randall remained on the New York stage until he was drafted in 1942. After serving four years in the Signal Corps, he returned to acting, first in Washington summer theater and then back in New York. In 1952, he scored his first hit on television with a supporting role on the situation comedy *Mr. Peepers*. Five years later, after his motion picture debut in the 20th Century-Fox film *Oh, Men! Oh, Women!*, he made a string of movies for that studio as well as for Universal and MGM. His most popular efforts include *The Mating Game*, *Pillow Talk* and *The Alphabet Murders*. Stardom finally came to him with the hit series *The Odd Couple*, in which he played Felix opposite Jack Klugman's Oscar from 1970 through 1975. In two subsequent seasons, he starred as a judge on his own series, *The Tony Randall Show*. Although his commercial success has been almost exclusively in comedy, his true devotion is to classical work such as Shakespeare, and he continues to apply himself to those plays at every opportunity.

Along with his wife of 40-plus years, Randall is an avid opera fan, has an extensive art collection and keeps in incredible physical shape with weight training and ballet lessons.

DAN RATHER

REAL NAME: Daniel Rather
DATE OF BIRTH: October 31, 1931
PLACE OF BIRTH: Wharton, Texas

EYE COLOR: Brown
HEIGHT: 6'

HAIR COLOR: Brown
WEIGHT: 180

"The central thing is fairness," says Dan Rather about his editorial credo. "You can include the hard news, weave in the background and even if necessary get in some analysis, but the main point is, are you fair and are you accurate?"

Son of a Texas oil rigger, Rather led a much-traveled childhood, but the family eventually put down roots in Houston. It was there that he got his first taste of politics by attending Democratic Party functions with his father and witnessed Texas-style hardball politicking. After high school, Rather enrolled at Sam Houston State College on a football scholarship, working part-time as a writer and sportscaster for a local TV station, and earned his degree in journalism in 1953. He went on to attend the University of Houston and South Texas School of Law for postgraduate work, then taught journalism for a year at his alma mater.

Dan honed his writing skills as a print reporter for the *Houston Chronicle* and UPI before joining the CBS radio affiliate in Houston, where he worked his way up from copy writer to news director in four years. During the latter '50s, he switched to television, again for CBS, covering Hurricane Carla in 1961 and the assassination of President John F. Kennedy in 1963. The next year, CBS made him its White House correspondent. From there, Rather worked for CBS in London and Vietnam before returning to Washington in time to cover the Nixon presidency and Watergate. When his reportorial aggressiveness rankled Nixon and his administration, presidential aide John Ehrlichman attempted unsuccessfully to have him fired, and Dan's Washington home was burglarized in search of certain sensitive files. "What burns me up," says Rather, "is that a certain amount of my check every month goes to pay these people's salaries."

In addition to his news duties, Rather joined the show *60 Minutes* in 1975 and remained until 1981, when Walter Cronkite announced his retirement and he was named to replace him as anchor of the *CBS Evening News*. He is also the host of *48 Hours*, a news show that premiered in 1988.

Although critics have derided his good looks, it doesn't hurt to be telegenic, and Dan is. With his 100-hour work week, he doesn't have much time for hobbies but enjoys an occasional fishing trip. He and his wife have two children to whom he would have this legacy left: "If a truck runs over me tomorrow, what I would really love to have someone tell my kids is that their father wouldn't buckle—not under Lyndon Johnson, not under Richard Nixon."

ROBERT REDFORD

REAL NAME: Charles Robert Redford Jr.
DATE OF BIRTH: August 18, 1937
PLACE OF BIRTH: Santa Monica, California

EYE COLOR: Blue   HAIR COLOR: Reddish blond
HEIGHT: 5'10"   WEIGHT: 159

Born just a few miles from Hollywood, Robert Redford moved to Van Nuys, California, when his father, a milkman, became an accountant with Standard Oil. Bored with the San Fernando Valley and disgusted with socially conformist classmates who displayed no desire to achieve anything, young Robert rebelled by stealing hubcaps and reselling them. Fortunately, he was a good enough baseball player to receive a scholarship to the University of Colorado in Boulder, but his first year was marred by the death of his beloved mother, who had been the one light of joy in his life. Devastated by the loss, he numbed himself by drinking and found that the life of a college jock and "groveling to win" did not appeal to him. He took up skiing and began skipping more and more practices to hit the slopes. In school, the only thing that interested him was art history, and after two years, he dropped out. A job in the oilfields of Los Angeles earned him enough money for a freighter ticket to Europe, where he spent thirteen months hitchhiking from country to country on a voyage of self-discovery. Eventually he enrolled in art school in Florence, but found that he lacked the self-discipline of a dedicated painter and came home.

Still hoping to study art, Redford thumbed his way around the country and landed again in Los Angeles in 1958. By this time, his drinking problem was nearly out of control, but when he met his future wife, Lola, a Mormon from Utah, he decided to pick up the pieces of his artistic ambition and enrolled at the Pratt Institute in Brooklyn. Redford's interest turned toward set design, and when a friend suggested that he join the American Academy of Dramatic Arts in order to learn more about the theater, he agreed. Enrolling in acting classes, he made his debut on Broadway as a basketball player in *Tall Story*. Throughout the late '50s and early '60s, Redford continued acting on the stage and appeared frequently on such TV shows as *Playhouse 90*, *Naked City*, *Route 66* and *The Twilight Zone*. Then, in 1963, he scored his first big triumph as the star of Neil Simon's *Barefoot in the Park*. After several less than successful films, Redford hit box office pay dirt opposite Paul Newman in *Butch Cassidy and the Sundance Kid*, and films such as *The Candidate*, *The Way We Were*, *The Sting* and *The Great Gatsby* soon elevated him to Hollywood's leading heartthrob. In 1980, he branched out into directing and won an Academy Award for his first film as a director, *Ordinary People*. His most recent directorial effort was 1992's *A River Runs Through It*.

In addition to his filmwork, Redford has spent a great deal of time and money on political and environmental causes, and he is the owner of a 4,000-acre resort community called Sundance in Utah, home of the prestigious Sundance Film Festival and the Sundance Institute, an organization dedicated to helping young moviemakers bring their ideas to film. His marriage to Lola produced three children, but the couple is now separated.

ROB REINER

REAL NAME: Robert Reiner
DATE OF BIRTH: March 6, 1945
PLACE OF BIRTH: New York, New York

EYE COLOR: Brown   HAIR COLOR: Brown
HEIGHT: 6'2"   WEIGHT: 220

The oldest of three children of the multitalented entertainer Carl Reiner, Rob Reiner was born in New York and spent his early years there, living for a time across the street from future wife Penny Marshall, later of *Laverne and Shirley* fame. As a boy, Rob had the luxury of hanging around in the family apartment while his father, who starred with Sid Caesar in *Your Show of Shows*, worked at home

with such world-class comics as Mel Brooks, Neil Simon and Norman Lear. Naïvely, Rob remembers that as a kid he thought "everybody had people like that over for dinner." When Rob was fourteen, his father moved to Beverly Hills to work on *The Dick Van Dyke Show*, and as his father's fame grew, Rob says, "For a long time, I lived my life not as myself, but as an extension of my father. He had this tremendous personality, so strong, and I kept thinking that's what I had to be when I grew up. But as a kid, I was painfully shy and sensitive—I always felt like I was competing with my dad, and losing." While attending Beverly Hills High School, Rob had few friends, but finally, in his senior year, he took a part in a school play just for the heck of it. "Suddenly I found acceptance. I had friends and a social life," he says.

At UCLA, he and some of his Beverly Hills High buddies founded an improvisational comedy group called The Session and performed in venues such as New York's Playboy Club. After one year of club work, Rob quit UCLA during his junior year, formed a comedy act with Larry Bishop and joined the San Francisco drama group The Committee. Soon he was landing small parts on television and in films and making headway on a writing career by way of *The Smothers Brothers Comedy Hour*, where he was teamed with Steve Martin.

He got his big break after making a guest appearance on a show called *Head Master*, where he was employed as a story editor. That appearance led to his star-making role on *All in the Family* as Mike Stivic, liberal son-in-law of superbigot Archie Bunker, who called him Meathead. He won two Emmys during that period and helped develop stories and scripts as well. "I think if I had just been an actor on the show, I would have been bored out of my mind," he says. After eight years with the show, Reiner turned down a chance to star in a spin-off and spent the next several years trying to raise the money for *This Is Spinal Tap*, a rock music documentary satire. When it was finally released in 1984, it became a cult hit and led to a distinguished directorial career that includes *The Princess Bride*, *Stand by Me* and *When Harry Met Sally....* Reiner is a founding partner of Castle Rock Entertainment, recently bought by Ted Turner.

Rob was married to fellow director Penny Marshall for ten years. In 1989, he married Michelle Singer and spends all of his free time putting together new projects.

BURT REYNOLDS

REAL NAME: Burt Reynolds Jr.
DATE OF BIRTH: February 11, 1936
PLACE OF BIRTH: Waycross, Georgia

EYE COLOR: Brown HAIR COLOR: Brown
HEIGHT: 6'1" WEIGHT: 178

Part Cherokee Indian and part Italian, Burt Reynolds grew up
with his brother and sister in Palm Beach, Florida, where his father

was the chief of police. An all-around athlete in high school, he went on to become an All-Southern Conference halfback at Florida State University. He was set to join the NFL Baltimore Colts when a knee injury in an automobile accident ended his career. Burt promptly left school—in his sophomore year—and moved to New York, where he drifted for two years, supporting himself working as a bouncer and a dishwasher. It was while hanging out in Greenwich Village with actor friends that he caught the acting bug and moved back to Florida to study drama at Palm Beach Junior College. His debut performance, in a school production of *Outward Bound,* won him the 1958 Florida Drama Desk Award for best actor and a scholarship to New York's Hyde Park Playhouse.

With the help of Joanne Woodward, he went on to land an agent, who got him a role in *Mister Roberts* on Broadway and an episode of the TV show *M Squad.* In 1959, he signed a seven-year contract with Universal Pictures television and appeared on 26 episodes of *Riverboat* before quitting after a conflict with another cast member. "Then I couldn't get a job," he recalls. "I didn't have a very good reputation. I did some things like *Pony Express,* the kind of shows they shoot with a Kodak and a flashlight. Those were depressing years." In the absence of other roles, he worked as an extra and a stunt man, and over the next several years made quite a few forgettable movies and appeared for almost three seasons as blacksmith Quint Asper on *Gunsmoke.* His big break came in 1972 with the release of *Deliverance* and his full-color centerfold in *Cosmopolitan* magazine. He then hosted his own short-lived *Burt Reynolds Show* and starred in two TV series, *Hawk* and *Dan August,* but it was his subsequent appearances on *The Tonight Show* as Johnny Carson's stand-in that established his reputation as a comic. Burt's popularity during the '70s and early '80s brought him his choice of scripts, most of them comedies, many of them hits such as *The Longest Yard, Smokey and the Bandit, Semi-Tough, The Man Who Loved Women* and *Best Friends.* But his luck ran out in the late '80s, and after a long string of turkeys, he returned to television, first in *B.L. Stryker,* and then in the popular sitcom *Evening Shade,* for which he won an Emmy.

Burt was married in the early '60s to actress Judy Carne, had long-term relationships with Sally Field and singer Dinah Shore, and was married to actress Loni Anderson in 1988, but after adopting a son, they were separated in June of 1993.

JOHN RITTER

REAL NAME: Jonathan Southworth Ritter
DATE OF BIRTH: September 17, 1948
PLACE OF BIRTH: Burbank, California

EYE COLOR: Blue   HAIR COLOR: Brown
HEIGHT: 6'   WEIGHT: 180

John Ritter was once described by a woman journalist as "the kind of guy you always wished had invited you to the junior prom."

The younger son of actor/singer Tex Ritter and actress Dorothy Southworth, John grew up in Los Angeles. Tex tried from the very beginning to discourage his two sons from entering show business, but both parents sensed that John was destined to become an actor. His mom remembers that "John was always playing a part, even as a little boy. By the time he was twelve, he and some other kids had already made their first movie, a parody of *Bonanza*." At Hollywood High School, he was active in student government and even served as president of the student body. "I wanted to be junior senator from California by the time I was 35," says John. "But I couldn't take myself seriously for that long. I realized I wasn't all sewed up mentally." After graduation, he majored in psychology at the University of Southern California, but during his sophomore year, he followed a girlfriend into one of Nina Foch's acting classes and caught the acting bug. He spent the following summer in Europe participating in Scotland's Edinburgh Festival and changed his major to theater arts. After earning his degree in 1971, John made his TV debut the same year with a guest-starring appearance on the series *Dan August*.

For the next several years, he did summer stock and appeared frequently on television. From 1972 to 1977, he appeared semiregularly as the Reverend Matthew Fordwick on *The Waltons*. But it was in 1975 that he landed his landmark part of Jack Tripper, a heterosexual who impersonates a homosexual in order to share an apartment with two beautiful women. During his 174 episodes on *Three's Company*, Ritter was one of the hottest stars on television and received an Emmy award. In 1984, he formed his own production company, Adam Productions, which is responsible for the popular sitcom *Anything But Love*. In 1992, John landed himself in another hit sitcom, *Hearts Afire*.

After completing his bachelor playboy period, John settled down in 1977 with actress Nancy Morgan, who had appeared with him in the film *Americathon*, and they have three children. He enjoys tennis and racquetball for exercise but especially likes collecting Beatles records and memorabilia. Explaining how he maintains his emotional equilibrium through the ups and downs of show business, John says, "If you take fame and success too seriously, you're going to be chronically disappointed, because there's always going to be someone bigger and more successful than you."

GERALDO RIVERA

Real Name: Geraldo Miguel Rivera
DATE OF BIRTH: July 4, 1943
PLACE OF BIRTH: New York, New York

EYE COLOR: Brown   HAIR COLOR: Brown
HEIGHT: 5'10"   WEIGHT: 155

Geraldo Rivera is not only a star—he's a media phenomenon.
And that's just the way he planned it.

One of five children born to a poor Puerto Rican immigrant
father and Jewish mother, he had a long way to go when he was
born. Living in the Williamsburg section of Brooklyn, Geraldo's dad
supported the family as a cab driver and dishwasher while his mother
helped out waitressing. Of his unusual mixed heritage, Geraldo says,
"These are two distinctive identities and it was very difficult for me as
a kid to handle them both. So I guess I compromised by being one or
the other at various times in my life." When the family moved to
Long Island in 1950, Geraldo leaned toward athletics and street gang
strife during his high school years. With his grades lagging, he took
remedial courses at a community college in order to gain entrance to
Maritime College at the State University of New York. After a short
time there, he left to serve two years in the Merchant Marines, but
rather than return to New York after getting out of the service, he
enrolled at the University of Arizona. Finding himself in a land of
WASPs for the first time, his ethnicity suddenly felt painful to him,
and he calls the years spent there the worst of his life. "Here I was,
this little hood from New York with the Brooklyn Spanish-American
accent," he remembers. "I wanted to be like them, to belong. So I
said my name was Jerry Rivers and I did everything I could to please
them. But they never accepted me."

In 1965, Geraldo took his B.S. degree with him back to New York
and Brooklyn Law School, working nights and weekends in a department store and clerking for the Harlem Assertion of Rights and the
Community Action for Legal Services. It was here that Geraldo practiced law defending the poor. After a year—and 50 court cases—he
decided he was just treading water and wasn't helping anyone. So in

1970, he joined the staff of New York's *Eyewitness News*, at first as a bilingual, soft-news reporter. But it didn't take long for Geraldo's passion and tenacious personality to start snagging provocative and timely stories. His first coup was a grim look at the realities of drug addiction in East Harlem through the eyes of three junkies. He continued his journalistic career in this vein and made a name for himself by throwing off the newsman's mantle of objectivity and replacing it with the cape of a crusader.

In addition to winning several prestigious journalism awards and Emmys, Rivera is best known for his controversial TV specials. After his much publicized dismissal from *20/20* in 1985, he struck out on his own with the first—and best remembered—of a series of specials, in which he ceremoniously opened Al Capone's secret vault (finding a few bottles and very little else). Although dismissed by critics as sensationalism, it garnered seismic ratings. In 1987, he ended up with his own syndicated talk show, *Geraldo*. Then, with the publication of his tell-all autobiography in 1991, Geraldo caused a stir by claiming affairs with female celebrities such as Chris Evert and Bette Midler and by revealing that he is a recovering sex addict.

Before his current wife, C.C., also the producer of his show, he was married thrice—once, during the '70s, to Kurt Vonnegut's daughter. The author of four books, Geraldo became a father in 1993.

JOAN RIVERS

REAL NAME: Joan Alexandra Molinsky
DATE OF BIRTH: June 8, 1937
PLACE OF BIRTH: New York, New York

EYE COLOR: Brown   HAIR COLOR: Blond
HEIGHT: 5'2"   WEIGHT: 102

Can we talk? Joan Rivers recalls her parents as "almost pathologically terrified of poverty." When they fled to this country from Russia, her father became a doctor and made a good living but could never quite attain the grandiose lifestyle his wife had left behind in the old country, and they never stopped fighting about it. In a kindergarten play, Joan took a fancy to acting and began dreaming of stardom, but her mother enrolled her in piano, violin and elocution lessons and upper-crust private schools with what she considered a higher goal in mind: entering society and marrying well.

At the Adelphi Academy preparatory school in Brooklyn, however, Joan demonstrated the strength and intelligence that would periodically fire up the rest of her adult life. Active in the drama club, she won second place in an acting contest, and after graduation, she got a small part in the film *Mr. Universe*. Though she was longing to pursue that path, she acquiesced to her mother's wishes and broke off her showbiz career to continue her education at Connecticut College for Women, then Barnard College, where she majored in English and anthropology, graduating Phi Beta Kappa in 1954.

Diving into the business world, she went to work for the publicity department of Lord & Taylor, then became fashion coordinator for the entire chain of the Bond clothing stores. The turning point came when she married a fellow employee who found her career ambitions unacceptable, and she shed both him and her parents and set off to do what she had wanted all along—become an actress.

After struggling for seven years in small parts in short-run plays off-off-Broadway, supporting herself mostly as an office temp, she tired of the grind and began earning better money doing stand-up comedy to support her acting efforts. Working the Catskills, strip joints and Mafia clubs, she learned that she really was a natural

comedienne. From 1962 until 1965, after a stint with Chicago's Second City, Joan worked the clubs and as a writer for such shows as *Candid Camera* and *The Ed Sullivan Show*. Then she was booked on *The Tonight Show* to talk about being a comedy writer, but her rapid-fire wit sparked with Carson's, and she soon became a regular stand-in host. After filling in for three years—sometimes doing better in the ratings than Johnny—Rivers signed a $10 million deal in 1986 with Fox to host her own show. After a brief run, the show bombed, and she moved on to daytime television as the host of *The Joan Rivers Show*, with solid ratings against Oprah Winfrey and Phil Donahue.

On her way up, Joan was dealing with personal angst. While her marriage to Edgar Rosenberg in 1965 brought her a daughter, his role as manager/architect of her career became increasingly heavy on their marriage, and months after the disappointment and humiliation of her being fired from the late-night show, he took his own life in a hotel room. But as Joan says, "I don't want to turn my career into anything maudlin or sentimental. Besides, I'm too short to be a tragic figure."

TIM ROBBINS

REAL NAME: Tim Robbins
DATE OF BIRTH: October 16, 1958
PLACE OF BIRTH: New York, New York

EYE COLOR: Blue   HAIR COLOR: Brown
HEIGHT: 6'4"   WEIGHT: 190

Tim Robbins acquired his social conscience before he began acquiring an appreciation for the art of acting. "My parents weren't

radicals or hippies," says Tim, "though they were a part of that scene. They worked for civil rights in the early '60s, made us aware of Martin Luther King and why he was important. They fostered an awareness in the family." His father—a folk musician who managed a Greenwich Village club—and his mother, who worked for a publishing company, raised him and his two older sisters in a one-bedroom apartment in Greenwich Village. By the time he was twelve, Tim was joining his older sisters in the Theater for the New City acting troupe. "We'd be trucked to different neighborhoods, set up a stage and do a play," he recalls. "It was a great place to learn how to act. You had to compete with trucks backfiring, mothers screaming out windows, junkies coming up on stage."

Tim received a Catholic school elementary education before entering prestigious Stuyvesant High, a public school with an emphasis on science and math and tough entrance requirements. Having learned hockey in the streets with a broom and a roll of electrical tape, Tim played the game in high school until he was kicked off the team for fighting. "It was a strange mix," says Tim, "a masculine, violent game on the one hand, and the '60's living theater, with its surreal plays and people naked on stage, on the other." Tim went on to UCLA, where he majored in drama and cofounded the avant garde theater group Actors' Gang, paying the rent with television and small movie parts. Finally, in 1989, his big break came as the wild pitcher in *Bull Durham*. Although co-star Susan Sarandon's main romantic interest in the film was Kevin Costner, she and Tim were developing their own love story off screen. They began living together and had a baby later that year.

Now that Tim had scored with the critics, he was able to be more selective in his work. *Miss Firecracker, Jacob's Ladder* and *The Player* followed. Then came *Bob Roberts*, a political satire that he had written and developed himself. With Robbins as director and star, on a $4 million budget, it was a critical and commercial success, and it's made Tim something of a "player" himself in Hollywood. But he and Susan, who had their second baby in 1992, maintain their homestead in New York. "If we lived in Los Angeles," says Tim, "it would be unbearable. And it's important to us that most of our friends are not in the business."

JULIA ROBERTS

REAL NAME: Julia Fiona Roberts
DATE OF BIRTH: October 28, 1967
PLACE OF BIRTH: Smyrna, Georgia

EYE COLOR: Brown   HAIR COLOR: Auburn
HEIGHT: 5'9"   WEIGHT: 115

Unlike her brother, Eric, and her sister, Lisa, Julia Roberts was slow to catch what their mother calls "the family disease": acting. Her siblings participated enthusiastically in plays at their parents' dramatic workshop, but Julia showed up only occasionally and said she intended to become a veterinarian when she grew up. Eric and Lisa were already working on their acting careers when she left home three days after graduating from high school and moved to New York to become an actress herself. "I had convinced myself that I had three choices. I could get married, I could go to college or I could move to New York. Nobody was asking me to get married, and I didn't want to go away to school, so I moved."

Supporting herself by working in a shoe store and an ice cream parlor, Julia took speech lessons to get rid of her Southern accent and made a brief run at acting classes before dropping out. But she eventually landed a guest-starring role as a child-abuse victim on the TV series *Crime Story*, and in 1986 played opposite her brother in the film *Blood Red*. After a crash course in playing the drums, she won a role as a musician in the film *Satisfaction* in 1988. Then came the string of featured roles—including *Mystic Pizza* and *Steel Magnolias* (for which she was nominated for an Oscar for best supporting actress)—that led to her breakthrough part as a golden-hearted prostitute opposite Richard Gere in the 1990 film *Pretty Woman*. One of the hottest actresses in Hollywood, she went on to command several million dollars per picture in *Sleeping With the Enemy*, *Dying Young* and *Hook*.

But Julia's shove into the spotlight, which put her love life under a microscope—including her ill-fated engagement to Kiefer Sutherland—drove her into a period of private solitude from which she emerged in July 1993 to marry country singer Lyle Lovett whom she met through her friend Susan Sarandon while in the midst of filming her newest film, *The Pelican Brief*. Still trying to keep a low profile, she spends most of her free time on her ranch in Montana, where she enjoys writing poetry.

MR. ROGERS

REAL NAME: Fred McFeely Rogers
DATE OF BIRTH: March 20, 1928
PLACE OF BIRTH: Latrobe, Pennsylvania

EYE COLOR: Blue   HAIR COLOR: Black
HEIGHT: 6'   WEIGHT: 155

With his genuine love for children as unique human beings, Mr. Rogers believes, "We must approach children's programming with a sincere respect for the child and his very existence."

The son of a brick manufacturer, Rogers and his sister grew up in Latrobe, Pennsylvania, where he served as student body president and editor of the yearbook in high school. Rogers studied briefly at Dartmouth before transferring to Florida's Rollins College, where he studied music composition and graduated in 1951. He was primed to become a minister, but after watching several children's TV shows, he realized what a wasteland existed for them and decided that his career lay in television.

A friend helped him land a job at NBC, and before long, he was working as an assistant producer on shows like *Voice of Freedom*, *The Kate Smith Hour* and *Your Lucky Strike Hit Parade*. It was in 1954 that he created his first children's show, *Children's Corner*, on station WQED in Pittsburgh. During its seven-year run, he earned his Bachelor of Divinity degree from Pittsburgh Theological Seminary and went on to become ordained by the Presbyterian church, accepting the mission of utilizing television to enhance the lives of children and families. It was while counseling and helping out at children's centers that he fully realized how little thought had been put into programming TV shows for children's emotional needs. Mr. Rogers explains, "I spent hours and hours observing and listening, and little by little something wonderful began to happen: I remembered the bewilderments, the sadnesses, the joys, the lonely times, the angers." Inspired, Rogers created a fifteen-minute show called *Misterogers* for the Canadian Broadcasting Corporation in 1962. It was syndicated in 1964, but when production funds ran out three years later, viewers protested the news that he had to be canceled, and the Sears Roebuck Foundation came forward with a $150,000 grant that saved the show. The expanded version, *Mr. Rogers' Neighborhood*, is still in syndication.

In addition to his TV work, Rogers is also the author of several books, including *Mr. Rogers Talks With Parents* and *Mr. Rogers Talks With Families About Divorce*. He has been married since 1952 to Joanne, a concert pianist, and has two sons.

KURT RUSSELL

REAL NAME: Kurt Vogel Russell
DATE OF BIRTH: March 17, 1951
PLACE OF BIRTH: Springfield, Massachusetts

EYE COLOR: Blue   HAIR COLOR: Sandy brown
HEIGHT: 5'11"   WEIGHT: 170

Kurt Russell describes his acting technique simply: "I was taught, as a hitter, to know the pitcher. Know what's going on in the game. Then when you step into the batter's box, you look for something white. That's all. That became ingrained in me, so as an actor, that's what I do. When the clapper bangs, I look for something white. That's all."

The second child and only boy of four children, Kurt spent his early youth in Maine with his grandparents, then moved to Los Angeles at age four. His father, Bing Russell, was a baseball player and an actor who appeared on *Bonanza* for fourteen years. Kurt followed his father's footsteps in both fields. When he was nine, his acting career began with a small role in the Elvis movie *It Happened at the World's Fair*, which led to a deal with Disney that cast him in such films as *The Horse in the Gray Flannel Suit* and *Follow Me, Boys!* At Thousand Oaks High School, he was mocked as the "Disney Boy" and became defiant. "I was pretty sarcastic," he says. "It got to a point where I sort of enjoyed, like all teenagers do, my out-of-the-crowd stature."

Sports became his outlet. Athletic and fiercely competitive, Kurt raced cars, won five national titles and was a world champion. He also began pursuing his father's second profession: baseball. After playing in high school, he moved on to the minor leagues in the '70s. As a second baseman for the California Angels organization in Class-AA, he was hitting .563 when he tore a shoulder muscle and was forced to quit. Quite the ladies' man, he says of his philosophy in those days: "Baseball is the only game played by men for women."

Kurt returned to acting in the late '70s but wasn't taken seriously as an adult actor until 1979, when his performance in the title role of *Elvis* won raves. He followed with a string of other films with director John Carpenter: *The Thing, Escape From New York* and *Big Trouble in Little China*. He also co-starred with such names as Sylvester Stallone in *Tango and Cash* and Mel Gibson in *Tequila Sunrise*, competing with each for leading-man status.

Kurt met live-in love Goldie Hawn while making *Swing Shift* in 1983, and in 1985 she had their first child, Wyatt. The two are content with their relationship as is, and because of their negative experience with the institution of marriage, don't plan to get hitched. He has a son, Boston, from his first marriage to actress Season Hubley. The group lives at their Home Run Ranch in Colorado's Elk Mountains with horses, cattle, dogs and other creatures, when not at their home in Pacific Palisades, California. Kurt is an avid hunter, seasonally stalking deer, elk, birds and other game.

MEG RYAN

REAL NAME: Margaret Hyra
DATE OF BIRTH: November 19, 1961
PLACE OF BIRTH: Fairfield, Connecticut

EYE COLOR: Blue   HAIR COLOR: Blond
HEIGHT: 5'4"   WEIGHT: 105

Meg Ryan grew up the daughter of two teachers and enjoyed writing and playing the piano. At Bethel High School, she was an honor student and was voted the school's homecoming queen. But when her parents divorced in her fifteenth year, Meg went into a deep funk. She says now, "I remember not talking about it for a year." To help Meg pull out of it, her mother, a part-time actress and casting agent, sent her on an audition for the role of Candice Bergen's daughter in the movie *Rich and Famous*. After graduation from high school, Ryan moved to New York to study journalism at New York University's night school. During the day, she spent two years on the soap *As the World Turns* and jokingly reflects, "God, you're famous when you're on a soap." In 1984, she quit school and the soap to take a hiatus in Europe.

Upon returning, she decided to give acting an all-out commitment and moved to California. Almost right away, she landed parts in a Disney series and a few small movies, but when she got a big movie with a small part, she garnered incredible attention. That movie was *Top Gun*. The next year, she starred with Dennis Quaid in *Innerspace*. More films followed, each one more clearly confirming her talent and appeal: *The Presidio*, *D.O.A.*, *Promised Land* and *The Doors*. But, in 1989, when the Rob Reiner film *When Harry Met*

Sally... became a blockbuster hit Meg had hit her stride. After *Prelude to a Kiss* with Alec Baldwin, she made *Sleepless in Seattle*, her most recent effort.

Meg and Dennis Quaid were inseparable after working together on *Innerspace*. After living together for a couple of years, they made it legal on Valentine's Day in 1991. Meg likes to recall her wedding day: "We just woke up that morning and said, 'Now we finally have to do it.' We were staying at the Bel Air Hotel and we just called the concierge. There was a reverend at a Rotary Club luncheon who came to our room." A year later, Meg and Dennis welcomed a baby boy.

WINONA RYDER

REAL NAME: Winona Laura Horowitz
DATE OF BIRTH: October 29, 1971
PLACE OF BIRTH: Winona, Minnesota

EYE COLOR: Brown	HAIR COLOR: Black
HEIGHT: 5'4"	WEIGHT: 105

A 100 percent pure offspring of radical '60s parentage, Winona Ryder can credit her godfather, Timothy Leary, for much inspiration: "He's great. We used to have long discussions, although I'm not sure I always understood what the hell he was talking about."

Winona's quirky, highly individualized personality strikes many as being affected. But with her free spirited antiwar activist parents, Winona is really the bizarre person we see and read about. Although the first years of her life were spent living in the Haight-Ashbury district of San Francisco, her parents set out trying to instill in her a sense of independence and open-mindedness. "They weren't hippies, though, which a lot of articles have said they were. They were much more involved with the political rather than the social side of the movement," Winona explains. When she was seven, the family left San Francisco and moved to rural Elk, California, where she lived for several years on a 300-acre farm with no electricity or television. After returning to civilization in Petaluma, California, her parents enrolled her in acting classes at San Francisco's American Conservatory Theater.

When she was thirteen, she was discovered by a talent agent who arranged for her to take a screen test that landed her a Hollywood agent. Winona's big break came when the producers of the film *Lucas* saw a video audition she had made for the movie *Desert Bloom*. Impressed, they hired her, and she shot her film debut in *Lucas* the summer before entering high school in 1986. Two years later, she starred as Lydia, the troubled teen in *Beetlejuice*. And in 1989, the same year she graduated from Petaluma High School with a 4.0 grade point average, she starred in the black comedy *Heathers*. After her well-received performances in *Welcome Home, Roxy Carmichael* and *Mermaids*, Winona declared, "I'm glad that I've fin-

ished doing the teen angst films because I've grown out of that personally. For a while I felt out of control and frustrated like my character in *Heathers*, but lately I've been more relaxed about acting and seeing dimensions in performing that I never imagined existed."

She certainly proved that last year as the star of Francis Ford Coppola's *Bram Stoker's Dracula*. Meeting her match in the mercurial Coppola, she recounts her experience in working with him: "He needs film to express this creative storm inside him. He's totally consumed by the process and you feel like you're tuned into this special wavelength when you work with him." Winona's most recent project was *The Age of Innocence* with another legendary director, Martin Scorsese.

Winona was engaged to her *Edward Scissorhands* co-star Johnny Depp, but the two later dissolved their marriage plans.

SUSAN SARANDON

REAL NAME: Susan Abigail Tomalin
DATE OF BIRTH: October 4, 1946
PLACE OF BIRTH: New York, New York

EYE COLOR: Brown   HAIR COLOR: Auburn
HEIGHT: 5'6"   WEIGHT: 106

"To me, the whole point of acting is to experiment and learn," says Susan Sarandon. "It's like living hundreds of lives in one lifetime."

Of Welsh-Italian lineage, Susan is one of nine children and received her early education at a Catholic school in Metuchen, New Jersey. Calling herself a "spacey child," she found relief from her parents' marital problems by participating in plays organized by the neighborhood kids. When she was junior high age, her family moved to Edison, New Jersey, where she enrolled in a public school and began to blossom. Because she could live for free off-campus with her grandparents, Susan chose Catholic University in Washington, D.C., where she earned tuition and pocket money by working in the drama department, modeling and cleaning apartments. Her varied academic interests ranged from drama, English and philosophy, to military strategy—and a graduate student named Chris Sarandon who was majoring in acting. Before long, they were living together—a bona fide sin in a Catholic school back then—and they were married in her junior year. Susan says, "I didn't think that much about it. The way I saw it, we would just renew every year; it was just one of those things you did for other people to make them comfortable."

When she graduated in 1968, she continued to model while Chris pursued theater along the East Coast. She actually was drafted into acting when she accompanied him to New York on a reading for an agent "so he'd have a warm body to play against." To her surprise, the agent asked her as well as Chris to come back. The couple moved to Manhattan, and the agent promptly sent her on an audition for the film *Joe*. She showed up with no idea what the film was, what the part was or what an audition was. "They asked me to do an improvisation," said Susan. "I asked them what that was and then did it, and they gave me the job on the spot. I thought, Gee, this seems easy;

maybe I'll try acting for a while."

For the next few years, Susan worked on soaps, then briefly on Broadway, before stepping up to TV movies. Then, in 1974, she moved up to the big time in *Lovin' Molly* with Anthony Perkins. In 1975, Susan accepted a part in the craziest cult movie of all time, *The Rocky Horror Picture Show*. The part required her to sing, which she couldn't, but she decided to gut it out and go for the challenge. "I was terrified," she recalls. "Since I'm basically lazy, I try for parts that frighten me or seem impossible. So to survive, I will have to learn something and overcome it."

Susan made poor film choices until her co-starring role opposite Burt Lancaster in *Atlantic City* in 1981. After retreating to the stage in the early '80s, she resumed her film career with *The Hunger* and kicked into high gear with a succession of hits: *The Witches of Eastwick*, *Bull Durham*, the controversial *Thelma and Louise* and her latest, the Oscar-nominated *Lorenzo's Oil*.

Divorced from Chris, she has been living with her *Bull Durham* co-star, Tim Robbins, since 1989. They have two children and continue to make their home in New York.

DIANE SAWYER

REAL NAME: Diane Sawyer
DATE OF BIRTH: December 22, 1945
PLACE OF BIRTH: Glasgow, Kentucky

EYE COLOR: Blue   HAIR COLOR: Blond
HEIGHT: 5'9"   WEIGHT: 124

Applauded for her insightful interviews with celebrities and her work as *60 Minutes'* first female correspondent, Diane Sawyer is unarguably on the first team of TV newswomen.

The second daughter of a judge and a teacher, she was raised in Louisville, Kentucky, where she proved to be an overachiever from the time she started school, pursuing every lesson and extracurricular activity offered: dance, voice, piano, riding and fencing. In high

school, she joined the school newspaper and expanded her interests to the arts. Deeply serious, Diane wanted to be more coquettish, and she remembers, "Part of me longed to be like the other girls, to wisecrack, flirt and ride in open cars, screaming with pleasure. But part of me wanted nothing to do with it, and I was something of a loner instead."

Kicking off her rise to the top, she took the crown as national Junior Miss, mostly on the strength of her essay and final interview, she claims. Although it was a frightening experience for her, she found "education in the terror" because she learned to think fast on her feet in public situations while touring the country as Junior Miss. After completing high school, Diane entered Wellesley College, where she carried a full academic load and continued her extracurricular development, singing with the Blue Notes, acting in student productions, and serving as student body vice president. Taking her B.A. in English in 1967 with a high grade point average, she returned to Louisville and joined the local ABC affiliate as a part-time reporter and weather girl, sprucing up what she thought were terminally boring weathercasts with quotes from her favorite poems.

Feeling the need for "an intellectual vitamin," she moved to Washington, D.C., in 1970. After working as assistant to Jerry Warren, the White House deputy press secretary, she worked her way up to staff assistant for President Nixon. After Nixon's resignation, she helped the former president research his memoirs "out of a sense of what was honorable. It was a human consideration," she says. When she was hired by CBS in 1978 as a reporter, she met hostile opposition all around because of her close association with Nixon, but she dug in and proved her journalistic ability by covering such stories as Three Mile Island and the Iranian hostage crisis. She joined Bill Kurtis as his co-anchor on the *CBS Morning News* in 1981, then was transferred to *60 Minutes* in 1984. Five years later she jumped networks to become a co-anchor, along with Sam Donaldson, of ABC's news magazine *Primetime Live*.

Having broken down virtually every barrier to success that she's encountered, she is admittedly obsessive about her job. Sawyer does, quite simply, whatever it takes to get the story.

Married since 1988 to director Mike Nichols, she finds time in her heavy schedule to keep in shape on her rowing machine and plays tennis on weekends.

ARNOLD SCHWARZENEGGER

REAL NAME: Arnold Alois Schwarzenegger
DATE OF BIRTH: July 30, 1947
PLACE OF BIRTH: Graz, Austria

EYE COLOR: Blue   HAIR COLOR: Brown
HEIGHT: 6'2"   WEIGHT: 214

In a few short years, Arnold Schwarzenegger has gone from being the world's premier body builder to the world's premier movie star. He is currently the most popular international box office draw, commanding upward of $10 million a film.

Born in Austria, Arnold remembers that he was raised a strict Catholic by a strict disciplinarian. "My father always acted like a general, checking to see that I ate the proper way, that I did my studies," he says. As a boy, he disliked his native country, so he spent a great deal of time watching movies featuring American heroes like Steve Reeves and dreamed of the day he could escape to America. He grew up playing sports and was especially adept at soccer. In fact, it was as a way to train for soccer that Arnold originally took up bodybuilding: "Once I decided I wanted to do it, I learned up about the body, how it works, how each muscle can be worked. I felt like Leonardo da Vinci;

I was a sculptor shaping the body." Soon, however, lifting weights became more than just a means to an end. Dropping out of other sports, he began training constantly, and the obsession grew so intense that his parents forbade him to go to the gym more than three days a week. Undaunted, Arnold built a gym at home and continued to train.

In 1965, after graduation from school, he enlisted in the Austrian Army: "The Army was a good experience. I liked the regimentation, the firm, rigid structure. The whole idea of uniforms and medals appealed to me." There, in addition to winning the Austrian Junior Olympic weightlifting championship and the Junior Mr. Europe competition, he also won several curling titles. After discharge, he became the manager of a Munich health club and continued to compete in weightlifting and bodybuilding competitions, winning Best Built Man of Europe and Mr. Europe, among others. Arnold says that this period of winning titles went to his head: "It was a bad time. Now, looking back on it, I'm embarrassed. I was nothing more than a punk, a big bully throwing my weight around. I had fights almost every day—all connected with my need to emphasize my masculinity, my superior size and strength." A friend helped him realign his sights, though, and Arnold focused on more lofty goals.

Right on cue, along came Joe Weider, the fitness entrepreneur, who brought Arnold to the United States for the Mr. Universe contest in 1968. Arnold placed second, but Weider took him under his wing, providing him with a Santa Monica apartment, a car and a salary in exchange for Arnold's training secrets. By the time he retired from bodybuilding, Arnold had taken seven Mr. Olympia titles and won the Mr. Universe competition three times. The following year—using his own name, Schwarzenegger, which means "black plowman"—he made his motion picture debut in 1976 as a bodybuilder in *Stay Hungry*. In 1983, after a series of mediocre films, he became a star as the fantasy hero in *Conan the Barbarian*. Currently, the star of such films as *The Terminator, Predator, Twins, Total Recall* and the disappointing *Last Action Hero* works out only an hour a day. In addition to acting and directing, Schwarzenegger was George Bush's chairman of the President's Council on Physical Fitness.

In 1986, Arnold married Maria Shriver, journalist and niece of JFK, they have two children. A multi-millionaire from his astute business dealings, Arnold is known for enjoying the good life.

JERRY SEINFELD

REAL NAME: Jerry Seinfeld
DATE OF BIRTH: April 29, 1957
PLACE OF BIRTH: Brooklyn, New York

EYE COLOR: Brown   HAIR COLOR: Brown
HEIGHT: 5'11"   WEIGHT: 150

After more than ten years of knocking them dead on the stand-up circuit, Jerry Seinfeld has finally hit the big time. Since 1989, he has starred in the offbeat, ultrahip show that bears his name, *Seinfeld*.

Raised in Massapequa, Long Island, with an older sister, Jerry was one of two funny men in the Seinfeld household. His father, Kalman, a sign-maker, inspired Jerry with his ability to make people laugh, and at age eight he began studying the comics on *The Ed Sullivan Show*, practicing material on friends and family and his pet parakeet. Like so many other comedians, Jerry was an introverted adolescent, but at Massapequa High School, he began to open up, entertaining himself and his classmates by wisecracking, passing funny notes and repeating jokes from *Rowan and Martin's Laugh-In*.

After graduation in 1972, Jerry enrolled in Queens College, completing his double major of theater and communications in 1976 as a dean's list student. His premiere as a stand-up came soon after at Manhattan's Catch A Rising Star. His first time on stage, Jerry was so nervous that he forgot his routine. Able to mutter only a few words: "The beach. Driving. Shopping. Parents," he walked off stage. To his surprise, the audience liked him and he continued performing, subsidizing his fledgling career by working odd jobs during the day. He sought the worst jobs possible, including selling light bulbs over the phone, so that he would force himself to succeed. He even sold costume jewelry illegally on the streets of New York and had to flee the police on several occasions.

After four years in New York, Jerry decided to try his luck in Los Angeles, auditioning for sitcoms and eventually winning a role as a joke writer on *Benson*. Showing up for a read-through of the fourth episode, he found no chair or script for him, and an assistant director finally pulled him aside and informed him that he'd been fired. Bitter from the experience, Seinfeld decided he was wasting time with television and returned to the stand-up circuit. Discovered by a talent scout for *The Tonight Show* at an L.A. comedy club, he made his first of dozens of appearances on that show. He also appeared regularly on *Late Night With David Letterman*. Over the next few years, Seinfeld toured the country, became one of the most well-known comedians around and then starred in his first solo TV special on HBO in 1987.

Taking advantage of his popularity, NBC offered him an opportunity to develop a show of his own. He and his good friend, comedian Larry David, sat down in a New York coffee shop and conceived the premise: following the life of a stand-up comic and how he comes up with the material for his routines. When it first aired in 1989 as *The Seinfeld Chronicles*, the show struggled but developed a cult following. It was added to the fall lineup in 1991 and has since become a solid hit. Despite its success, Jerry still prefers the energy and unpredictability of stand-up, and hits the stage whenever he can.

In his grooming and living habits, Jerry is meticulous, and some say he borders on obsessive/compulsive. His home is devoid of clutter, and he's always impeccably dressed in a uniform of jeans, sport shirt and athletic shoes, of which he owns several dozen pairs, including a custom set of "Air Seinfelds" from Nike. He has practiced yoga for the past twenty years and is a strict vegetarian.

TOM SELLECK

REAL NAME: Thomas William Selleck
DATE OF BIRTH: January 29, 1945
PLACE OF BIRTH: Detroit, Michigan

EYE COLOR: Brown   HAIR COLOR: Brown
HEIGHT: 6'4"   WEIGHT: 200

Although born in Detroit, Tom Selleck and his three siblings
grew up in Sherman Oaks, California, where their father was an
investment counselor. Having thrived in a secure, happy household,
Tom says, "My parents raised us by example, but I wouldn't say they
were strict. And I wasn't a totally square high school kid. I was in a
pretty crazy club called The High Hats, which had an initiation ceremony where you got the hell beaten out of you with paddles. They
used to drink at parties and kid me. But I never had any problems
getting along." Tom resisted smoking, drinking, and cursing in order
to receive the gold Rolex watch his father awarded each child at 21
who did so. An all-around athlete, Selleck excelled in high school
sports and earned a basketball scholarship to the University of
Southern California. There, in addition to hoops, he played baseball
and football. While studying for his bachelor's degree, he worked for
United Airlines as a campus representative. On the advice of his
drama teacher, he began modeling and acting in commercials.
Shortly before graduation, Tom had to choose between finishing the
year or signing a contract with 20th Century-Fox. "I decided if I
didn't try acting, I'd wonder ten years later how I would have done,"
he says, and he chose the contract.

He began with small roles in a variety of films that included *Myra
Breckenridge* (he was personally hand-picked by Mae West for this
role), *The Seven Minutes* and *Daughters of Satan*. His big break
came when he was given a recurring role on the soap opera *The
Young and The Restless*. After that he won guest spots on such TV
shows as *The Rockford Files*, then starring roles in the TV movie
Returning Home and the miniseries *The Sacketts*. It wasn't until
after a string of unsuccessful TV pilots that he landed the role of
detective Thomas Magnum on *Magnum, P.I.* in 1980. During his

eight years as Magnum, Selleck won an Emmy and a Golden Globe and became one of television's brightest stars. He was also considered one of the sexiest men in the world and awarded the title by *People* magazine in 1987. After the series was canceled, Selleck jumped into producing with the Burt Reynolds action series *B.L. Stryker*. He also revived his movie career—which had suffered through such bombs as *High Road to China, Lassiter* and *Runaway*—with the megahit *Three Men and a Baby*.

Tom was divorced in 1982, and then married dancer Jillie Mack in 1987; they have one child. Still athletic, he plays volleyball in the over-35 division for the Outrigger Canoe Club in Hawaii where, he says, "No one cares if I'm on TV. I'm off the team if I don't perform. It's nice to get away from business, and it's a neat way to get stuff out of your system." He was also the honorary captain of the 1984 and 1988 U. S. Olympic volleyball teams. Tom enjoys acting but tries to keep it in perspective with other, more meaningful aspects of life: "I don't like to get too reverent about it. I don't think we're curing cancer."

WILLIAM SHATNER

REAL NAME: William Shatner
DATE OF BIRTH: March 22, 1931
PLACE OF BIRTH: Montreal, Canada

EYE COLOR: Brown   HAIR COLOR: Brown
HEIGHT: 5'11"   WEIGHT: 165

"No actor wants to be tied to one part, but despite everything else I've ever done, it's the role they always remember... and I may as well face the fact that, for better or worse, I am Captain Kirk."

William Shatner was the only son of a well-to-do Jewish clothing manufacturer, and he remembers, "I always had the best. My parents

were not particularly well off but my father provided us with every-thing we needed." It was during his yearly visits to a French Canadian summer camp, where he eventually became a counselor, that he did his first acting in camp plays. In high school, William divided his extracurricular time between football and acting, endur-ing jeers from his fellow jocks when he went off to rehearsals. But his positive stage experiences overshadowed all else in college at McGill University, and he soon found he was spending "eighteen hours a day producing, directing and writing college musicals."

In his junior year, William informed his father that he was going into acting and would not be taking over the family business as his father had always planned. This led to much battling, but William stood his ground. After finishing college with a B.A. in 1952, he start-ed out touring with repertory companies in Shakespeare revivals. While he was doing nothing more than carrying a chair in a play on Broadway in 1956, a 20th Century-Fox scout saw something special in him and offered him a seven-year contract at $500 a week. Starving though he was, William turned him down: "I wanted to be independent, to choose my own roles. I thought there was nothing to be gained from signing and everything to lose. Mainly my youth."

So he went to New York for a try at television and theater, and stayed busy making the rounds of TV dramas such as *Playhouse 90*. He was in Hollywood for more TV work in 1957 when he was finally persuaded to sign with MGM and was cast in *The Brothers Karamazov*. Over the next ten years, William went back and forth between coasts for movies and theater. After considering and being rejected for many series, he finally settled on *Star Trek*—which debuted as *Where No Man Has Gone Before*—in 1966. The series lasted only three years, but it spawned a following that would become a new subculture with its own name: Trekkies. William attempted to wiggle out of his Captain Kirk image with films such as *The Devil's Rain* and *Dead of Night* and starred in a new series, *T.J. Hooker*, as a cop, but none of it really took. Accepting the old saying, "If you can't beat 'em, join 'em," he signed up with the rest of the TV cast and made six *Star Trek* films.

From his first marriage, William has three daughters. He married actress Marcy Lafferty in 1973. A passionate outdoorsman, he enjoys skiing, flying and canoeing, but his first love is horseback riding and horse breeding.

CHARLIE SHEEN

REAL NAME: Carlos Irwin Estevez
DATE OF BIRTH: September 3, 1966
PLACE OF BIRTH: New York, New York

EYE COLOR: Brown   HAIR COLOR: Brown
HEIGHT: 5'10"   WEIGHT: 160

Charlie Sheen grew up in Malibu, one of four children of actor Martin Sheen, hanging out with guys like his brother Emilio Estevez, Rob and Chad Lowe and Sean Penn. Together, these future stars made hundreds of Super 8 films written by, directed by and starring themselves. Charlie made his TV debut at the age of nine opposite his father in *The Execution of Private Slovik*, but for the most part, he preferred sports to acting. At Santa Monica High School, he rarely showed up for class but was a good enough pitcher to earn a baseball scholarship to the University of Kansas. Unfortunately, his hopes of playing college ball fell apart when he was

kicked off his high school team on the last day of his senior season for skipping so many school days. Another distraction was his fast-track lifestyle in Malibu, where he went through a drug phase and a few scrapes with the law. Now that baseball was gone, he found no more reason to go to school, and Charlie dropped out before graduation to give acting a try.

He soon landed a role in the forgettable film *Grizzly II: The Predator.* Although it was never released, the experience turned him on to acting, and he went on to prove himself with starring roles in several films, including the hit *Red Dawn.* Then Sheen landed the role of Charlie Taylor in *Platoon,* a part originally offered to brother Emilio. As fame came hurtling at him, he became an active member of the now defunct Hollywood Brat Pack. But he began to take acting seriously after holding his own in *Wall Street* opposite such screen veterans as Michael Douglas and his own dad, and the leading roles that started coming his way sparked an awe in him. He explains, "It's kind of a load to carry a big film at this age. But I love the pressure. I love being trusted—you know you took the risk and you accepted the challenge."

Charlie got a chance to consummate his love for baseball in the film *Eight Men Out* and starred in a western, *Young Guns,* both in 1988. He has hardly missed a year on the big screen since then and has worked with his brother Emilio and his father in *Men at Work* and *Cadence,* respectively. In 1991, as the tongue-in-cheek super-hero of *Hot Shots!,* he revealed an engaging talent for making fun of himself, and this year did it again in the Rambo parody *Hot Shots! Part Deux.* Charlie will be very busy in 1993 with parts in three movies: *The Chase, Major League II* and *The Three Musketeers.*

After an engagement to actress Kelly Preston and one child out of wedlock by another girlfriend, Charlie is settling down with actress Ginger Allen, who is making a transition from adult films to main-stream acting. He completed a stay in rehab for drugs and alcohol in 1991. Understanding the pressures of instant success and the highs and lows that are inherent to show business, Charlie is able to speak from experience when he says, "The set is a very confined, private world where you can make a ton of mistakes and if you get it right once, you've done your job. When I leave the set is when I have the problems. Suddenly, there's no script, no director, no producers. Nothing controlled. It's all real."

MARTIN SHEEN

REAL NAME: Ramon Estevez
DATE OF BIRTH: August 3, 1940
PLACE OF BIRTH: Dayton, Ohio

EYE COLOR: Gray   HAIR COLOR: Brown
HEIGHT: 5'10"   WEIGHT: 175

"People think acting is an accident. It's not. It's calculated, planned, scrutinized, rehearsed. A performer has to know what he's doing every instant, to invent and improvise and feel, to bleed a little or else there's no growth.... God, how I love to act!" So says the patriarch of one of acting's most famous families.

One of ten children, Martin Sheen was the product of a Spanish father and Irish mother, both immigrants who met in an English-language school. Born with a left arm three inches shorter than his right, he was an industrious child and by the age of nine was earning

extra money as a caddy at a local country club. All along, Martin had his sights set on becoming a professional golfer like his idol Arnold Palmer, until he spoke three lines in a high school play. Feeling that he had seen his life in a whole new perspective, he threw all his energies into acting from that day on. It paid off, because when he was eighteen, he won an amateur drama contest, and the prize was a trip to New York City. Though his father was proud of his son's award, he wasn't terribly impressed and insisted that Martin get a college education. Rather than disobey his father's wishes, Martin deliberately flunked the entrance exam and set off to New York on a bus.

Once in Manhattan, he worked as a shipping clerk at American Express and joined the Living Theater Group. With no formal acting training, he soon began appearing on the New York stage and scored his first triumph as a drug addict in the controversial play *The Connection*. It was during this period that he adopted the name Sheen from Bishop Fulton Sheen, a Catholic orator he had long admired, and took as his first name, Martin, as a tribute to casting director Robert Dale Martin, who had encouraged him during his early years in New York.

In 1961, he got married and babies started coming. With little income from acting, he supported his family with part-time jobs as a soda jerk, theater usher, busboy and messenger boy. And all the while, they were moving into cheaper and cheaper apartments. But persistence finally paid off with a Broadway debut in 1964. The play ran only eight days, but he went on to land bigger and better parts and began the transition to TV movies, usually in the role of an angry misfit or lowlife.

Pursuing his TV career, he moved to Los Angeles in 1969, and before long starred in *That Certain Summer* and was nominated for an Emmy award for his performance. In 1970, he played Lieutenant Dobbs in the hit film *Catch-22*, and has since dazzled audiences in a series of hits that includes *Badlands*, *Apocalypse Now*, *The Dead Zone* and *Wall Street*.

In addition to acting, Sheen is extremely visible in supporting political and social causes that include military aid to foreign countries and domestic aid to the homeless, and in 1989, he was appointed honorary mayor of Malibu. Still married to his first wife, he is the proud father of four children, two of whom—Charlie Sheen and Emilio Estevez—are also renowned actors.

JACLYN SMITH

REAL NAME: Jaclyn Ellen Smith
DATE OF BIRTH: October 26, 1947
PLACE OF BIRTH: Houston, Texas

EYE COLOR: Brown	HAIR COLOR: Brown
HEIGHT: 5'7"	WEIGHT: 115

With a successful career in modeling, then acting, then clothing design to her credit, Jaclyn Smith's greatest goal is to make sure that her son and daughter have the warm, satisfying memories of childhood that she holds so dear herself. "I used to run barefoot through the grass, roller-skate on the sidewalks, skip rope, play jacks," she remembers.

Jaclyn and her older brother were born in Houston, Texas, to a successful dentist father and a housewife mother. And until her beloved grandfather's death at the age of 101, he was the center of their close-knit household. Remembering her childhood as "uncomplicated, free-spirited," Jaclyn began taking ballet lessons at the age of three and attended Pershing Junior High School and Lamar High School before studying drama and psychology at Trinity University. But after a year at Trinity, she dropped out and moved to New York City to study ballet, first with George Balanchine and then with Patsy Swayze, Patrick Swayze's mother, along with classmates Tommy Tune and Lisa Hartman.

It was while dancing in a Central Park production that she was spotted by a modeling agent and quickly became a highly paid print and TV model. Making commercials for such big-gun companies as Breck, Wella Balsam and Max Factor brought her to the attention of Hollywood, and in 1968, she landed a small role in TV's *The Adventurers*. In 1976 she became Kelly Garrett, one of the original three angels on *Charlie's Angels*, and kept the role through 1981. That successful run, although pure fluff, brought her bankability in television. Since then, she has gradually assumed the title of queen of TV movies and miniseries with *The Users*, *Rage of Angels*, *Jacqueline Bouvier Kennedy* and *Florence Nightingale*, among numerous others. Having found her niche artistically, Jaclyn has rejected many big-screen offers: "I have been offered Hollywood parts, but they were as an armpiece or a decoration. Or there was nudity. And they were just not as good as the parts I get in television. I'm happy in TV. It's a wonderful medium, and I started there."

In 1990, Jaclyn was divorced from her third husband, with whom she had two children. She keeps her model's figure in shape by exercising six days a week, stretching and practicing yoga.

WESLEY SNIPES

REAL NAME: Wesley Snipes
DATE OF BIRTH: July 31, 1963
PLACE OF BIRTH: Orlando, Florida

EYE COLOR: Brown   HAIR COLOR: Black
HEIGHT: 6'   WEIGHT: 170

"I'm just thankful that I realized this is what I'm supposed to be doing," says Wesley Snipes of his occupation. He loves acting and appreciates the luck that enables him to make money doing something that comes so easily to him.

Although Wesley was born in Orlando, he grew up in the Bronx, New York. Wesley never lived with his father, who had moved to South Carolina with four of Wesley's six brothers and sisters after a divorce. After taking singing, dancing and acting lessons throughout his youth, he began studying in earnest upon enrolling in New York's High School of the Performing Arts. Before he could finish there, his mother moved the family back to Florida, and for a time she washed windows at Disney World to support the family. After finishing high school in Miami, he began touring with a local troupe called Struttin' Street Stuff, which performed street and puppet theater. To pursue his emerging dream of becoming an actor, he returned to New York and the State University at Purchase to study drama, and earned a B.F.A. degree in theater arts. While there, he also began to develop a political consciousness; he fell under the spell of Malcolm X in 1980 after seeing a documentary on the civil rights leader.

After graduation, he installed telephones to earn a living while he took more acting classes and pursued stage roles, including Puck in *A Midsummer Night's Dream*, and eventually made it to Broadway in *Execution of Justice*, in which he played drag queen Sister Boom-Boom. He made his film debut in *Wildcats*, then went on to win parts in *Streets of Gold* and *Major League*, and in Michael Jackson's extended video "Bad." In 1989, he won an ACE award for best actor in HBO's *Vietnam War Story*, then garnered enormous critical praise for his portrayal of the ruthless drug mogul in *New Jack City* in 1991. Since then, he's become one of the hottest actors in Hollywood

and put his starpower to work in a couple of controversial films: *Jungle Fever*, dealing with interracial dating, and *Rising Sun* with Sean Connery, about relations between the United States and Japan.

Since his youth, Wesley has studied martial arts, especially the African/Brazilian version called Capoeira. He believes this training has given him great discipline in every facet of his life, including acting. He has the ability to stop a conversation to begin a scene, then return to the conversation as if there was no pause, then pour himself back into the scene he'd been working on. "I enjoy being in unpredictable and strange situations and not knowing how the hell I'm going to get out of them," he confides. "I suspect acting is really a minor form of schizophrenia." His discipline and natural athleticism extend to his role preparation as well. He trained as a boxer for *Streets of Gold*, mastered the saxophone for *Mo' Better Blues*, learned to operate a wheelchair for his role as a paraplegic in *The Waterdance*, used his martial arts skills in *Passenger 57*, *Rising Sun* and the upcoming *Demolition Man* with Sylvester Stallone, and, although he hadn't picked up a basketball since he was fifteen, he looked like a pro in *White Men Can't Jump*.

Now single, Wesley has a son from a previous marriage.

SISSY SPACEK

REAL NAME: Mary Elizabeth Spacek
DATE OF BIRTH: December 25, 1949
PLACE OF BIRTH: Quitman, Texas

EYE COLOR: Blue   HAIR COLOR: Blond
HEIGHT: 5'2"   WEIGHT: 95

Although her real name is Mary Elizabeth, her two older brothers affectionately tagged her Sissy, and the nickname stuck. Growing up in a tiny town northeast of Dallas, where her father was a county agent for the Department of Agriculture, Sissy was an avid horsewoman as well as the winner of the Fiesta Dogwood Pageant. A cheerleader at Quitman High School, she kept her social calendar full by working on the school paper, serving as fire marshal and participating in the local 4-H club. In her early teens, she bought a guitar through the Sears Roebuck catalog and learned to play it well enough to give lessons to other kids for 50 cents an hour. Sissy had been accepted by the University of Texas in her senior year of high school and was heading in that direction until Robbie, one of her brothers, was diagnosed with leukemia. Rather than have Sissy witness his slow demise, her parents sent her to spend the summer with a cousin, actor Rip Torn, in New York.

Living in Greenwich Village with Rip and his wife, actress Geraldine Page, Sissy was thrown into a world of actors, singers and artists, and she fell in love with it. Deciding that she wanted to become a singer, she made the rounds of clubs and agents and was booked on Johnny Carson's *Tonight Show*, but stage fright got the best of her, and she canceled three appearances in a row. Returning to Quitman and her brother's death, Sissy says she gained a new perspective on life and saw that "there isn't all the time you thought there was supposed to be." After studying at the University of Texas for two years, she went back to New York with a new determination and supported herself by singing background vocals for commercials, performing in bistros and working in a boutique. Under her new name of Rainbo, she cut a record about John Lennon and Yoko Ono, but when it didn't sell, she gave up singing and switched to acting.

In her 1972 film debut, *Prime Cut*, as a teenager trying to escape from white slavers, she earned generally good reviews, and soon afterward moved to California. After appearing in the film *Badlands*, she made guest appearances on television before rising to stardom as the telekinetic teenager in Brian De Palma's 1976 chiller, *Carrie*. She has long since outgrown disturbed-teen roles and distinguished herself in a string of dramatic roles in films such as *Three Women*, *Raggedy Man* and *The Long Walk Home*. She was seen most recently as Liz Garrison in Oliver Stone's controversial *JFK*. During an acting career that spans 30 years, she has been nominated for five Oscars and won as best actress in *Coal Miner's Daughter*.

Sissy married art director Jack Fisk (who directed her in *Raggedy Man*) in 1974. Between films, they take their children back to Quitman for reality checks, where Sissy still enjoys riding horses. She also jogs and enjoys working in her garden at their home in Virginia. Knowing the value of roots, Sissy explains, "Texas is the place that keeps me most grounded. When I get real nuts, I can go back there and walk in the woods and swim and water ski and go riding. It's a little cocoon. It's great."

STEVEN SPIELBERG

REAL NAME: Steven Spielberg
DATE OF BIRTH: December 18, 1947
PLACE OF BIRTH: Cincinnati, Ohio

EYE COLOR: Brown	HAIR COLOR: Brown
HEIGHT: 5'10"	WEIGHT: 175

"Making movies is an illusion, a technical illusion that people fall for. My job is to take that technique and hide it so well that never once are you taken out of your chair and reminded of where you are," says Steven Spielberg. As the director of some of the most successful movies of all time, including *Jaws*, *E.T.*, *Close Encounters of The Third Kind*, *Raiders of the Lost Ark* and *Jurassic Park*, he must be one of the champion illusionists of all time.

Steven had a nomadic childhood following his electrical engineer father around the country from job to job. From nine to sixteen, though, he lived in Phoenix, Arizona, a shy child who preferred the solitary confines of his bedroom, venturing outside only for Little League baseball or scouting. Fearing that their son might be frightened by television, his parents forbade Steven to watch anything on the tube but the most innocuous shows, and they kept an eye on what movies he got to see as well. But when the family went on vacations, Steven served as the family photographer, and he soon graduated to making short 8 mm and 16 mm films using family and friends as actors and developing elaborate sets and scripts, usually horror stories. Sometimes the only cast available were his three sisters, and Steven has joked, "I killed them all several times."

Throughout high school, his interest in film grew to be so all-consuming that he had no interest in studies and financed his hobby with a part-time job. He also caught his father's passion for astronomy and made himself a reflecting telescope at which he would spend hours each night. It became the subject of his first feature-length movie, a science-fiction film entitled *Firelight*; at sixteen years old, he actually persuaded a Phoenix movie house to show it. Soon afterward, the Spielbergs moved to San Jose, California, where his parents divorced and Steven finished high school. Rejected by all of the

major film schools after graduation, he ended up studying English at Cal State Long Beach. And while he was in school, he made a habit of driving up to Los Angeles and sneaking into the major studios, where he took in all he could before being kicked off the lot.

He gained entree into the entertainment business when his short film, *Amblin'*, was paired with *Love Story* for national exhibition and Universal Studios liked him enough to sign him to a seven-year contract. The studio started him out directing episodes of such TV shows as *Night Gallery*, *Columbo* and *Owen Marshall* and, in 1971, gave him his first film, a made-for-TV movie called *Duel*. Several more TV movies followed, and then came Spielberg's first feature, *The Sugarland Express*. It was a box office yawner, but the producers admired his work and signed him to direct the film adaptation of a bestseller by Peter Benchley called *Jaws*. Although Spielberg brought the film in over budget, it became a monster hit and made him, at 27, the most sought-after director around. After serious work in *The Color Purple*, *Empire of the Sun* and his latest, *Schindler's List*, he still is.

Steven has a son by his former wife, actress Amy Irving, and he and present wife, actress Kate Capshaw, have two children.

SYLVESTER STALLONE

REAL NAME: Sylvester Gardenzio Stallone
DATE OF BIRTH: July 6, 1946
PLACE OF BIRTH: New York, New York

EYE COLOR: Brown   HAIR COLOR: Brown
HEIGHT: 5'10"   WEIGHT: 175

Like his alter ego, Rocky Balboa, Sylvester Stallone has gone from rags to riches, fought the good fight and come out on top.

Sly was born in the Hell's Kitchen section of Manhattan, the son of a chorus girl mom and an Italian immigrant dad studying to be a hairdresser. When he was born, the forceps that pulled him from the womb also severed a nerve in his face and partially paralyzed his lip, chin and half of his tongue. While his parents struggled to scratch out a living, Sylvester lived in a foster home until the age of five, and though he was later reunited with his parents and younger brother, it was a troubled household. He was constantly running away because of the constant arguments between his parents and says, "I was not an attractive child. I was sickly and even had rickets. My personality was abhorrent to other children, so I enjoyed my own company and did a lot of fantasizing."

Never the best student, Stallone got into quite a bit of trouble and was kicked out of a host of schools. Even his name, Sylvester, with its cartoon associations, got him into fights, and in the interest of self-preservation, he turned to weightlifting. At age ten, his parents divorced, and he moved to Philadelphia with his brother and their mother and new stepdad. While attending Devereaux High School, a school for students with behavior problems, he played football, fenced and threw the discus. He also found satisfaction by acting in school plays. After graduation, he landed a work scholarship to the American College of Switzerland, and it was there, while he served as a girls' athletic coach, that he played the part of Biff in a school production of *Death of a Salesman*.

Returning to the United States, Stallone went on to study drama at the University of Miami but dropped out before earning his degree. In 1969, determined to become an actor, he moved to New York.

Working a variety of odd jobs that included sweeping out the lion's cages at the Central Park Zoo, he made the rounds of auditions and eventually began landing roles in off-Broadway plays like *Rain* and *Score*. To make ends meet, he even appeared in a couple of soft-porn flicks, *Party at Kitty's* and *Studs*.

The turning point came in 1974, after selling several script treatments, when he and his wife moved to Los Angeles. The idea for *Rocky*, the film that would make his career, was inspired by a prizefight he saw in which an unknown named Chuck Wepner went fifteen rounds before being knocked out by Muhammad Ali. Although he himself was an unknown with no clout in the entertainment industry and desperately needed the money, Stallone turned down huge offers for the script until he was given the right to direct and star in the picture himself. It went on to make $250 million, earn ten Oscar nominations and win the Academy Award for best picture of the year. Stallone followed it up with four more *Rocky* movies, three *Rambo* flicks and a host of other less commercially successful films, including a couple of misbegotten comedies—that threatened to eclipse his career. But his latest release, *Cliffhanger*, has soared into a megahit that helped to re-establish him, at the advanced age of 47, as an action-adventure superstar. Sylvester's next project will be *Fair Game*. His paintings have been featured in prominent galleries.

Sly hasn't been so lucky in love. His marriage to his first wife, Sasha, by whom he has two sons, ended in 1985. Then he married Brigitte Nielsen, only to divorce three years later in tabloid hell.

SHARON STONE

REAL NAME: Sharon Stone
DATE OF BIRTH: March 10, 1958
PLACE OF BIRTH: Meadville, Pennsylvania

EYE COLOR: Green	HAIR COLOR: Blond
HEIGHT: 5'5"	WEIGHT: 108

"Masculine men are an endangered species. We've endangered them not by experiencing our equality as women but by trying to be like men. It's an enormous mistake." This could be Sharon Stone's basic analysis of why she has surfaced as the long-awaited sex symbol who could fill Marilyn Monroe's sheets.

The daughter of a tool-and-die manufacturer, Sharon started out as a beauty pageant contestant. While breezing through school and skipping grades with a 154 IQ, she entered and won many contests as a young girl. At fifteen she was taking college courses and at seventeen competed in the Miss Pennsylvania Pageant. Sharon had begun doing some acting during high school and enjoyed it enough to enroll in the theater department at Edinboro State University. When she was nineteen, she persuaded her mother to go with her to New York City to see if she could get work as a model. She ended up meeting Eileen Ford and within the week was being sent out on jobs. As one of Ford's most popular models, Sharon spent several years traveling the world on photo shoots for such magazines as *Elle* and *Vogue*.

Determined to move on to acting, she took drama lessons with a variety of coaches and began auditioning for roles. Her big break came in 1980 when Woody Allen picked her out of a line of extras for a bit part in his film *Stardust Memories*. From there, Stone went on to star in almost twenty B-movies such as *Deadly Blessing*, *Action Jackson* and *Allan Quartermain and the Lost City of Gold*. But it wasn't until after almost a decade of work that people began to notice her when she appeared as Arnold Schwarzenegger's combative wife, Lori, in the 1990 film *Total Recall*. Asked what it was like to drop-kick Arnold, Sharon responded, "It was great. I get a wonderful response from women. They tell their boyfriends, 'I'm gonna do that to you.' Let's be honest, we're all pissed about something." Within

days of wrapping that film, Sharon posed for a *Playboy* layout, but that was prudish compared to her portrayal of a bisexual ice-pick murderer in the 1992 hit *Basic Instinct*. The originality with which she "exposed" herself in that film has put her in a white-hot spotlight. The filming and release of 1993's *Sliver*, another graphic sex flick, was a banquet for critics and the press. Sharon's next film will be *The Quick and the Dead*.

Sharon's love life is, of course, under a magnifying glass: Who she dates and who she dumps makes headlines. She's been married twice, to TV director George Englund and TV producer Michael Greenburg, and is engaged to Bill MacDonald, the executive producer of *Sliver*. No date has been set, but it will probably be announced once Bill is divorced from his current wife.

MERYL STREEP

REAL NAME: Mary Louise Streep
DATE OF BIRTH: June 22, 1949
PLACE OF BIRTH: Summit, New Jersey

EYE COLOR: Brown   HAIR COLOR: Blond
HEIGHT: 5'6"   WEIGHT: 110

By her own admission, Meryl Streep was not a glamorous child. The only daughter of three children born to her mother, an artist, and her father, a pharmaceutical company executive, she was "pretty ghastly," according to one brother. Outside the home, she tyrannized

the neighborhood kids, and as if that wasn't bad enough, she claims, "With my glasses and permanented hair, I looked like a mini-adult. I had the same face I have today, and the effect wasn't cute or endearing." She did have a wonderful singing voice, however, and when she was twelve, she began taking lessons with New York vocal coach Estelle Liebling, who had also taught opera diva Beverly Sills. During high school, determined to become "the perfect *Seventeen* magazine knockout," she bleached her hair blond, got rid of her glasses and braces and blossomed into a cheerleader, swimming star and homecoming queen. She also appeared in campus theater productions and after graduation enrolled at Vassar to study drama. There, she found relief from the social structure of her hometown: "I remember feeling: I can have a thought. I can do anything, because everything is allowed."

During her sophomore year, Meryl also studied costume design and playwriting in an honors program at Dartmouth University. Looking for "an edge," as she has said, she went on to earn her M.F.A. at the Yale School of Drama while making money waitressing. Feeling she was finally properly prepared to present herself to the acting community, she moved to New York and made her debut as the ingenue lead in a Lincoln Center production of *Trelawny of the Wells*. In her first eighteen months in New York, she appeared in a total of eight plays, including a Tony-nominated appearance as Flora in *27 Wagons Full of Cotton*.

In 1977, she made her motion picture debut in *Julia* and promptly followed it in 1978 with an Oscar-nominated portrayal of a lonely wife in *The Deer Hunter*. Since then, she added to her laurels in films such as *The French Lieutenant's Woman, Silkwood* and *Out of Africa*. Unquestionably the most critically acclaimed actress of her generation, she can change the cadence of her speech, convincingly pull off any foreign accent, and alter her physical appearance for any given role. Nominated for eight Academy Awards, she has won Oscars for her performances in both *Kramer vs. Kramer* and *Sophie's Choice*. She continued to broaden her range when she starred—and sang—in the comedy *Postcards From the Edge*. Meryl's latest film is *The River Wild*.

Meryl has been married since 1978 to sculptor Don Gummer, and they have three children. They make their home primarily on a large estate in Connecticut.

BARBRA STREISAND

REAL NAME: Barbara Joan Streisand
DATE OF BIRTH: April 24, 1942
PLACE OF BIRTH: Brooklyn, New York

EYE COLOR: Blue   HAIR COLOR: Brown
HEIGHT: 5'4 1/2"   WEIGHT: 125

When she was fifteen months old, Barbra Streisand's father, an English teacher, died, and she and her brother and sister were raised by their mother in the poor Williamsburg section of Brooklyn. Barbra likes to say, "We weren't poor poor, but we didn't have anything." At four years old, Barbra informed everyone that she planned to become a famous actress, but throughout her school days, she was neither outgoing nor popular. Then, when she was fourteen, she found herself a summer job working in a theater. In every spare minute, she was either watching a movie or television or reading fan magazines, reinforcing her determination to become a star. After graduation from Erasmus High School at fifteen—two years early with a grade average of 93—Streisand left home on her own and moved to Manhattan to become an actress.

While sleeping on a cot in a friend's office, she made the rounds of casting agents, worked temp jobs and began singing in gay bars and nightclubs. Refusing the pleas of agents to change her name, fix her nose and conform, she made one concession and dropped the "a" from Barbara. Her singing career was launched by accident one night when she entered a talent contest as a singer in a Greenwich Village bar. Barbra had never sung in front of an audience before, and to her amazement, she won. The prize was a regular singing job at another bar that paid $108 a week.

Confidence soaring, she took advantage of every minute at the microphone and started ad-libbing and joking. That exposure got her onto TV shows and a shot at Broadway in 1961 when she made her stage debut in the musical revue *Another Evening With Harry Stoones*. The engagement lasted only one night, but it was long

enough to catch the eye of producer David Merrick, who signed her for a part on Broadway in *I Can Get It for You Wholesale*. Three years later, she scored a resounding hit in the title role in *Funny Girl*. After her Oscar-winning film debut in the motion picture version of *Funny Girl*, Streisand rose to stardom in a string of popular films: *The Owl and the Pussycat, What's Up, Doc?, The Way We Were, Funny Lady* and *A Star Is Born* for which she received a best song Oscar for "Evergreen." She expanded her talents to writing, directing and producing in *Yentl* and the recent *The Prince of Tides*. But even her impressive screen credits are surpassed by the sales from her Grammy-winning albums, many of them soundtracks to her movies.

Until 1971, Barbra was married to actor Elliott Gould; their teenage son, Jason, played Barbra's son in *The Prince of Tides*. Later during the '70s, she had a lengthy relationship with hair dresser-turned-super-producer Jon Peters.

DONALD SUTHERLAND

REAL NAME: Donald McNichol Sutherland
DATE OF BIRTH: July 17, 1935
PLACE OF BIRTH: St. John, New Brunswick, Canada

EYE COLOR: Blue   HAIR COLOR: Blond
HEIGHT: 6'2"   WEIGHT: 185

The man whose boyhood hobby was making puppets considers himself the ultimate puppet of directors. Explaining his acting methodology, Donald Sutherland says, "In movies it's not my charac-

ter I'm creating. It's the character in the director's head. My job is to figure out what he wants and give it to him."

Donald lived on a farm until the age of ten, when he moved to Bridgewater, Nova Scotia, with his salesman father and math teacher mother. A sickly child, he didn't participate in sports, and when he outgrew puppet-making, he became interested in sculpting and radio broadcasting. Entering junior high school at fourteen, he was featured as a disc jockey on his own radio program. After graduation, he entered the University of Toronto as an engineering major, but quickly switched to English, acting in local theater and spending two summers acting professionally with the Straw Hat Theater in Ontario. He took his English degree in 1956 and, convinced that his future lay with acting, moved to England to study at the London Academy of Music and Dramatic Arts.

Soon he began to appear on the London stage and on British television. In 1964, he made his film debut in the dual role of a soldier and a witch in the Italian horror film *The Castle of the Living Dead.* More horror films followed before he made his American debut in the successful war film *The Dirty Dozen* in 1967. For the next three years, he honed his talent with co-starring roles on television and in movies before becoming a household name as Hawkeye Pierce in the movie version of *M*A*S*H.* While he played that character with "a dry martini bite," as one critic described, his own political views were perfectly in synch with Hawkeye's. Outspokenly against the Vietnam War, he joined forces with another visible activist, Jane Fonda, and performed politically satirical programs for servicemen. In one of his many antiwar statements, Sutherland said, "We must understand that war is finished. War is like capital punishment."

Considered to be either a director's dream or a director's nightmare, Donald never gives a half-way performance. Of his more than 50 films, the more memorable ones include *Klute, The Day of the Locust, The Eagle Has Landed, Ordinary People, Eye of the Needle, A Dry White Season* and the controversial *JFK.*

Donald's son, actor Kiefer Sutherland, is from his second wife, whom he long ago divorced. He has been living with French Canadian actress, Francine Racette, since 1974, and they have two sons. He enjoys working more than idling but will take time to watch a baseball game or go sailing and rarely neglects his daily jogging.

KIEFER SUTHERLAND

REAL NAME: Kiefer William Frederick Dempsey George Rufus
Sutherland
DATE OF BIRTH: December 18, 1966
PLACE OF BIRTH: Los Angeles, California

EYE COLOR: Blue   HAIR COLOR: Blond
HEIGHT: 5'10"   WEIGHT: 155

Belying his Brat Pack image and helter-skelter bachelorhood, Kiefer Sutherland explains himself: "I try to maintain an equilibrium in my life. Balance is the key to almost everything—a good performance, a good film, a good life. It's the middle of the road I find complex."

The son of actor Donald Sutherland, Kiefer is one of his generation's most promising young actors. During his short yet successful career, he has distinguished himself as both hero and villain in a string of films that includes *Stand by Me*, *Bright Lights*, *Big City* and *Flatliners*.

Kiefer comes from a political family. His father was an antiwar activist, his grandfather, T.C. Douglas, was the Socialist premier of Saskatchewan from 1944 to 1961, and his mother, actress Shirley Douglas, was blacklisted in the United States because of her left-wing politics and for a time was unable to work in television or in films. Kiefer's parents divorced when he was four, and he spent his early years with his mother in Beverly Hills. In 1975, at the age of nine, he made his starring theatrical debut in an Odyssey Theater production of *Throne of Straw*. Soon afterward, he moved with his mother to Toronto, where he attended theater workshops and appeared in local productions. When he was fifteen, Sutherland quit school, got an apartment, landed a job at a restaurant and set out to forge an acting career for himself. "No one would take me seriously," he recalls. "I was only lucky to run into a drummer I once knew who let me stay at his place until I could find acting roles."

In 1984, he made his film debut in the Canadian film *The Bay*

Boy, for which he won a Genie award. Two years later, he moved to New York, and although he was immediately offered a role on a soap opera, Kiefer turned it down and spent the next year basically unemployed. Moving to Los Angeles, he lived on the beach and soon began making it in films and TV movies. In 1986, he scored big as a bad guy in *Stand by Me*. The next year, he scored again as the leader of a coven of teenage vampires in *The Lost Boys*. His resume ever since is full of complex parts in well-reviewed movies such as *Bright Lights, Big City*, *Young Guns*, *Young Guns II* and *Flashback*. He will add *The Three Musketeers* to his credits when it is completed in 1993.

For a while, in 1991, Kiefer was the most envied guy in America while he was living with and engaged to Julia Roberts. However, the romance ended when an extracurricular girlfriend, a stripper, made her presence known. Kiefer now devotes much of his free time bonding with his daughter from a previous marriage to actress Camelia Kath, which ended in 1988.

PATRICK SWAYZE

REAL NAME: Patrick Swayze
DATE OF BIRTH: August 18, 1954
PLACE OF BIRTH: Houston, Texas

EYE COLOR: Blue HAIR COLOR: Brown
HEIGHT: 5'10" WEIGHT: 170

"I want to be Gene Kelly, Errol Flynn, Spencer Tracy, Robert De Niro, Dustin Hoffman, John Gielgud and Katharine Hepburn all rolled into one." That's Patrick Swayze's goal.

The third son of four children of *Urban Cowboy* choreographer Patsy Swayze, Patrick grew up dividing his time between sports and dancing lessons at his mother's studio. His Irish father, a design engineer, held down most of the domestic duties at home. From age three, he was a permanent student in his mother's studio and looked up to her as his icon of success. "On a certain level, I always did feel I had to compete for my mother's love with all of her students and company members. My mother's a very intense lady. On certain levels, I felt ripped apart as a kid. I wanted to please my mother because she was so good at everything, and I wanted to be like her," Patrick says.

Often teased by the other kids about his dancing, Swayze spent a lot of time fighting in order to convince his peers that he wasn't a wimp. In addition to his morning paper route, he took up football, track and gymnastics during high school and was so proficient at the latter that he was given a scholarship to San Jacinto College in Pasadena, Texas. But with dancing in his blood, he dropped out to tour for a year with Disney on Parade as an ice skater and then moved to New York to dance. First came a stint with the Buffalo Ballet Company, then the Harkness Ballet Company and the Joffrey.

His dancing career hit its peak when he danced as a featured performer with the Eliot Feld Dance Company. When an old knee injury, suffered during his high school football days, began acting up, Swayze hung up his dance shoes and turned to acting.

His big break came in 1978 when he spent eight months on Broadway as Danny Zuko in the musical *Grease*. The next year, he made his movie debut in *Skatetown U.S.A.* His credits since then include *The Outsiders, Youngblood,* his star-making role in *Dirty Dancing, Road House,* the blockbuster romantic hit *Ghost,* and the ambitious but unsuccessful *City of Joy.*

Patrick met his wife, dancer Lisa Niemi, when she was fifteen and a student at his mother's studio. For both, it was love at first sight, and they married in 1975.

JESSICA TANDY

REAL NAME: Jessica Tandy
DATE OF BIRTH: June 7, 1909
PLACE OF BIRTH: London, England

EYE COLOR: Blue HAIR COLOR: Silver
HEIGHT: 5'4" WEIGHT: 110

Every year, Jessica Tandy seems to top herself, astounding critics and audiences with the power of her work. The range and number of her roles alone—around 160 on stage, screen and television—stand as a monument to her talent.

For Jessica, the road to international stardom was not smooth. Her father died when she was twelve, leaving her and two brothers to be raised by their mother, who taught night school to supplement her salary as a headmistress in a school for retarded children. Deprived though they were, Mrs. Tandy knew the value of culture, exposing her children to museums, plays and literature, and they responded by staging plays for her at home. At the age of fifteen, Jessica announced her intention to become an actress, and began tutoring sessions with a drama coach on weekends, then studying Shakespeare before entering the Ben Greet Academy of Acting.

Three years later, Jessica debuted in a small theater in *The Manderson Girls*. From her salary of two pounds a week, she was expected to provide her five costume changes—elaborate period gowns that she couldn't afford, so she sewed them herself. For the next ten years, Jessica performed practically nonstop, with Shakespeare as her forte. During that time, she married a fellow actor and had a daughter, but they broke up around the time of World War II and she emigrated to the United States. Arriving in New York in 1940 with ten pounds and a six-year-old to support, she found little work. Having gone through her nest egg with no job in sight, Jessica remembers being on the edge of quitting: "It mattered terribly that I should make a living, and I couldn't. I got to that stage where I felt I'd made it all up, I never could act, I didn't act well, I'd lost it."

Fortunately, she had fallen in love with another actor, Hume Cronyn, and they moved to Hollywood. Under a five-year contract with 20th Century-Fox, Jessica was introduced to the world of film. But it was her performance on stage with Marlon Brando in *A Streetcar Named Desire* that brought her the critical notices that led to the meatier screen roles she longed for. Besides her best actress Oscar-winning role in *Driving Miss Daisy* in 1989, her other, more memorable film credits over the past five decades have ranged from *Forever Amber* and *September Affair*, to *The World According to Garp*, *Cocoon* and *Fried Green Tomatoes*.

She and Hume, married since 1942 with three children, have acted on stage and screen together almost twenty times, and many stand in awe of the strength of their marriage. Jessica says, "The reason we can live and work together is that in no way do we threaten each other. We're safe: I can't play him, and he can't play me. That's basic."

ELIZABETH TAYLOR

REAL NAME: Elizabeth Rosemond Taylor
DATE OF BIRTH: February 27, 1932
PLACE OF BIRTH: London, England

EYE COLOR: Violet	HAIR COLOR: Black
HEIGHT: 5'6"	WEIGHT: 135

In her 60 years, Elizabeth Taylor has experienced enough notoriety and tragedy to fill five lifetimes.

Elizabeth's American father was running an art business in London when she was born. Her American mother had been a stage actress before marriage, and Elizabeth also has an older brother. Until she was seven, Elizabeth went to a private school, took dance lessons beginning at age three, and went riding on her own pony at her godfather's estate in England. When World War II began, the Taylor family relocated in Beverly Hills, where Elizabeth's astounding beauty caught the attention of movie producers. In 1941, she signed a contract with Universal and played a small part the next year in *There's One Born Every Minute*. While attending the MGM school, she appeared in several more small roles and graduated from University High School. It was her experience as an equestrienne that made her so desirable for the lead in *National Velvet*, but at twelve, she was still too small for the character, so she put herself on a four-month diet and exercise regimen to increase her size. The resulting extra three inches—and her magnetic performance—elevated her to top billing.

Elizabeth got her first stage kiss in her first adult role in 1947 in *Cynthia*, and her career started snowballing. She recalls that the first film that required her to reach inside and pull out some real acting was 1951's *A Place in the Sun*. At this point, Elizabeth was considered the jewel of Hollywood and turning out a film a year, including *Cat on a Hot Tin Roof*, along with such epics as *Giant* and *Raintree County*. In 1958, after two divorces, Elizabeth's partnership with pain took hold: Her third husband, producer Michael Todd, was killed in a plane crash. The next year, she landed in the hospital at death's door with pneumonia. Shortly after her recovery, she won an

Oscar for her role in *Butterfield 8*. The scandals in her life began in 1963 with the film *Cleopatra*. The huge budget of this extravaganza, along with her $1 million salary, the highest that had ever been paid an actor, was big enough news. But Elizabeth was married to singer Eddie Fisher, and her flagrant affair with co-star Richard Burton shocked Americans. Splitting up with Fisher, she married Burton and they shared stage and screen together many times. Their better remembered films are *Who's Afraid of Virginia Woolf?* and *The Taming of the Shrew*. In a surprising change of roles, Elizabeth will be featured in the film version of the cartoon classic *The Flintstones*.

Her first battle with pneumonia left Elizabeth a frail woman, and she has never regained a strong constitution. After several more bouts of pneumonia, she suffered a back injury and became addicted to painkillers. Along with many years of drinking, they sent her to the Betty Ford clinic twice.

Elizabeth is the only actress to top Zsa Zsa Gabor's matrimonial record. In 1992, when she married Larry Fortensky, whom she met on her second visit to Betty Ford, she hit the nine mark (although she did marry Richard Burton twice). But this mother of four children and many grandchildren claims to be an eternal romantic: "I think I ended up being the scarlet woman partly because of my rather puritanical upbringing and beliefs.... I always chose to think I was in love and that love was synonymous with marriage. I couldn't just have a romance; it had to be marriage."

JOHN TESH

REAL NAME: John Tesh
DATE OF BIRTH: July 9, 1952
PLACE OF BIRTH: Garden City, New York

EYE COLOR: Blue   HAIR COLOR: Blond
HEIGHT: 6'6"   WEIGHT: 210

He may be the successful co-anchor of America's most popular
entertainment news program, but it's a mere second fiddle to his
career as a music composer.

John Tesh is one of three children born to a nurse mother and a
chemist father who also played the violin. He assimilated his father's
love for music. From early childhood, John was experimenting with
electronic variations on sound and music. "When I went to clean his
room," his mother recalls, "I thought I was going to hang myself
with all the electrical wires in there." In high school, John was proficient in piano, electric organ, trumpet and trombone, and while
majoring in music and communications at North Carolina State
University, he doubled as a disk jockey on the college radio station.
The resonance of his voice impressed the manager of a local Durham
TV station, and he was recruited to be the weekend news anchor.
When the opportunity arose to assume the plum weekday spot, John
quit college and began a broadcasting career.

Promotions took him to stations in Orlando and Nashville and
culminated at CBS Sports in New York. With music still in the fore-
front of his consciousness, John got permission to score the theme
song for the 1985 Tour de France bicycle race while covering it as
sportscaster. Just as his music career was jump-starting, along came
Entertainment Tonight in 1986 with an offer to become the new co-
anchor. The chemistry between he and Mary Hart seemed to be the
ticket to pull up *ET*'s ratings, because it's still going as strong as ever.

Meanwhile, John has used his *Entertainment Tonight* earnings to
install a $1 million music and recording studio in his home. After

turning in his four hours a day at *ET*, John works into the night composing music. In addition to five albums already in stores, he has scored numerous theme songs for TV series, NBC sports events, his own *ET* program, the 1992 Olympic Games and six Tour de France races. "I try and use the word 'powerful' when describing my style of music," says John. "I can only write aggressively. Even my ballads use kettle drums and lots of heavy strings and timpani rolls. The way I hear music is really the way I live my life, which is like being plugged into 240 volts."

Divorced in 1991, John married actress Connie Sellecca in 1992 and is adapting to his newest career role as stepfather to her son from a previous marriage. His fourth album includes a song he wrote for and named after his wife: "Concetta," which is Italian for Connie.

EMMA THOMPSON

REAL NAME: Emma Thompson
DATE OF BIRTH: April 15, 1959
PLACE OF BIRTH: London, England

EYE COLOR: Blue   HAIR COLOR: Chestnut
HEIGHT: 5'4"   WEIGHT: 110

An elegant, talented lady who won an Oscar without having to disrobe, Emma Thompson says, "There is a problem at this moment with women and their sexuality being demonized. I don't think there are many women out there thinking, "Hey, I really want to be made to look stupid and take off all my clothes in a film."

She was born into an acting family: Both parents were Shakespearean actors, her father was a director, and her sister, Sophie, is an actress who has appeared with her on British television. After graduation from the Camden School for girls, she was studying English literature at Newnham College in Cambridge when her father had a stroke, and Emma took time off from her studies to nurse him back to health so he could speak again. When he died five years later, she joined a troupe called Cambridge Footlights, the home of John Cleese and Eric Idle of *Monty Python* fame.

After college, Emma made stabs at television and stage, some successful, some not. But then she got her break on a BBC mini-series and found success and love on the same set. She met the "young lion," as she calls him: Irish actor Kenneth Branagh. Since their marriage in 1989, they have built their careers in tandem with appearances together on stage and in film projects that have included his own productions of *Dead Again*, *Peter's Friends* and their most recent triumph, *Much Ado About Nothing*. Emma's solo appearances on the screen have brought her accolades as well. Her radiant performance in *Howards End* won her a 1993 Oscar for best actress, and she completed another film with her *Howards End* co-

star Anthony Hopkins, called *The Remains of the Day,* shortly thereafter. Her next release will be *In the Name of the Father.*

As with many couples who work together and stay married,
Emma has found the one ingredient that seems to make it stick: "I've
been earthed. One of the most attractive male qualities is the capaci-
ty to earth a volatile woman. With Ken and me it's symbiosis.
Together you're stronger, one and one make three."

JOHN TRAVOLTA

REAL NAME: John Joseph Travolta
DATE OF BIRTH: February 18, 1954
PLACE OF BIRTH: Englewood, New Jersey

EYE COLOR: Blue   HAIR COLOR: Brown
HEIGHT: 6'   WEIGHT: 170

"At once mean-looking and pretty, he conveys the kind of threatening sexuality that floors an audience," wrote critic Frank Rich in *Time* after watching John Travolta in *Saturday Night Fever*.

The youngest of six children of drama coach Helen Travolta and a former semiprofessional football player who owned a tire store, John started out early as a performer, taking tap lessons when he was three years old. He would entertain the Travolta brood with his song-and-dance renditions of musicals such as *Yankee Doodle Dandy*, so it was no surprise that, when he was twelve, he landed a role in an Actor's Studio production of *Who'll Save the Plowboy*. While attending Dwight Morrow High School, he was a mediocre student and spent much of his free time appearing in various local plays. "I was a bit of a clown in school, only an average student," John remembers. "I was inhibited by a lot of the people there. My reality was different from theirs. I was interested in show business, and they weren't." At sixteen, he dropped out of school and, with the help of agents, soon began appearing in commercials.

A year later, he moved to Manhattan and broke into stage work with an off-Broadway production of *Rain* at the Astor Place Theater. He toured with the national company of *Grease*, made guest appearances on TV shows and made his Broadway debut in the musical *Over Here!* In 1975, he appeared in his first motion picture with a small role in the horror film *The Devil's Rain*. It was after leaping to TV stardom as "sweathog" Vinnie Barbarino on the hit show *Welcome Back Kotter* that he scored as Tony Manero in the smash hit *Saturday Night Fever*. More film roles followed, including the movie version of *Grease* and *Urban Cowboy*. After a long fallow period, he made a comeback in *Look Who's Talking* and *Look Who's Talking Too*.

John lost his lover, actress Diana Hyland, to cancer in 1977, and remained a bachelor until 1991, when he married Kelly Preston, with whom he has a son. An avid pilot for fifteen years, he likes to take the throttle of his own DC-3.

KATHLEEN TURNER

REAL NAME: Mary Kathleen Turner
DATE OF BIRTH: June 19, 1954
PLACE OF BIRTH: Springfield, Missouri

EYE COLOR: Blue   HAIR COLOR: Blond
HEIGHT: 5'9"   WEIGHT: 123

Anyone who was captivated by Kathleen Turner's sizzling sensuality in *Body Heat* or watched in amazement as she made love with a man's big toe in *Crimes of Passion* may be tempted to write Kathleen Turner off as nothing more than a supercharged sex kitten. But she has been compared in star power with Lana Turner and Ava Gardner.

One of four children born to a U.S. foreign service officer, she remembers being a tomboy in a very competitive household. After early years living in Canada, Cuba, Washington, D.C., and Venezuela, her family settled at the American consulate in England. "I think I learned a lot about adjusting quickly, about presenting a picture of myself, because you go to a new school and right away kids are challenging you," she says. "I think that had a lot to do with acting; you went in there showing people something. You felt you could redo yourself; nobody knew what you were."

In London, she became enthralled with the performances of such fine actors as Christopher Plummer, Diana Rigg and Angela Lansbury during her weekly visits to the theater. Longing to join them, she supplemented her school days with classes at the Central School of Speech and Drama. Her father's death in 1973 sent the family back to the United States, and they settled in her mother's hometown of Springfield, Missouri. Kathleen continued her quest by taking voice lessons at Southwest Missouri State University. But Kathleen found Springfield a cultural wasteland and the college even worse, so she bought a $300 used car, drove to Baltimore and enrolled at the University of Maryland, where she obtained her B.A. as a theater major in 1977.

She wasted no time in heading for New York and securing an agent. Working as a waitress, she earned her wings in TV commercials and off-off-Broadway plays before a two-year stint on a soap

opera. Anxious to break into film, she flew to Hollywood to test for a part as a female wrestler. Turned down, she bumped into the casting agent for a film called *Body Heat*. He got her a reading with the producer, and Kathleen remembers, "I went in dressed to the nines: I put on my highest heels and a slit skirt and all the makeup I could muster." It worked: With absolutely no film credits, she landed the lead in that hot movie, and stardom was within reach. Refusing to be typecast as a vamp, she immediately started picking roles that not only stretched her professionally but challenged her intellectually. After *Peggy Sue Got Married*, she went on to appear in *Romancing the Stone, Crimes of Passion, Prizzi's Honor, The Accidental Tourist, The War of the Roses* and more. *Undercover Blues* is her most recent film. She also lent her deep, sexy vocal chords to the cartoon character of Jessica in *Who Framed Roger Rabbit?* Kathleen lives with her real estate agent husband and their daughter in New York, goes to Mets games, spends weekends at the Hamptons and is, by her own admission, deliriously happy.

MIKE WALLACE

REAL NAME: Myron Leon Wallace
DATE OF BIRTH: May 9, 1918
PLACE OF BIRTH: Brookline, Massachusetts

EYE COLOR: Brown   HAIR COLOR: Brown
HEIGHT: 5'10"   WEIGHT: 160

Though he's mellowed a bit with age, Mike Wallace is still considered—at 75—to be a tenacious and intimidating interviewer. Summing up his own personal technique, he says, "You role-play to a certain degree. If you succeed in persuading your object of scrutiny that you know a great deal more about him than you do, he opens up all that more easily. You try to establish a chemistry of confidentiality. You want to give him a psychological excuse to reveal himself."

When his father arrived in this country from Russia early in 1900, his surname was Wallik, but an immigration official misunderstood

the pronunciation and recorded it as Wallace. Soon the senior Wallace married, became a grocer and had four children, including Mike. Throughout school, Mike was a diligent student and pursued ambitious extracurricular events: school newspaper, drama, public oration and tennis. By this time, Mike's father had become an insurance broker, and they lived in Brookline, a few houses away from where JFK was born. "This town was a middle-American dream," says Mike. "You were taught to strive. You paid attention to what your folks said, and there was a sense that you darn well better achieve." Mike set that goal into motion by earning his B.A. degree in 1939 from the University of Michigan, paying his way through by washing dishes and waiting tables.

His initiation into journalism took place at a radio station in Grand Rapids, Michigan, where he learned the business by doing a little of everything. Moving on to Detroit and Chicago, he continued doing radio work—announcing, narrating and acting on shows such as *The Lone Ranger*. In 1943, Mike began a three-year tour of duty in the Navy, then returned to Chicago and resumed his radio career. During the late '40s, he married Buff Cobb, and the couple teamed up to broadcast a live entertainment program from a posh nightclub. They were wooed to New York by CBS-TV, and their national *Mike and Buff* show lasted until their divorce in 1954. By now, Mike was an established TV figure, hosting numerous educational and family series. He even had a part in the 1954 Broadway play *Reclining Figure* and received decent reviews.

Mike originated the in-depth interview format when he and Ted Yates Jr. developed the news department for a New York TV station in 1955. The unconventionality of Mike's focus on grilling famous people led to his own show, *Night Beat*, in 1956. Mike incorporated his interview style into hard-news programs as anchor of *The CBS Morning News* in 1963. When CBS News producer Don Hewitt conceived *60 Minutes* in 1968, Wallace was his first choice to co-anchor with the low-key Harry Reasoner. He's been on it ever since, still trying to build into every story a "value conflict."

Now in his fourth marriage, Mike has two sons from his first marriage. One son was accidentally killed while mountain climbing in 1962, and the other, Chris, is in broadcasting. Although he was forced to have a pacemaker installed in 1991, Mike insists that retirement is not in his plans.

BARBARA WALTERS

REAL NAME: Barbara Walters
DATE OF BIRTH: September 25, 1931
PLACE OF BIRTH: Boston, Massachusetts

EYE COLOR: Green   HAIR COLOR: Brown
HEIGHT: 5'5"   WEIGHT: 120

A great interview, says Barbara Walters, is "one that brings out something concerning a guest that he hasn't revealed about himself before." She may not be the only journalist in the business who can ask the most intimate and provocative questions without alienating her subjects. But she's certainly the best.

From babyhood, she was no stranger to celebrities and a whirlwind lifestyle. Her father, Lou Walters, was the founder of the legendary New York Latin Quarter and owner of other glamorous nightclubs. His business took the family to live in such cities as Boston, New York and Miami, where colorful people and celebrities floated in and out of the Walters home. Barbara attended high school in Miami, finished at the Fieldston School and Birch Wathen School, both private schools in New York, and took her B.A. degree in English at Sarah Lawrence in 1954.

Intent on becoming a teacher, she began working on her master's degree in education while working as a secretary. But, when she accepted another job as a publicity assistant in a CBS affiliate TV station, all thoughts of teaching evaporated. She left graduate school, moved right into a training program for producers and was soon producing shows on women's topics. For the next few years after leaving CBS—which Barbara refers to as her "dark ages years"—she worked behind the scenes writing material for Dave Garroway on the *Today* show in 1961. While others such as Lee Meriwether, Florence Henderson and Maureen Sullivan came and went as *Today* girls, Barbara campaigned for and got the chance to co-host the show herself in 1974. After producing and writing stories for two years, she began conducting interviews herself, and in 1976, aired her first interview show, *The Barbara Walters Special*. Sixty top-rated specials have been aired since then, and she joined *20/20* as Hugh Downs' co-host in 1984.

She has received enough honors and awards—including her induction into the Television Hall of Fame in 1990—to qualify her as one of the most respected and accomplished women of our generation. Barbara has been married twice and has a daughter from her first marriage.

DENZEL WASHINGTON

REAL NAME: Denzel Washington
DATE OF BIRTH: December 28, 1954
PLACE OF BIRTH: Mount Vernon, New York

EYE COLOR: Brown   HAIR COLOR: Black
HEIGHT: 6'   WEIGHT: 170

"I like my work to speak for me," says Denzel Washington. "I don't like to speak for my work." A self-described "regular guy," he shuns interviews and despite his immense talent and box office popularity, his friends, fellow actors and co-workers all agree that he has

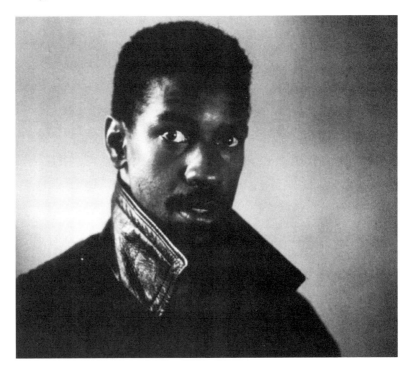

no ego and that he is one of the friendliest and most polite people in the business.

Born to a Pentecostal minister and a beautician, Denzel was raised in middle-class Mount Vernon, New York, and left his neighborhood to attend mostly white public schools, where he threw himself into sports: football, baseball and basketball. When he moved on to Fordham University in the Bronx, he tried out for and earned positions on both the football and basketball teams. Seeking a creative outlet, Denzel wrote poetry until he decided to turn his talents toward acting. At Fordham, he dabbled in drama, but because there seemed to be little chance of making it as an actor, he pursued other employment. Although he made his film debut in 1980 with the forgettable film *Carbon Copy*, he almost traded his dream for a nine-to-five government job and a steady paycheck in Washington, D.C., but turned it down when he won the role of Malcolm X in *When the Chickens Come Home to Roost*, about a fictional encounter between Malcolm and Elijah Muhammad. This breakthrough led to other stage roles, including the Ensemble production of *A Soldier's Play* and then the film version of the play, *A Soldier's Story*. He spent six seasons on television as Phil Chandler on the Emmy award-winning *St. Elsewhere*, then moved back into films.

Thrice nominated for Academy Awards, Denzel believes that he was destined to portray Malcolm X on the big screen. "Everything I have done as an actor has been in preparation for this," he says of the role that earned him his third nomination. Because he wanted to do justice to Malcolm's life, he attended Fruit of Islam classes, watched videos and read FBI and prison records, and even learned to lindy hop. He's also played romantic leads in *The Mighty Quinn, Mo' Better Blues* and *Mississippi Masala*, and characters infused with politics in *Cry Freedom* and *Glory*, for which he won an Oscar. His upcoming projects are *The Pelican Brief* with Julia Roberts and *Philadelphia*, in which he portrays a homophobic attorney who represents a gay AIDS victim.

With his wife, Pauletta, who is a professional singer, and their two children, Denzel resides in Los Angeles.

SIGOURNEY WEAVER

REAL NAME: Susan Weaver
PLACE OF BIRTH: New York, New York
DATE OF BIRTH: October 8, 1949

EYE COLOR: Brown   HAIR COLOR: Brown
HEIGHT: 5'11"   WEIGHT: 125

"I was a privileged, pampered, sheltered child. It was as though every day had a happy ending. I thought everyone's father was head of a network." Sigourney is referring to her father, Pat Weaver, president of NBC from 1949 to 1956 and one of the co-founders of cable television. Her mother, Elizabeth Inglis, was a British actress who appeared in several American films, and her father had been a comedian who worked in Bob Hope movies. Sigourney also has an older brother.

She was floating through her fairy-tale childhood, being educated at the elite Chapin and Brearley schools in New York and then the Ethel Walker School in Simsbury, Connecticut. Then she hit 5'11" at age thirteen, and she became so self-conscious and intimidated by her height that she turned into the class clown at school and an introvert at home. At fourteen, feeling that such a tall girl needed a more imposing name than Susan, she officially changed her name to Sigourney after being inspired by a character in *The Great Gatsby*.

Sigourney entered Stanford University and majored in English with the intention of becoming a teacher, but once she started acting with an activist "guerrilla theater" group, she abandoned her future as a teacher, much to her parents' dismay. During her last year at Stanford, she dressed bizarrely on campus—elf costumes and the like—and lived in a treehouse with her equally bizarre boyfriend.

After graduation, she was accepted by the Yale Drama School under the name of Mr. Sigourney Weaver. She recalls her three years there as miserable, mostly because her wacky appearance and demeanor were not considered amusing on campus. "It was pretentious and terribly pseudo-serious," she recalls. "For six months, they wouldn't cast me even in a tiny role. I had to work in a cabaret." After graduation in 1974, she went straight to New York and, while her

father reluctantly supported her financially, found one door after another closed in her face by agents because of her height. Eventually Dad's patience and support ran out, and Sigourney supported herself for several years making TV commercials, working briefly on a soap opera and picking up small parts in off-Broadway plays.

Sigourney's first film appearance was a bit part in *Annie Hall*, but just two more film parts later she landed in the huge success *Alien* in 1979. The film made loads of money, and she got great reviews, but Hollywood didn't proceed to besiege her with new scripts. For the next five years, she commuted between New York and Hollywood, appearing in dark, experimental plays on the stage, and making a film every other year, but still unable to capture any real notoriety. Her role in the huge hit *Ghostbusters* in 1984 finally established her as a star, and a series of hits has followed ever since: *Aliens* in 1986, then *Working Girl, Gorillas in the Mist* and *Ghostbusters II*. In 1993, she co-starred with Kevin Kline as the wife of the president in the political satire *Dave*.

In 1984, Sigourney married director Jim Simpson. No longer the awkward teen, she says, "I think my greatest asset as an actress has been my height because it's forced people to think of me for distinctive roles. You can't hide me onstage—I take up a lot of room."

BETTY WHITE

REAL NAME: Betty Marion White
DATE OF BIRTH: January 17, 1924
PLACE OF BIRTH: Oak Park, Illinois

EYE COLOR: Blue   HAIR COLOR: Blond
HEIGHT: 5'4"   WEIGHT: 115

"My greatest talent is being able to be natural in front of the camera," says Betty White. The only child of an electrical engineer father and a housewife mother, Betty got her start in acting at Beverly Hills High School, but she wrote so many school plays that she was plan-

THE OFFICIAL CELEBRITY REGISTRY

ning on becoming a writer at first. Those plans changed after graduation when she went right into acting in local theater and radio productions. By this time, the late '40s, television was beginning to be the place to be, and Betty went from guest spot appearances on regular shows like *Hollywood on Television* to becoming the full-time host of that show.

She launched her comic career and won an Emmy at the same time, in 1952, as the star of the TV sitcom *Life With Elizabeth*, which revolved around her character as a ditzy housewife. "We didn't worry about relevance in the early days. We were trying to be funny. We were more two-dimensional cartoon characters than three-dimensional real people," she remembers. In spite of Betty's popularity and decent ratings, one show after another was canceled over the next five years. So she threw in the towel on sitcoms and became a professional game show panelist on *I've Got a Secret* and *Password*, among other shows, for a dozen years. "It's like stealing money," she said of that experience. "You sit down and play games." During summer hiatuses, Betty kept in form by acting in informal theater productions.

In 1973, when Betty was offered the role as the vixen in lamb's clothing, Sue Ann Nivens, on *The Mary Tyler Moore Show*, she hit her stride as a performer. "So many people knew me as that nice lady. It was great fun for them to see that nice ladies sometimes have claws. For me, it was like being born again," she said. By the time the show shut down in 1977, Betty had won four consecutive Emmys as best supporting actress in a comedy series. Then she tried her hand at a series of her own and showed up in miniseries and TV movies for eight more years until she struck gold again with another Emmy for *The Golden Girls*.

After a divorce in 1949, Betty broke her vow of singlehood and married actor Allen Ludden in 1963. Although Betty has no children of her own, she has three stepchildren from her marriage to Allen, who died in 1981.

As the years have gone by, Betty has devoted more and more time and money to the cause that's dearest to her: animals. She has served on the board of directors of the Los Angeles Zoo and numerous foundations researching animal diseases. As one of her stepchildren has said, "Animals are her real work. Acting is just a hobby."

ROBIN WILLIAMS

REAL NAME: Robin Williams
DATE OF BIRTH: July 21, 1952
PLACE OF BIRTH: Chicago, Illinois

EYE COLOR: Blue   HAIR COLOR: Brown
HEIGHT: 5'9"   WEIGHT: 170

A critic has described Robin Williams as "an astonishing lunar wild man out of Jonathan Winters by way of Lenny Bruce, with a touch of Richard Burton thrown in." And Robin himself has called it "legalized insanity." His father, a Ford Motor Company vice president, was 50 at Robin's birth, so his childhood was a lonely one. Though both parents had grown children from previous marriages, he was the only child living at home with his mother, whom he describes as "a crazy Southern belle," on their 30-room estate in

Bloomfield Hills, Michigan. With no playmates nearby, Robin spent most of his time with his 2,000 toy soldiers, building battle scenes and acting out the characters. His idol was Jonathan Winters, whose routines he taped and then re-created for his own amusement. "My imagination was my friend, my companion," he remembers.

While his father continued to advance with Ford, the Williams family moved six times in eight years. Attending exclusive private schools, overweight and always the new kid, Robin was picked on and beaten up a lot. He finally discovered that he could circumvent the ridicule by making the other kids laugh. During his senior year in high school, when his father retired from Ford, they moved to Tiburon, California, in Marin County, a very progressive, hip community, and Robin found himself liberated. "Everyone was on acid," he remembers, "and they had gestalt history classes." Joining the fray, he lost weight, took up athletics and was voted "funniest" and "most likely to succeed."

After high school, he moved south to study political science at Claremont Men's College. It was there that he discovered acting, and soon he was back in Northern California studying Shakespeare at the College of Marin. He was so talented that he won a scholarship to the Juilliard School in New York, where he studied for three years, and for extra money performed mime routines on weekends in Manhattan. Returning to California in 1976, Robin stopped off in San Francisco long enough to meet his future wife and develop a stand-up comedy routine. Moving to Los Angeles, he was soon appearing at clubs like the Comedy Store and within six months had landed a continuing role on the zany TV show *Laugh-In*. He got his big break after appearing as space alien Mork from Ork on *Happy Days* and was given his own show, *Mork and Mindy*. The huge success of *Mork* led to movie offers, and in 1980, he made his motion picture debut in the title role of *Popeye*. He has since gone into orbit with three successful comedy albums and Academy Award nominations for his performances in both *Good Morning, Vietnam* and *Dead Poets Society*. In 1986, along with Whoopi Goldberg and Billy Crystal, Robin founded Comic Relief, an annual comedy show that benefits the homeless.

His first marriage, from which he has one son, ended in 1988. He was wed to his son's nanny in 1989, and together they have a daughter. When he's not on stage, he maintains his sanity through jogging, yoga and skiing.

BRUCE WILLIS

REAL NAME: Walter Bruce Willis
DATE OF BIRTH: March 19, 1955
PLACE OF BIRTH: Idar-Oberstein, Germany

EYE COLOR: Brown   HAIR COLOR: Brown
HEIGHT: 5'10"   WEIGHT: 170

The son of an Army serviceman, Bruce Willis was born on a military base in Germany. When Bruce was two, his father returned with his son and German bride to Carneys Point, New Jersey, where three more children were born. In the predominantly blue-collar community, his father went to work in a shipyard and machine repair shop. During high school, Bruce reigned as the school prankster and, to

the teachers' chagrin, was elected president of the student council. Popular in student productions as well, particularly comedies, he found that the stammer he'd had since childhood disappeared whenever he had someone to perform for, on stage or off. During his senior year, Bruce was expelled after participating in a racial disturbance and was able to graduate only because his father hired an attorney to get him reinstated.

After high school, Bruce worked at a Du Pont chemical plant for a time before quitting to take a string of odd jobs, including security guard and playing harmonica in a blues band. Deciding to go back to school, he selected Montclair State College because of the low tuition and exceptional drama department. He quickly took acting to his bosom and began spending more time commuting to New York to audition for off-Broadway parts than he spent concentrating on school. Before long, he landed a role in the 1977 play *Heaven on Earth*, dropped out of Montclair and moved to New York. Taking an apartment in the Hell's Kitchen district, Bruce started getting work on the stage as well as in TV commercials. But to pay the rent during the early '80s, he worked mainly as a bartender in a trendy hangout for showbiz types. One fellow bartender remembers, "He was outrageous. He used to roller-skate into the place dressed in huge parachute pants, headbands and ripped T-shirts.... He was into punk years before its time." He is fondly remembered as spicing the atmosphere with his impromptu blues and harmonica serenades for patrons at the bar.

Bruce's big break came when he was picked to take over the lead role in *Fool for Love* off-Broadway in 1984. That same year, while on vacation in Los Angeles, he auditioned for a new TV show called *Moonlighting* and won out over 3,000 competitors for the role of the wisecracking, finger-popping private eye David Addison. He played Addison from 1984 through 1987 and even won an Emmy for his work. Although his first two films were only marginally successful, his third, *Die Hard*, was a huge success, and he has followed that up with *Die Hard 2*, *Bonfire of the Vanities*, *The Last Boy Scout* and other action films. In addition to acting, Willis has released two albums, *The Return of Bruno* and *If It Don't Kill You It Makes You Stronger*.

Bruce married actress Demi Moore in 1987, and they have two children, Rumer and Scout.

OPRAH WINFREY

REAL NAME: Oprah Winfrey
DATE OF BIRTH: January 29, 1954
PLACE OF BIRTH: Kosciusko, Mississippi

EYE COLOR: Brown   HAIR COLOR: Black
HEIGHT: 5'4"   WEIGHT: 140

"Dishing the dirt and meddling in other folks' business is what I do best," says Oprah Winfrey.

We'd be watching the *Orpah Winfrey Show* instead of the *Oprah Winfrey Show* today if the midwife who delivered her hadn't accidentally transposed two letters in her biblical name when she was filling out the birth certificate. Soon after Oprah's birth, her parents, who were not married, broke up. Both parents left Mississippi, and Oprah remained on the farm with her grandmother, who taught her to read when she was a mere toddler. With farm animals for playmates and a corncob doll as her only toy, Oprah retreated into her fantasy world for entertainment. She demonstrated the loquaciousness for which she would become famous when she delivered an Easter sermon to her church congregation when she was two years old. Oprah skipped kindergarten and second grade and at six was being invited to recite poetry at church and social functions in Milwaukee, where she now lived with her mother and stepbrothers. During a visit to her father in Nashville, Oprah earned her first paycheck, at age twelve, for delivering a speech in church. With $500 in her hand, she informed everyone that when she grew up, she was going to be "paid to talk."

Returning to the Milwaukee ghetto where her mother was subsisting on a domestic help's salary and welfare, Oprah found herself left alone most of the time, and at the hands of male friends and relatives. Having suffered their sexual abuse since she was nine, Oprah's frustration and rage began surfacing in the form of violent outbursts and running away. She once approached Aretha Franklin as Aretha was stepping out of a limo and convinced her that Oprah had been abandoned. Aretha gave her $100 to get home, and Oprah used it to stay in a hotel until the money ran out. When she finally went home, she was sent off to live with her father and stepmother in Nashville.

"My father saved my life," Oprah recalls. He had become a barber and a respected member of the city council, and he nurtured her back to good habits with loving sternness and required her to read a book a week and increase her vocabulary. As she blossomed under his care, she excelled academically and in the drama and debate clubs. Entering Tennessee State University on a scholarship, she won the title of Miss Tennessee and competed in the Miss Black America contest. In 1971, while still a sophomore, Oprah accepted an offer to be the first black news co-anchor on a local TV station. "Sure, I was a token," she recalls. "But honey, I was one happy token."

After graduation from TSU in 1976, she moved to Baltimore to report and co-anchor for the ABC affiliate station. It was a year later that she discovered her professional forte as a co-host on the local talk show *Baltimore Is Talking*. Seven years later and several ratings points higher, Oprah was recruited to work her magic on the *A.M. Chicago* show, and within a year, it was renamed *The Oprah Winfrey Show*. Her personal warmth, unpredictable questions and sometimes out-of-character responses made Oprah a lovable and respected hostess. When her show went into national syndication in 1986 and she took over as the show's producer, Oprah had become one of the wealthiest women in television. As an actress, her first film role, in 1985's *The Color Purple*, won her an Oscar nomination; and she has starred in *Native Son* and the miniseries *Women of Brewster Place*.

Oprah is engaged to be married to former basketball player Stedman Graham, and they have set 1993 for the big event.

PHOTO CREDITS